A SENSE OF THINGS

A SENSE
OF THINGS

The Object Matter
of American Literature

BILL BROWN

THE UNIVERSITY OF CHICAGO PRESS
CHICAGO AND LONDON

The University of Chicago Press, Chicago 60637

The University of Chicago Press, Ltd., London

© 2003 by The University of Chicago

All rights reserved. Published 2003

Printed in the United States of America

12 11 10 09 08 07   5 4 3 2

ISBN (cloth): 0-226-07628-8

ISBN (paper): 0-226-07629-6

Library of Congress Cataloging-in-Publication Data

Brown, Bill, 1958–

   A sense of things : the object matter of American literature / Bill Brown.

      p.   cm.

   Includes index.

   ISBN 0-226-07628-8 (cloth : alk. paper) — ISBN 0-226-07629-6 (pbk : alk. paper)

1. American fiction—19th century—History and criticism.   2. Material culture in literature.
3. Economics and literature—United States—History—19th century.   4. Material culture—
United States—History—19th century.   5. Production (Economic theory) in literature.
6. Consumption (Economics) in literature.   7. Possessiveness in literature.   I. Title.

PS374.M39B76   2003

813'.409355—dc21   2002010611

FOR MARY, DIANA, AND FRASER,
who see into the lives of things

CONTENTS

CONTENTS

ILLUSTRATIONS

ACKNOWLEDGMENTS

As I worked on this book, I rediscovered many long-standing intellectual debts: to René Girard, Russell Berman, Wanda Corn, Theodore Brown, Laura Rigal, Diana Young, and to Jay Fliegelman, whose commitment to apprehending the importance of things in the cultural history of America will always be an inspiration.

For the resources (the time and the money) to complete the project I am indebted to two deans at the University of Chicago: Philip Gossett, Dean of Humanities, and John Boyer, Dean of the College. For their unflagging commitment, I am particularly indebted to three research assistants, whose assistance went beyond mere research: Noel Jackson helped me to establish some of the groundwork for the enterprise; Nicholas Yablon both helped to build its archive and brought a historian's questions to the claims I was trying to make; and Thomas Kim helped me to refine several conceptual details and to overcome countless details in the editorial and production process. Their energy often kept the project afloat. With nothing short of grace, Norah O'Donnell kept my own adminstrative office in order as she struggled to produce the time in which I brought the book to a close. As an editor at the University of Chicago Press, Alan Thomas—always engaged, always patient yet persuasive—has lived up to his remarkable reputation.

An earlier version of chapter 1 appeared as "The Tyranny of Things (Trivia in Karl Marx and Mark Twain)," *Critical Inquiry* 29 (winter 2001): 442–69; a portion of chapter 3 appeared in "Regional Artifacts (The Life of Things in the Work of Sarah Orne Jewett)," *American Literary History* (winter 2002), 195–226, and is reprinted by permission of Oxford University Press; and a fragment of chapter 4 appeared in "A Thing about Things: The Art of Decoration in the Work of Henry James," *The Henry James Review* 23, no.3 (2002); reprinted with permision of The Johns Hopkins University

Press. Responses from these journals helped me to clarify several points. Because the basic topic of this book seems to be generally compelling, I've had the chance to learn from different conversations, casual and professional, and I want to thank the many people with whom I've talked about "things." In particular, the finished product has benefited from the generous responses of Jonathan Auerbach, Homi Bhabha, Mitchell Breitwieser, Jessica Burstein, Bradin Cormack, Frances Ferguson, Chris Gair, Jonathan Goldberg, W. J. T. Mitchell, Robert Kaufman, Michael Moon, Lisa Ruddick, Jay Schleusener, Eric Slauter, Julia Stern, Lesley Stern, and William Veeder.

Janel Mueller, the current Dean of Humanities at Chicago, performed the extraordinary feat of remaining, in the midst of her deanship, one of my very best readers, sparing the time and taking the trouble to comment at length and in depth on several chapters. Miriam Hansen has been the colleague with whom I've shared the topic of "things" (and taught about "things") for many years now. I continue to rely on James Chandler more than anyone: he has suffered through many drafts, and his critical intelligence, as always, cornered me into thinking as well as I can. I recognize the lively presence of such colleagues throughout this book.

I can legitimately be held to know only
in so far as objects exist to make me know.
Take away, consequently, the object of
knowledge (or thing known) . . . and you a
fortiori take away the subject: for the subject
in existence is logically constituted only by
the object for which and to which and
by which he lives.

Henry James Sr., *Society, The Redeemed Form
of Man and the Earnest of God's Omnipotence in
Human Nature: Affirmed in Letters to a Friend* (1879)

The Idea of Things and
the Ideas in Them

When none of us had much to offer the workshop, Ken Fields would bring in some xeroxes (a range of work: Andrew Marvell and Adrienne Rich, Derek Walcott and Theodore Roethke) and we would talk about enjambment, say, or synecdoche—about the formal and figural craft of poetry. But at times like these he was also given to offering general advice or admonishment. "Remember," Ken said one afternoon, sitting idol-like on the sofa, glancing somewhat beyond the faces that expressed belief in poetry as a kind of calling, "It's not no ideas. 'No ideas but in things' doesn't mean no ideas."

William Carlos Williams always hovered in our midst as the poet most responsible for making poetry what it was in the twentieth century, and no less responsible than Whitman for making poetry American. He also seemed responsible, however unwittingly, for fostering a kind of neglect—a refusal to assume responsibility for ideas, a willingness to be satisfied with mere things.

And yet, no matter how much common sense convinces us that things are matter-of-fact and mute, concrete and self-evident, apprehending the *mereness* of things can become a difficult task. As a forgotten psychologist of mind, Mark Baldwin, put it in 1895, "this 'mereness'" hardly offends idealist thought because an idealist posits a "real thing" that has its phenomenal expression in the "mere thing."[1] Materialism does not always offer an obvious alternative. As the Objectivist poet Louis Zukofsky put it, paraphrasing Marx, "The labor process ends in the creation of a thing, / Which when the process began / Already lived as the worker's image."[2] Within these accounts of idealism and materialism, then, the idea of the thing seems to lie elsewhere—in some imagined place of origin, whether in the worker's mind (and only *then* in the act of manufacture), or in, say, the mind of God. Both accounts employ a temporal structure wherein the mereness of the thing, its present physical presence, is inseparable from its metaphysical past. But such accounts would thus find it difficult to fathom the idea that an idea could ever be fully present in a thing.

They hardly begin to suggest how difficult it is to "think thingness" in the abstract—as abstract physicality. "A thing cannot be a lump," Baldwin argued, for that "would make it impossible that we should know it as a thing" (552). In his diagnosis of the "allergies to entity," Theodor Adorno argues that there can be no "primeval history of the object," only a history "dealing with specific objects."[3] The experience or history of specific objects, though, depends on a generalizable experience of the very thingness of both natural and man-made objects, which itself depends on our ideas— about thingness—no less than it depends on our senses (and our understanding of them). Such a point seems to digress readily toward the idea *of* things, and away from the ideas *in* them. "No things but in ideas"—that is an old Hegelian saw.[4] But can we think about the ideas *in* things without getting caught up by the idea *of* them? Probably not.

The idea *of* things assumes some clarity in Williams's prose. *A Novelette* (1932), for instance, argues that preconceptions have prevented any human appreciation (indeed recognition) of the simplest physical details that surround us: "A tree with a split that admits water will show fresh wood when it freezes. A stone is darker when wet than when dry. . . . When these things were first noted categories were ready for them so that they got fast in corners of understanding. By this process, reinforced by tradition, every common thing has been nailed down, stripped of freedom of action and taken away from use."[5] This is an account of how our ideas prohibit our senses from offering any access to new knowledge. Adorno would align it with the way in which "philosophical imperialism" (both epistemology and phenomenology) "bewitche[s] what is heterogeneous to it," subordinating sensation to cognition (194).

And yet when Williams celebrates Juan Gris in *Spring and All* (1923), he seems to understand the process of wresting things away from life and experience to be the essential dynamic of the artist's endeavor. The "things" in Gris's paintings are "still 'real'" and as recognizable as if photographed "as things touched by the hands during the day," but they are "detached": "Things with which he is familiar, simple things—at the same time to detach them from ordinary experience to the imagination."[6] In the early part of Williams's career, there is a dynamic contradiction between the epistemological and the aesthetic, between knowing the world in its thingness and turning the work of art into a thing. The artist, he proclaims, is "AT WORK MAKING OBJECTS" (112). Writing, he powerfully (if paradoxically) explains, "by being actually itself would be in itself a general idea of the most

2

concrete."[7] This effort to fathom the concrete, and to imagine the work of art as a different mode of mimesis—not one that serves to represent a thing, but one that seeks to attain the status of a thing—is a fundamental strain of modernism, as characteristic of Stein as it is of Malevich, of Picasso as it is of Zukofsky.[8] The question of things becomes a question about whether the literary object should be understood as the object that literature represents or the object that literature has as its aim, the object that literature is.

Can there be ideas without things? Williams certainly thought so. Rather, he thought that other poets thought so. That, of course, was the problem— the abstractness of our ideas—which convinced Williams, as it had T. E. Hulme and Ezra Pound, that modernism must demand a new idiom. In Emerson's terms: the poet should not (as he himself wished) "conform[ ] things to his thought," but should act as the "sensual man [who] conforms thought to things."[9] More exactly: the poet should recognize things as the necessary condition for ideas. The modernist's point, as Ken tried to emphasize, wasn't that things should replace ideas, but that ideas and things should somehow merge. This was Williams's anti-Emersonian effort to achieve what is, after all, an Emersonian effect: overcoming the subject/object opposition, and contesting the ontological distinction between thoughts and things.[10]

When I began to work on what became *A Sense of Things,* I was convinced that cultural theory and literary criticism needed a comparably new idiom, beginning with the effort to think with or through the physical object world, the effort to establish a genuine sense of the things that comprise the stage on which human action, including the action of thought, unfolds. I wanted criticism to avoid succumbing to the state of affairs described by Georges Bataille, where the very fact that capitalism is "an unreserved surrender to *things*" means that capitalist cultures "place what is essential" beyond or outside "the world of *things*."[11] I imagined a kind of cultural and literary history emanating from the typewriter, the fountain pen, the light bulb—component parts of the physical support for modern literary production.[12] However much I shared the new historicist "desire to make contact with the 'real,'" I wanted the end result to read like a grittier, materialist phenomenology of everyday life, a result that might somehow arrest language's wish, as described by Michel Serres, that the "whole world . . . derive from language."[13] Where other critics had faith in "discourse" or in the "social text" as the analytical grid on which to reconfigure our knowledge about the present and the past, I wanted to turn attention to things—the objects that are materialized from and in the physical world that is, or had been, at hand.[14] I presumed that I would find in them—as had Georg Simmel and

Gaston Bachelard, Siegfried Kracauer and Walter Benjamin—not just the physical determinants of our imaginative life but also the congealed facts and fantasies of a culture, the surface phenomena that disclose the logic or illogic of industrial society.[15] I presumed that I would be adhering to Adorno's dictum that "we are not to philosophize about concrete things; we are to philosophize, rather, out of these things" (33). The project would thus come on the heels (or the coat tails) of important anthologies that, from different disciplines and from the space between them, have summoned us to attend to things: *The Social Life of Things* (1986), *History from Things* (1993), *The Sex of Things* (1996), *Material Cultures: Why Some Things Matter* (1998).[16] These volumes denaturalize consumer practices and trace (within and between cultures) the *work* of exchange and consumption: the way value is created in specific social formations and lodged in specific material forms, the way that people code, recode, and satisfy their material wants and needs.

And yet I began to wonder whether such work had not, in a different way, left things behind, never quite asking how they become recognizable, representable, and exchangeable to begin with. Rather than beginning with the fountain pen, I began all over again by re-reading some literary texts that seemed to pose those questions, whether or not they meant to. These are texts that, as I understand them, ask why and how we use objects to make meaning, to make or re-make ourselves, to organize our anxieties and affections, to sublimate our fears and shape our fantasies. They are texts that describe and enact an imaginative possession of things that amounts to the labor of infusing manufactured objects with a metaphysical dimension. And, not incidentally, they are texts published in the era when the typewriter and the fountain pen and the light bulb began to flourish, an era of unprecedented invention in the nation known, since the Civil War, for its manufacturing ingenuity and capacity—an era when the invention, production, distribution, and consumption of things rather suddenly came to define a national culture.

"The war," as one of the first industrial historians put it in 1886, "was unquestionably a powerful stimulant to the manufacturer by creating a new and enormous demand for things."[17] This demand for things did not subside after the war, in large measure because the manufacturer had new and no less powerful stimulants on which he could depend. Even a character penned by Henry James could be so crass as to declare: "They invent everything all over again about every five years, and it's a great thing to keep up with the new things."[18] In the closing decades of the nineteenth century, the U.S. enjoyed the fastest growing market of any industrial nation. The revolutions in transportation and communication, evolving from the war, fueled postwar revolutions in production and distribution, all of which were part of an "organizational revolution," as Alfred Chandler has called it, that fundamentally changed people's relation to agricultural and manufactured goods.[19] As an example of the new pace of production, he refers to the Diamond Match Company: in 1881 Diamond began deploying a machine that produced and automatically packed matches by the billion (250). Such unprecedented mass production (achieved before its explicit conceptualization) was coupled with new forms of mass distribution, most notably new retailing institutions: mail-order houses, chain stores, department stores. By 1900, the Montgomery Ward catalogue swelled to five hundred pages, and it arrived in more than one million homes.[20] The complex phenomenon that goes by the name of the "industrial revolution" in America transformed the economy, politics, and law; it produced a struggling and embittered labor population, increasingly made up of immigrants; it also changed daily life by, on the hand, increasing industrial employment and thus the purchasing power of the working population, and, on the other, exponentially increasing the number and kind of goods for sale.

One could quite simply declare, after the century turned, that Americans lived in an "age of things." But the effort to sell things, to purchase things, and to accumulate things had an inevitable result: "We realize that we do not possess them; they possess us." The point wasn't just that Americans were "stifled with the sense of things," but that they now lived life peculiarly possessed.[21] The tale of that possession—of being possessed by possessions—is something stranger than the history of a culture of consumption. It is a tale not just of accumulating bric-a-brac, but also of fashioning an object-based historiography and anthropology, and a tale not just of thinking with things but also of trying to render thought thing-like. Even as the prose fiction of the nineteenth century represents and variously registers the way commodity relations came to saturate everyday life, so too (despite those relations or, indeed, intensified by them) this fiction demonstrates that the human investment in the physical object world, and the mutual constitution of human subject and inanimate object, can hardly be reduced to those relations. Whereas William James believed that "reality, life, experience, concreteness, immediacy, use what word you will, exceeds our logic, overflows and surrounds it,"[22] my gambit is simply to sacrifice the clarity of thinking about things as objects of consumption, on the one hand, in order to see how, on the other, our relation to things cannot be explained by the cultural logic of capitalism. As Ishmael put it, "some certain significance lurks in all things, else things are little worth, and the round world itself but an empty cipher, except to sell by the cartload, as they do hills about Boston."[23]

There were some days when, after the workshop, I walked around trying to notice whether this thing or that—a crushed Styrofoam cup, a stone bench, a horse chestnut—might have an idea in it. Then—honestly—I started to write a poem, a Christmas poem: a joke, composed as a child's letter to Santa Claus that asked for things with ideas in them. The poem closed with the image of a small boy wildly unwrapping a package, then unwrapping the thing within the package, tearing away layers of plastic, wild-eyed to get to the idea.

At the time I knew that my lyric humor didn't amount to much. The poem would never be good enough to show the workshop, let alone coax into print. I have successfully repressed particular lines. I have some lingering memory, though, of how pleasantly perplexing this great cliché of modernism, this idea of there being ideas in things (really *in* them), could actually be when it became part of daily life. Do those socks rolled up there have ideas in them, somewhere inside them? Perhaps they do.

At the time, when I talked to people about the poem (amusing enough in conception, if not on the page), someone told me that I'd been scooped—that Baudelaire had already written a version of it. Indeed, Baudelaire explains, in his "Philosophy of Toys," that the "overriding desire of most children is to get at and *see the soul* of their toys." The desire becomes an "infantile mania": "When this desire has implanted itself in the child's cerebral brow, it fills his fingers and nails with an extraordinary agility and strength." Rather than finding such a desire blameworthy, Baudelaire considers it a "first metaphysical tendency"—by which he means a will-to-metaphysics that provokes remarkable physical changes in the child's body. This is the very tendency, the desire, that initiates the child—once the toy has been destroyed, once it has been opened up—into the "melancholy and gloom" that characterizes the human response to the soulessness of modern life.[24] It is a lesson in the insufficiency of the desired object. For of course there is no soul within the toy, not even the mechanical toy. Not even the worker's image of the thing really lurks there *in* it, however convinced Walter Benjamin was, in the case of the hand-crafted toy, that children could still feel the hand of the worker *on* it.[25]

At the time I didn't know that Toni Morrison had already written a far more engaging, chilling, version of my poem in the opening pages of *The Bluest Eye*, a version that translates Baudelaire's "first metaphysical tendency" into a first sociological tendency. Before she endures her "unsullied hatred" of Shirley Temple, Claudia suffers the "gift of dolls" at Christmas, perennially confused by the "big, blue-eyed Baby Doll": "I was bemused by the thing itself." Unable to understand why everyone in America agrees "that a blue-eyed, yellow-haired, pink-skinned doll was what every girl child treasured," Claudia has "only one desire": to "dismember" the doll, to "see of what it [is] made," to "discover the dearness, to find the beauty, the desirability that . . . escape[s] [her], but apparently only [her]."[26] What she cannot find there, let us say, is the thing that makes the object special, the thing that makes Shirley Temple iconic, the idea that is in fact an ideology scripting beauty to maintain a social hierarchy, the cultural psychology that makes part-objects—yellow hair, blue eyes—sacred to a culture. She doesn't find the thing, or the idea in the thing, because it is everywhere and nowhere. If the idea had been there she could have junked the toy, gotten on, and lived her childhood outside its power.

The very idea of ideas in things—literalized by the child's search—is repeatedly revealed as a fantasy doomed to exposure. Alternatively, André Breton's Nadja adores her daughter "particularly because she resembles other children so little, 'with their mania for taking out their dolls' eyes to see *what's there* behind them.'"[27] The girl succeeds, as other children do not, in accepting the object without projecting on it—or into it—an animating spirit. Modernity's child is sated by surface alone.

And yet, even an American as infatuated with surfaces as Whitman can be heard proclaiming that "Only the kernel of every object nourishes; / Where is he who tears off the husks for you and me?"[28] Indeed, as Nabokov came to believe, it seems impossible to grant things their superficiality and opacity—impossible, that is, not to read them as transparencies: "When we concentrate on a material object, whatever its situation, the very act of attention may lead to our involuntarily sinking into the history of that object."[29] It is far more than history, though, that lies somehow within, somewhere within, the object materialized by human attention. It is not the worn, hard surface of the jug, after all, but the void constituted by the jug where Heidegger discovers the thingness of the thing and its gathering of earth and sky, divinities and mortals.[30] It is not the elegant form of the vase but the void created by the vase where Lacan discovers the Thing that names the emptiness at the center of the Real.[31] And it is all those spaces within—the inside of the chest, the inside of the wardrobe, the inside of the drawer—that, by Bachelard's light, enables us to image and imagine human interiority.[32]

Taken literally, the belief that there are ideas in things amounts to granting them an interiority and, thus, something like the structure of subjectivity. (When you "isolat[e] a thing," Fernand Léger explained, "you give it a personality.")[33] It amounts to asserting a kind of fetishism, but one that is part of the modernist's effort to arrest commodity-fetishism-as-usual: that is, an effort to interrupt the habit of granting material objects a value and power of their own, divorced from, and failing to disclose, the human power and social interaction that brought those objects into being. And yet one way that Marx means to give us a sense of commodity fetishism is by depicting ideas in things: when the table "emerges as a commodity . . . it stands on its head, and evolves out of its wooden brain grotesque ideas."[34] What may be most grotesque about this table is its ability to anticipate and appropriate an aesthetic project of the subsequent century even as it seems to locate us in a dream. (In Nabokov's novel, Hugh Person dreams "that his bedside table, a little three-legged affair [borrowed from under the hallway telephone] was executing a furious war dance all by itself" [21].) Still, the modernist's fetishized thing—excised from the world of consumer culture, isolated, re-focused, doted upon, however momentarily—is meant to be saved from the fate of the mass-produced object. It is saved from the humiliation of homogeneity; and it is saved from the tyranny of use, from the instrumental, utilitarian reason that has come to seem modernity's greatest threat to mankind. Williams first wrote his dictum—"no ideas but in things"—as part of an early lyric, "Paterson," in the year, 1926, when Henry Ford published his (ghost-written) article on "Mass Production" in both the New York Times and the Encyclopaedia Britannica, thereby transforming his industrial success into a new American ethic, defining a topic that captured national and international attention.[35] American poetry's best-known decree appears as the inverse (or perhaps the specular completion) of American industry's best-known managerial contribution. The decree later became the refrain for his epic Paterson (1946).[36]

Without ever imagining ideas in things, Paul Strand, the photographer who belonged to the same Manhattan art scene as Williams, demonstrates this process with particular clarity. Strand was fortunate to have grown up (like Frank Lloyd Wright) playing with Froebel blocks, to have had Lewis Hine as a photography teacher in high school, to have been exposed to Modernist painting at Alfred Stieglitz's 291 gallery and at the Armory show of 1913, and to have found a place among Stieglitz's Photo-Secession group and in the pages of Camera Work. As Strand traveled across the country in 1915, his work shed its lingering pictorialism and he abandoned both soft focus and multiple-gum printing. In the medium of photography he increasingly felt that America could be "expressed in terms of America without the outside influence of Paris."[37] Mesmerized by the flatness of Texas, he shot photographs that were increasingly geometric and that increasingly impressed Stieglitz, back in New York.[38] Then, as Strand himself tells the story, in the summer of 1916, on the porch of the Twin Lakes cottage in Connecticut, he began to experiment more intensely with his commitment to abstract shapes. Using some bowls from the kitchen as his subject matter—"maybe *object matter* would be a better term"—he stood above them and produced the first abstract photographic still-life, which soon appeared in *Camera Work* (see fig. 1).[39]

It is obvious that, by fragmenting the objects, Strand has shed them of their associations; freed them from their domestic, human context; and enabled them to achieve a formalism that obfuscates any exchange or use value that the objects may have. He nonetheless confers on them an aesthetic value, transforming them into both something less (fragments) than the objects they were, but also something more (forms), discovering a kind of thingness obscured by their everyday use as objects. Moreover, whether or not you agree with Fernand Léger's belief that fragmenting an object frees it of atmosphere even as enlarging the fragments gives them a life of their own, you can hardly deny that the objects in Strand's photograph, which seem suspended in a fragile balance, have curiously become organic or animate, have at least emerged out of their ontological status of being mere inanimate objects.[40] This is the photographer's version of suffusing those objects with warmth, the warmth not of the hand but of the eye. Strand makes it clear that although, as Benjamin would have it, photography emancipates objects from aura by rendering them reproducible and proximate (by eradicating their uniqueness), photography can nonetheless also invest objects with an aura they never had, a luminosity that gives them, even in their particularity, a kind of doubleness.[41] When, addressing his photography of the bowls, Strand describes the effort to "make a two-dimensional area have a three-dimensional character so that the eye of the person beholding the picture remain[s] in that space and [goes] *into* this picture and [doesn't] go off to the side," he describes an effort to give the photograph itself an extra dimension, to make it more object than image, and to grant the image itself an interior.[42]

And yet, insofar as *literary* modernism structures the doubleness of objects by the inside/outside dichotomy—"no ideas but in things"—it illuminates the material specificity of reading, of engaging with things—books— that have ideas in them. And given that the very act of reading seems to depend on a hermeneutic model of surface and depth, how can literary criticism resist this impulse to see into things, to scratch through the surface of them? Whenever Georges Poulet came upon a statue, he circled the object

FIGURE 1

Paul Strand, *Photograph* ("Abstraction–Bowls"). Printed in *Camera Work,*
December 1916.

in order to detect some interior, to find "the entrance to a secret chamber."[43] But that urge derived, he says, from the habit of reading—from the operation by which the reader delivers a book from its "materiality" and "immobility," and makes the "object qua object" disappear: "You are inside it; it is inside you; there is no longer either outside or inside" (56–57). Indeed, from his point of view, the "omnipotence of fiction" resides in the way reading overcomes the "incompatibility" between "consciousness and its objects" (58).

Benjamin makes a related point about reading in his Proustian meditation on "The Sock," where he describes himself as a child opening his chest of drawers to begin the adventure of reaching into the farthest corner for his socks, rolled up there "in a traditional way": "Nothing was more pleasurable than to sink my hand as deeply as possible into their insides. . . . It was 'the Possession' *(Das Mitgebrachte)* that I held always in the rolled-up interior in my hand, which drew me into their depths." But after he retrieves "the Possession" within the sock—the "soft, wooly mass"—and after he unwraps it from its woolen pouch, he is surprised to discover that the pouch has disappeared. "I could not do the test using this method often enough. It taught me that form and content, veil and veiled, are the same. It instructed me to pull truth cautiously from literature *(Dichtung)*."[44] All told, then, Poulet's assertion of fiction's power, like the moral of Benjamin's compulsively repeated experiment (his version of the *fort/da* game), imagines, deep within the surface/depth dichotomy, overcoming it. However intriguing the inside might be, a sophisticated intelligence will make it disappear.

If the idea of an object's spiritual insides seems so jejune, and if the idea of there being ideas in things seems illustrated most clearly by accounts of children, this may be because we come to learn that the very idea of things exerts what force it has only in opposition to the idea of images or of impressions or, above all, of ideas. "Things are what we encounter, ideas are what we project," as Leo Stein schematically put it.[45] How is it, then, that such a fantasy—of ideas in things—sustains one version of what we name American modernism?

The answer, of course, is that this literalization of Williams's creed violates his own poetic practice of rendering things—"a red wheel / barrow"—in their opacity, not their transparency. "No ideas but in things" should be read as a slip of the pen: a claim—on behalf of replacing abstractions with physical facts—that unwittingly invests objects with interiority, whereas Williams meant to evacuate objects of their insides and to arrest their doubleness, their vertiginous capacity to be both things and signs (symbols, metonyms, or metaphors) of something else. On the one hand, that slip may be read as a mark of the limitation of language, for how else could one put the matter—"no ideas but in things"—so epigrammatically? On the other hand, it may be read as the mark of a limit within modernism's effort to accept opacity, to satisfy itself with mere surfaces. In his essay on "Things" (1916), Max Weber, for instance, claimed that "culture will come when every man will know how to address himself to the inanimate simple things of life. A pot, a cup, a piece of calico, a chair, . . . " But he goes on to argue that "culture will come when people touch things with love and see them with a penetrating eye," and he concludes by insisting that "it is only through things that one discerns himself."[46] What first reads like the effort to accept things in their physical quiddity becomes the effort to penetrate them, to see through them, and to find . . . within an object . . . the subject.

It is at—or *in*—this limit where modernism, whatever its intentions, can help to focus attention not just on things as such, but on the place things occupy in daily life; the place they occupy, if you will, in the history of human-being; the pressure they exert on us to engage them as something other than mere surfaces. Imagined literally, this idea of the idea in things prompts questions that are inseparable from questions about the modern fate of the object in America, by which I mean both the history of production, distribution, and consumption, *and* the complex roles that objects have played in American lives. What desires did objects organize? What fantasies did they provoke? Through what economies were they assigned new value? Through what epistemologies were they assigned meaning? Today, how do we ask material objects to represent us, to comfort and help us, to change us? Today, do we collect things in order to keep the past proximate, to incorporate the past into our daily lives, or in order to make the past distant, to objectify it (as an idea in a thing) in the effort to arrest its spectral power? Today, why do you find yourself talking to things—your car, your computer, your refrigerator? Do you grant agency to inanimate objects because you want to unburden yourself of responsibility? Or because you need to mark how overwhelmed you are by your material environment? Or is it simply because you're lonely? Because, unlike a child, you don't have a toy to talk with?

Engaging as these questions are, and as much as they implicitly inform the following pages, this is not a book about how we occupy our contemporary material culture. And it is not a book about William Carlos Williams, about Imagism's "direct treatment of the 'thing,'" about Objectivism or modernism more broadly understood.[47] Rather, it takes what I understand to be a fundamentally modernist question (Williams's question, Léger's question, Heidegger's question, Sartre's question), the question of things and their thingness (variously understood), and it asks how a prior generation had begun to think some versions of the question, without ever explicitly appropriating thingness as a new status for the work of art, without participating in what would become art's drive to reify itself and thus to resist commodification.[48] The answers I propose are generated in readings of three novels from the mid 1890s: Frank Norris's *McTeague* (written in 1895, published in 1899); Sarah Orne Jewett's *The Country of the Pointed Firs* (composed of sketches that appeared in the *Atlantic* in 1896); and Henry James's *Spoils of Poynton* (serialized as *The Old Things* in the *Atlantic* that same year). They are answers that emerge within a story that is not modernism's story but the story of possessions and possession, which is nonetheless a story of isolating and cherishing certain objects within an evaluative context that is not the market-as-usual—the story of a kind of possession that is irreducible to ownership.

I frame these readings, in chapter 1, by trying to introduce a somewhat different account of the potency and "tyranny of things" in America, an account staged as mirror readings of Karl Marx and of Mark Twain: Marx writing about an apparently "trivial thing," the commodity, and Twain organizing the plot of *The Prince and the Pauper* around the disappearance of a very different "trivial thing," the monarch's Great Seal. I try to establish the basic stakes of asking about the role of objects in America in relation both to "commodity fetishism" and to what Léger would come to call "the *advent of the object*" (by which he meant the commercial world's new appreciation for, and production of, an aesthetics of the commodity).[49] But here, as elsewhere, I contend that the human interaction with the nonhuman world of objects, however mediated by the advance of consumer culture, must be recognized as irreducible to that culture. This is a book about something other than the "consuming vision," "the culture of consumption," the "fables of abundance," the "market" or "mass markets" that have come to dominate studies of the Gilded Age and the Progressive Era just as they dominated that age and era themselves.[50] It nonetheless concerns the slippage between *having* (possessing a particular object) and *being* (the identification of one's self with that object). It is a book about the indeterminate ontology where things seem slightly human and humans seem slightly thing-like. In other words, this is a book about humans and things that tracks the metamorphosis of the one into the other, but not a metamorphosis fully explained by the so-called reifying effects of a society permeated by the commodity form. Indeed, the doubleness of the commodity (its use value and exchange value) might be said to conceal a more fundamental difference, between the object and itself, or the object and the thing, on which the success of the commodity, the success of capitalism, depends. Put differently: value derives from the appropriation of a pre-existing surplus, the material object's own excessiveness.

If I end up providing a prehistory of the modernist fascination with things, this should be understood as something other than a coherent and continuous genealogy, something other than the link between, on the one hand, George Santayana's claim that the poet's art is "the art of intensifying emotions by assembling the scattered objects that naturally arouse them," and, on the other, T. S. Eliot's "objective correlative."[51] Still, this book can be read as an account of the twentieth century should we adopt Gertrude Stein's nationalized chronology: "The United States began a different phase when, after the Civil War, . . . they created the Twentieth Century." That creation had everything to do with material history, "the conception of assembling the whole thing out of its parts, the whole thing which made the Twentieth Century productive."[52] How do we explain how this long twentieth century moved away from Emerson's "evanescence and lubricity of all objects, which lets them slip through our fingers when we clutch hardest," and towards Williams's ideas in things?[53] From Whitman's account of the intimate proximity of things, wherein "the house chairs, the carpet, the bed and counterpane of the bed" are no less a part of you than the "pulses of your brain," to the insuperable distance between you and your physical environment?[54] From Poe's "Philosophy of Furniture" to Willa Cather's "Novel Démeublé"? Is there an afterlife to Thoreau's conviction that Americans should expropriate themselves of their possessions, or to his claim that things themselves write a history in "proof-sheets which need no correction"?[55] At times it seems that the physical object world, once breathtakingly legible, has become opaque; that man-made objects, once subordinate to nature, have come to transform the natural world; or that human possessions, once disclosing character, have been exorcised on behalf of character. Such transformations hardly add up to a single story of things in American literature. Yet I understand the novels I read in the following pages as windowsills on which to lean and to look out, to catch a glimpse of how the materialized world begins to shift.

After reading Twain's romance both as a response to anxieties provoked by his new house in Hartford and as an allegorical theorization of things in democracy, I examine three different literary registers—naturalism, regionalism, and realism—to determine, first off, how they dramatize the role of objects in American lives, and how they dramatize the role of humans in the life of American objects. The stage sets for those roles are built within the generic space established by Balzac, for whom, as James put it, the "mise-en-scène" is no less significant than an "event," and through whom the novel of contemporary life becomes inexorably associated with the "passion for *things*—for material objects, for furniture, upholstery, bricks and mortar."[56] And yet Norris seems to write with no faith in the reality-effect established by Balzac, and one of his obvious objectives is to work relentlessly at rendering human subjects and inanimate objects convincingly physical. Jewett works instead to render objects legible, showing how human history can be found within both human artifacts and the natural world. And James replaces the physical world with a psychological world while transposing thoughts into things, giving substance to thinking. To call Norris a materialist, Jewett a culturalist, and James a psychologist would be to grossly simplify their literary projects but also to begin to understand something of the relation between them.

Chapter 2 argues that the competing, incompatible, and excessive modes of repetition in *McTeague* result from a confusion of epistemology, phenomenology, and biology that prompts Norris (as it did much of pragmatism) to imagine that human subjects and nonhuman objects are what they are, and are knowable as what they are, from their habits. For all his attention to habit, Norris seems to lack anything like an understanding of custom, or culture, the intuitive grasp of which is precisely what the American regionalist shares with the folklorist and ethnologist of the 1890s, before "culture" attained its full anthropological theorization. Chapter 3 tracks the materialist epistemology of *The Country of the Pointed Firs* in relation to the object culture of the 1890s, but it also points to where Jewett stages the limits of the meaning of things. Just as Franz Boas abandoned museum work in 1907, unconvinced that the social and psychological aspects of culture could ever be rendered artifactual, so Jewett, for all her attention to meaningful objects, recognizes what they fail to disclose about the human condition. And, as I argue in chapter 4, James, seemingly caught up in a milieu where so much depends on things, works systematically to attenuate that milieu to the point where objects all but disappear, or where they circulate foremost as figures. The fire that concludes *The Spoils of Poynton*, consuming the things around which the plot has revolved, literalizes the Jamesian break with a realist tradition's representation of the physical object world, the break with Balzac. The fire allegorizes the consummation of realism as an avant-grade project of the sort that W. D. Howells spent much of his career defending. It is the fire that necessitates a new relation between the material world and the work of art—Imagism's "direct treatment of the thing," Cubism's *papier-collées*, Dada's *objet trouvé*, to take the most obvious examples.

The questions I pose in this book could be addressed through other texts, indeed somewhat more obvious texts (by Howells, Thedore Dreiser, and Edith Wharton, for instance), and the fate of the object could be tracked in many other media: photography and pre-classical cinema, trompe l'oeil still life, advertising, proto-mass production. But though I will address those media intermittently, my overall aim is to concentrate on literary texts precisely to determine what literature does with objects (or how literature produces its objects), for although I have learned a great deal from interdisciplinary approaches to culture, and though I'm as undisciplined as anyone in my engagement with other fields, this is meant to be a disciplined, self-disciplinary experiment in returning to some fundamental questions of literary form, questions about the rhetorical grammars on which these novelists depend. Norris strives to materialize the referent through repetition. The success of Jewett's fiction depends on metonymy, where human touch invariably leaves a legible trace, and on synecdoche, where an isolated object is meant to stand for the environment. And when James turns his full attention to things, in *The American Scene* (1907), he does so through an elaborate use of prosopopeia and the pathetic fallacy. Still, asking how literature represents objects—which is really, after all, the question that Auerbach asks of Homer, that Kenneth Burke asks of Keats, that Lukács, Barthes, and Jameson ask of Flaubert, and that Elaine Scarry asks of Hardy—tells us something both about literature and about objects, about the way objects and subjects animate one another.

The disciplinary juxtapositions that prompt portions of the book—literary naturalism and pragmatist philosophy, literary regionalism and museal anthropology, literary realism and interior design—are not meant to blur the difference between literary and non-literary discourse. Nor, however, do I imagine this difference to be one where the literary exposes the contradictions of bourgeois ideology, or a difference that composes a utopian alternative to the status quo because, say, of the text's inherent ambivalences and ambiguities. Instead, I am interested, for instance, in the way that objects become figures of thought and of speech, and in the way that narrative form reinvests the subject/object dialectic with its temporal dimension. That is why this is not a book about lyric poetry or about painting or about photography, but a book about narrative fiction. I recognize, nonetheless, that with one eye on the extraliterary referent, and one on the text, I mean to effect something like a stereoscopic effect, wherein our knowledge about how human subjects interact with material objects assumes a different dimension.

In a previous book, *The Material Unconscious: American Amusement, Stephen Crane, and the Economies of Play,* I tried to show how the material culture of the American 1890s impressed itself on the literary imagination, how it remains subliminally present no matter how underdetermined the apparent references to it. I tried to show how the material everyday—by which I meant the daily sensuous encounter with the physical world, from rollercoasters to freak shows, from Kodak cameras to toy stoves—had left textual residues that help us to reconstruct cultural history even as they test what we mean by "culture" and "history." In *A Sense of Things* I want rather to explore the imaginative technologies for lifting and redeeming that substratum. Thus, reading Twain, my concern is not with how the trivia of the era work their way into the rhetorical fabric of his fiction, but with how what gets termed a "trivial thing" (indeed, an absent thing) becomes monumental in *The Prince and the Pauper,* how it comes to disclose a kind of thingness that cannot be confused with physicality. The effort to redeem things results in a subjectification of objects that in turn results in a kind of objectification of subjects, which is why, arguably, James comes to abjure the idea of the precious object.

As a phrase, "a sense of things" can designate the sensation of thingness. It can also designate meaning, or the understanding (often the intuitive discernment) of an existing set of relations. ("So, do you have a sense of things?" "What's your sense of things?") It is the convergences of, or the disjunctures between, that sensation and that understanding (between the senses and our cognitive sense-making) that serve as the focal points of my reading. The question I am asking is no longer about an unconscious logic that can explain a peculiar, barely perceptible cultural reference. (The effort to explore the "unconscious" of a literary text is invariably an effort to discover the inside of the critically constituted object—that is, the exploration is the critic's extension of the child's quest to find ideas in things.)[57] It is more about the logic of reference as such within one period of literary history. What are the rhetorical strategies by which fiction works to convince us not just of the visual and tactile physicality of the world it depicts but also of that world's significance?

Though the literary criticism of the past decade has been newly attuned to image culture and the logics of vision, it has hardly begun to bring material culture into full view. (And though cultural studies has helped to put material culture on the critical map, it has generally done so when it relegates literature, or the literariness of the literary, to the periphery.) The criticism of the past decade has been profoundly successful in showing how literary texts exhibit multiple modes of fashioning the identity of subjects (national subjects, gendered subjects, hybrid subjects), but the identity of objects has hardly been voiced as a question. We might say, as has François Dagognet in his "eulogy of the object," that "we remain the prisoners of 'subjectivity.'"[58] Or, more theatrically, we might say, as has Jean Baudrillard, that the object, because it is considered "only the alienated, accursed part of the subject," has been rendered unintelligible, "shamed, obscene, passive."[59] But I mean to ask questions that are not quite Dagognet's or Baudrillard's questions: What are the poetics and the politics of the object? How do objects mediate relations between subjects, and how do subjects mediate the relation between objects? How are things and thingness used to think about the self? Epigrammatically: along with the subject matter of any novel there is its "object matter"—an understanding of the phenomenal object world through which human subjects circulate. Not to forestall doubts about how addressing such "object matter" might distract attention away from the ethical center of recent criticism, let me nonetheless recall Theodor Adorno's claim— made very late in his career, as yet another answer to Hegel and Heidegger, and in belated concert with Benjamin—that granting the physical world its alterity is the very basis for accepting otherness as such.[60]

This book is an experiment, then, to see what happens when we objectify literary texts so that they become for us objects of knowledge about physical objects. In this respect, I hope that a study with a very narrow historical focus will provide a much broader perspective on the "object matter" of American literature *tout court*. Asking what amounts to two rather simple questions—How are objects represented in this text? And how are they made to mean?—results in rather complex, partial, and provisional answers. I have been compelled when the answers, for predictable and not so predictable reasons, swerve off track; the experiment has been recast into essays that do not always maintain a focus on things, but that nonetheless show how the question of things has been integral to what the text at hand is trying to get said. Just as the child of Baudelaire's imagination expresses his first "metaphysical tendency" while playing with a toy, so too the texts I read, even while drawing attention to a particular object, can evoke the place that particular objects, like billiard balls and sealing wax, have had in Western philosophy. The critical recourse to things may seem like an effort to evade philosophy, but these novels adamantly make "things" not a solution to a problem, but a problem in their own right.

To understand these novels from the 1890s within a longer trajectory, I also locate their aspirations and inclinations between other models. Thus, for instance, I try to understand Norris's repetitiveness in relation to Stein's subsequent fixation on repetition as an impossibility (a variant of the point made by Friedrich Nietzsche, Marcel Proust, and Gilles Deleuze) that is nonetheless the only possible way of understanding identity. I locate Jewett's artifacts in relation to those objects in *Moby Dick* that have too little or too much meaning, and in relation to the role of artifacts in Cather's *The*

Professor's House, the status of things in Williams's poetry, and the sudden Melville revival in the 1920s. I think backwards from *The Spoils of Poynton* and *The Golden Bowl* to one of the great French novels of collecting, Balzac's *Cousin Pons,* and forwards toward Cather's effort to rid the novel of unnecessary bric-a-brac. In "The Novel Démeublé," she argued against the novelist as "interior decorator," against the way "the importance of material objects and their vivid presentation have been so stressed" in the novel.[61] "How wonderful it would be," Cather writes, seeking to purify modern fiction, "if we could throw all the furniture out of the window" (51). Instead of throwing it out, James, in *The Spoils of Poynton,* had already burned it up.

And yet, as I read *The American Scene* (1907) in a Coda, the exorcised physical object world returns in James, and it does so by being granted its own voice, a voice that declares the rights of things which are not (as they are in English law) the rights of subjects to their property, but rather the rights of buildings to house multiple generations, to remain durable despite the vicissitudes of human life. In his effort to show how modernism develops from the fin de siècle, Hugh Kenner centralized this autobiographical masterpiece as a forerunner of Williams's claim on behalf of things.[62] Seductive as Kenner's lead may be, I describe instead the discrepancy between *The American Scene* and Williams's modernism. For James prefigures instead a certain postmodern fate of the object, both the artistic reproduction of "objects as they're felt, not as they are," and a reconceptualization of the difference (or sameness) of human subjects and nonhuman objects.[63] The implicit point is to circle back to ask why literary critics, historians, and anthropologists might have turned their attention to things in the midst of the "abstraction [that] increasingly determines our lives"—an updated, intensified version of the abstractness said, by Simmel and others, to characterize modernity.[64]

I n response to Ken's admonishment—"'No ideas but in things' doesn't mean no ideas"—I remember lighting a cigarette, toying with the green plastic lighter and shoving it down inside the front pocket of my jeans, there with some change and a ring of keys. Within our rules of reference, the right sort of drag on a cigarette could register the right complexity of consent.

Already, whatever we were writing or trying to write, we had begun to inhabit a postmodernity that had too little sense of things. In fact, we found the idea of things hard to think about, let alone the idea of ideas in them. Already, the long twentieth century seemed almost over. Still, that drag was meant as a sign of vague agreement. Also, as a mark of follow-up questions to come.

The Tyranny of Things

Hamlet: *The king is a thing*—
Guildenstern: *A thing, my lord?*
Hamlet: *Of nothing.*
—William Shakespeare, *Hamlet* 4.2.27–29

There every thing is frozen—kings and *things*—formal,
but absolutely *frozen:* here it is *life.*
—P. T. Barnum, quoted in
the *Brooklyn Daily Eagle,* 1846

Should you begin to think about things in late nineteenth-century America, it won't be long before you stumble over Mark Twain's House in Hartford, Connecticut. It's a toe-stubber if there ever was one. Monumental and lavish, it was an architectural novelty (to some eyes, a nightmare) designed by Edward Tuckerman Potter in what you could call a German gothic style (fig. 2). The nineteen-room house became a local attraction even before its completion in 1874. That, obviously, was the idea—Twain's idea about stamping an indelible impression of his status as the nation's most widely read and best paid writer. As though performing a pastiche of the "conspicuous display" that Thorstein Veblen would describe in 1899, Twain bought the adjacent Hartford property in order to have the shrubs pruned, the trees felled, and thus his mansion properly viewed by the whole neighborhood. Ostentation, of course, was really his second career.

Within the house, as his biographers lament, Twain and his wife Olivia decorated and redecorated. In 1880, they installed the treasures they had amassed while touring Europe (six thousand dollars worth) as Twain gathered material to write *A Tramp Abroad* (1880), meant as a sequel to the lucrative *Innocents Abroad.* Among the treasures, Twain was especially taken by an enormous Venetian bed, carved mahogany, complete with serpentine columns and baroque *puti* (fig. 3).[1] The following year they hired Tiffany to renovate the interior: the Associated Artists painted the public rooms in salmon pink, peacock blue, and silver; they stenciled Native American, Turkish, and Chinese motifs onto the walls and ceilings; they draped the windows with imported muslin and velvet; they installed stained and leaded glass.[2] In the library—which Suzy and Clara used as a theater to perform

FIGURE 2
Mark Twain's house in a recent photograph, after the restoration. The Mark Twain
House, Hartford, CT.

The Prince and the Pauper, for instance, which Twain himself originally conceived as a play—the girls nightly begged their father to tell them stories about the objects arranged on the mantel. For the library was itself dedicated to theatricalizing those "things in the way of *bric-à-brac*" that Clarence Chatham Cook had recommended in his guide to modern decorating, *The House Beautiful: Essays on Beds and Tables, Stools and Candlesticks* (1878).[3]

Whatever pleasure Twain took in the objects, though, and whatever pleasure the girls took in the stories emanating from them, he was patently ambivalent about the decorating aspiration *tout court*. He mercilessly caricatured Cook's apostles in the House Beautiful section (chapter 38) of *Life on the Mississippi* (1883).[4] And his letters express frustration and exhaustion with the very projects that enthralled him. During the Tiffany remodeling, he declared the need not for carpenters and decorators but for "an incendiary": "If the house would only burn down, we would pack up the cubs and fly to . . . the crater of Haleakala and get a good rest." Especially alarmed by the strain of the house on Olivia—"I think my wife would be twice as strong

22

FIGURE 3

Twain at work in the Venetian bed (moved to his home on Fifth Avenue), 1906.
Printed as a frontispiece in *Mark Twain's Autobiography*, vol. 1.

as she is, but for this wearing and wearying slavery of house-keeping"—he thought of himself, too, as hideously bound by "house-keeping slavery," from which he could only imagine the "wild independence" he might achieve by living in a boarding house.[5]

Twain seemed to suffer from what one commentator called, in the pages of the *Atlantic*, a new national pathology, "The Tyranny of Things": the "passion for accumulation is upon us," the author proclaimed; we "make 'collections,' we fill our rooms, our walls, our tables, our desks, with things, things, things." The inevitable result of this passion—which for subsequent generations has seemed the quintessence of so-called Victorian taste—was that Americans ended up "overwhelmed by the invading host of things."[6] Alexis de Tocqueville had once worried that "democratic liberty" would become "democratic tyranny," by which he meant the tyranny of the majority or the tyranny of a despot; by the middle of the century, Emerson foresaw a "fearful extent and multitude of objects," intensified by both the production of new objects and the new proto-mass production of objects; by the century's turn, those objects themselves seemed to tyrannize the subjects of democracy.[7] The problem was not simply that, as Charlotte Perkins Gilman put it, the American woman, "debarred from any free production," had become "the priestess of the temple of consumption, as the limitless demander of things."[8] Everywhere, Thoreau would have found that man he had denounced: the man "harnessed" by the "trumpery which has accumulated from long housekeeping, which he has not the courage to burn," the men who haven't considered "what a house is" and spend their lives being "needlessly poor" to impress their neighbors.[9] For Twain, the harness was tightened by financial pressure; in 1891, the combination of slack book sales (by his standard) and mounting debt forced him to close the house and to go on an extended speaking tour. Still, in the spare Villa Viviani (outside Florence), he came to mourn the loss of the "objects without number" that made "the American house . . . the most satisfying refuge yet invented."[10] Clearly, those objects were for Twain objects of fascination and repulsion, modes of self-definition and self-obliteration, sources of safety and threat.

Where in Twain's writing do we stumble across a sense of things that can help to explain his ambivalence and the source of such tyranny? Not, I think, in the culture of consumption and speculation that he and Charles Dudley Warner satirized and irrevocably named in *The Gilded Age* (1873). And not in the satirical accounts of décor in the European travel books, in *The Adventures of Huckleberry Finn* (1885), or in *Life on the Mississippi*. Rather, it is in the royal court of *The Prince and the Pauper* (1881) where Twain strives to imagine, within history but also (as it were) beyond history, one dialectic by which human subjects and inanimate objects may be said to constitute one another. He dislodges the question of things—the status of things and the value of things and the meaning of things—from the "tyranny of things" in America, even as he discloses a tyranny of the Thing that helps to explain both the power of monarchy and the problems of democracy. Twain wrote his first notes for *The Prince and the Pauper* in 1877; he was interrupted by the European tour and his enraging struggle to complete a *Tramp Abroad*. When he returned to *The Prince* in 1880, he did so jubilantly, and when he finished the novel in 1881, in the midst of the decorating nightmare, it remained a source of intense pleasure. That pleasure derived, I want to speculate, from his exquisitely perverse exposition of how an object's capacity to materialize identity remains contingent beyond the bounds of democracy and its consumer culture.

Twain thought of his house as "not unsentient matter."[11] If it thus makes some sense to say, casually, that he fetishized his Hartford house, projecting onto it a life of its own, nonetheless his inexorable preoccupation can hardly be explained by "commodity fetishism" as Marx defined it, or by the "consuming visions," the "culture of consumption," or the "fable of abundance" that historians see emerging in the U.S. around 1880.[12] Still, to establish the stakes of *The Prince and the Pauper* as I understand them, I want to address that fetishism and that culture. I also want to juxtapose a reading of Marx on the commodity with a reading of Twain's romance to portray them as rival yet twinned efforts to explain the tyranny of a "trivial thing."[13] The juxtaposition is meant to exhibit something about both the subjects and the objects of American democracy. But I am especially interested in how Mark Twain shares with Karl Marx a logical, structural understanding of this tyranny, and how the "trivial thing" lurking in Twain's most widely read and least studied romance is explicable neither by the "object lessons" *in* the period nor cultural histories *of* the period, neither by the paradigms of consumption provided by novelists like Zola and Dreiser nor by historical accounts of consumerism.

Fetishisms

To gather some sense of these things, you could begin with George Santayana's *The Sense of Beauty* (1896), for Santayana's understanding of aesthetic value, and of the fetish character of the work of art, helps to clarify what Marx does not and cannot say in his theory of commodity fetishism, where "an extremely obvious, trivial thing" famously turns out to abound in "metaphysical subtleties and theological niceties" (1:163). Santayana did not share William James's antipathy toward the "grotesque stuff called Aesthetics in the systems of German philosophers, from Baumgarten and Kant downwards."[14] But *The Sense of Beauty* is nonetheless clearly, if unexplicitly, written as an interruption of the *Third Critique*. To begin with, Santayana refuses to believe that our appreciation of beauty is, unlike pleasure, disinterested—an idea which could "seem[ ] satisfactory only to the least aesthetic minds."[15] For we might simply say that all pleasure is disinterested, being an end in itself, if we don't also insist that aesthetic pleasures are indeed interested because the beautiful object is coveted, as a presence if not as a possession. Such a formulation shows how quietly yet tenaciously Santayana returns the object to aesthetics, from which, according to one reading of Kant, it had been summarily exorcised.[16] Whether or not one concurs with Santayana's fundamental definition—"Beauty is pleasure regarded as the quality of a thing" (39)—it is clear that he means to contest the *Third Critique* with a basic psychological observation (initially shared by Kant yet argued beyond): "an element of sensation" is transformed "into the quality of a thing" (35). Thus beauty, in Santayana's reformulation, "is constituted by the objectification of pleasure. It is pleasure objectified" (41). In his effort to retrieve aesthetics as the study of sensation and perception, he describes beauty as reified pleasure, emphasizing less the quality of the feeling, more the quality (the thingness) of its apparent source.

Although his argument does not wholly square with the basic doctrine of physiological aesthetics—that the sense of beauty has a "purely physiological origin"—his emphasis on sensation and pleasure does away with the idea that judgment plays any role in aesthetic perception.[17] For although the assessment of beauty may be made with the conviction of its universal validity, that conviction, in Santayana's view, is meaningless; it can only mean that someone with the same senses, "associations and dispositions" would produce a comparable assessment. In sum, "the frailty and superficiality of our own judgements cannot brook contradiction" (33, 34); like any value, aesthetic value is contingent. Whereas, when it comes to calling something beautiful, Kant argues that a man "judges not merely for himself, but for all men, and then speaks of beauty as if it were a property of things" (52), Santayana argues that it is because he considers beauty a property of things that a man speaks of judging for all men: "If we say that other men should see the beauties we see, it is because we think those beauties *are in the object*, like its colour, proportion, or size" (35). Santayana wants to extend Humean epistemology, declaring that our experience of beauty resides in perception and thus cannot be separated from the apperceptive act by which the "chaos of impressions [is] framed [into] the world of conventional and recognizable objects" (36). Emotions, no less than impressions of sense, can be objectified; they can be experienced as objects.

The unreasonableness of such a claim is very much to the point, for beauty, Santayana argues, is "a species of value" that, like all other values, derives from the "irrational part of our nature" (17). And this is why he finally takes recourse in an analogy to the "primitive and inexperienced consciousness" that peoples the world with its projected "terrors and passions" (37). Beauty is a projected value, phantasmatically experienced as integral to the perceived object. Insofar as the experience of beauty is "the survival of a tendency originally universal to make every effect of a thing upon us a constituent of its conceived nature," the study of aesthetics, rather than following Kant's rationalization, must engage the "animistic and mythological habit of thought" (37–38, 37).

Such habits of thought supplied Marx with his analogy for the fantasy of autonomous value. Marx, too, was (debatably) making a psychological point about the human perception of value—though not about perception, not about sensation. In *Capital,* however aesthetically ambitious his account of the commodity may be, the aesthetics of the commodity itself are utterly beside the point. Nothing would have seemed so perverse to Santayana, who proclaims all value to be fundamentally aesthetic and begins his "outline of aesthetic theory" by pointing to the aesthetics of the everyday, the way we live our daily lives through our "aesthetic senses" (3). These are the senses that play no part in Marx's account of commodity fetishism.

Or almost no part. For within the famous opening chapter of *Capital* it is hard not to sense an especially poignant contradiction. Marx's vivid portrayal of the commodity's vivacity—the imagery with which he portrays the commodified object-come-to-life—does not quite square with his theoretical presentation of the commodity's fetishization. His explanation of the commodity's structure, its bifurcation into use-value and exchange-value, makes it clear that the phantasmatic social life of things depends on their abstraction—more precisely, on their abstractability, their fungibility, their capacity to have a relation to each other that is mediated by the abstracting measure of value. And yet, at the very outset of his account of the fetishism of the commodity, explaining how a material object "transcends sensuousness" once it appears as a commodity, Marx provides a surreal image of a table that by no means etherializes the object. This table, when understood as an object of use, is "wood, an ordinary, sensuous thing," and it becomes, when it "emerges as a commodity," something else: "It not only stands with its feet on the ground, but, in relation to all other commodities, it stands on its head, and evolves out of its wooden brain grotesque ideas, far more wonderful than if it were to begin dancing of its own free will" (1:163–64).[18] What I want to mark as a contradiction—or, more fairly, a productive antinomy—is the way that the table, despite its transformation, retains much of its material form and force: its brain is wooden, it comes to life acrobatically, its very ideas (call them the ideas in things) are understood in relation to physical recreation. This is Marx's way of representing a metaphysical condition as a physical event.

In contrast, at the close of his account of fetishism, Marx's more famous commodities that speak seem to illustrate—precisely because they are disembodied voices of apparently generic commodities—the very abstractness about which they speak, which is their lively relation to one another "merely as exchange-values" (1:177). The unruly table seems the more unruly because of its unwillingness to abandon its physicality. Perhaps the table alone exemplifies the contradictory doubleness of commodities as such, their materiality and immateriality both, their status as "sensuous things which are at the same time suprasensible" (1:165). And yet the point about commodity *fetishism* is that the commodity-form has "absolutely no connection with the physical nature of the commodity and the material *[dinglich]* relations arising out of this" (1:165). In other words, whereas the commodity as such is characterized by a kind of doubleness, the fetishism of commodities (their animation into autonomy) amounts to the eradication of this doubleness; it arises from the singleness of value, from the assumption that value inheres in objects irrespective of their relation to human history. If, then, the deranged table violates the very dynamic it is meant to illustrate, how should we account for this violation? What sort of sense can we make of this surreal supplement?

Does this table linger as a prop in a theoretical scene where it does not belong because its animation evokes the kind of aesthetic fascination that Marx never mentions explicitly, however much such fascination has become part of the accounts of fetishism within various strains of Marxist and post-Marxist thought (and thus to have become, retrospectively and phantasmatically, part of the original account)? The scene itself, of course, is prompted by Marx's momentous and far from intuitive decision to begin his multivolume history and theory of the capitalist system with the commodity. (In 1844, he had begun, in the *Economic and Philosophical Manuscripts*, with "alienated labor"; in 1848, he had begun, in the *Manifesto of the Communist Party*, with the class conflict between the bourgeoisie and proletariat; in 1857 he had begun, in the *Grundrisse*, with production. The story of Capital can be told from many points of origin. There are many possible points of access into its mystery.) Does the wealth of capitalist society really appear as an "'immense collection of commodities'" (as he states in 1867, at the outset of *Capital*) (1:125)?[19] To begin *in medias res*, rather than to begin with the evolution of capitalism, is one sort of challenge; to begin *in medias res*, in the midst of *things*, is quite another.

The rhetorical power of this uninevitability lies in Marx's capacity to read the whole system of capitalism out of the structure of the commodity—which means to write the whole of *Capital* as a reading of this structure. To the degree that he is able to elaborate the system by concentrating on the structure he can also justify his decision to begin with the commodity, a starting point that gradually achieves what we might call an inevitability-effect. Marx presents *Capital* as a hermeneutic enterprise: an extended interpretation of one structural fact, the fact that the commodity is both a thing and not a thing at all, "its sensuous characteristics . . . extinguished" (1:128). Value turns "every product of labour into a social hieroglyphic" that, once genuinely deciphered, turns out to be the value of congealed labor (1:167).[20] The rhetorical force of the declared and richly described mystery lies in its capacity to convince us that there is truth—the whole truth of Capital understood as a system—lurking at the bottom of the mystery, lingering there, right there in the commodity.

This mystery story, predicated on the difference between the commodity's apparent and actual source of value, never begins to address the mystery of consumer desire, without which capitalism (in any of its stages) cannot be sustained.[21] Marx's story of the linen and the coat, the account of how amounts of coffee, corn, gold, and iron can be related to linen as a general form of value—these serve to explain how objects become generally exchangeable, how they are fungible, in relation to one another. As objects they could not be more banal; Marx even makes gold uninteresting. (What is "dazzling" is the money *form*.) Within his opening chapter, only the unruly table can be said to captivate our pictorial imagination, and indeed to frustrate that imagination as we try to picture a table not upside down but, rather, standing on its head. Only the table emerges out of the first chapter of *Capital* as an object worth imagining or an object worth having, as an object personified while remaining very much an object. It is the moment where Marx intimates not the fetishism he theorizes but the more pedestrian, not to say less powerful, fetishism through which objects captivate us, fascinate us, compel us to have a relation to them, which seems to have little to do with their relation to other commodities. This is a social relation neither between men nor between things, but something like a social relation between human subject and inanimate object, wherein modernity's ontological distinction between human beings and nonhumans makes no sense. This relation, hardly describable in the context of use or exchange, can be overwhelmingly aesthetic, deeply affective—it involves desire, pleasure, frustration, a kind of pain. Among the many profundities in the first chapter of *Capital*, the profundity of Marx's capacity to illustrate something in excess of his structural point attests both to a residual humanism of *Capital* and to the text's, if not the author's, recognition that a human fascination with objects subtends the resplendent success of the commodity form.

Object Lessons

Within this recognition—call it the recognition of bourgeois experience lived in the physical world—lies the alternative fate of "commodity fetishism" as a concept, which you can track most readily by juxtaposing Lukács's exposition and elaboration of commodity fetishism in *History and Class Consciousness* with Benjamin's catachretical (though hardly casual) use of the concept in the published portion of his *Passagenwerk*, "Paris, Capital of the Nineteenth Century." Invoking and extending Marx's claim that "the solution to the riddle of commodity-*structure*" illuminates capitalism in its totality, Lukács insists that this structure can be made to "yield a model" of all the objective and subjective forms of bourgeois society because the "fetish character of commodities" ramifies in both the objective and subjective registers.[22] The requisite abstraction of the object, from which Marx derived abstract labor, eventuates in a culture of rationalization and calculability that "conceals above all the immediate—qualitative and material—character of things as things" (92). Lukács never discloses this character of things as things because, let us say, the commodity understood as structure necessitates no attention to the physical object world at hand, no empirical attention to the world of consumer culture.[23]

In contrast, Benjamin cites Marx's notion of fetishism in the midst of his analytical collage of historical events, quotations, and institutions of lived life. When he writes that "world exhibitions are the sites of pilgrimages to the commodity fetish," he confuses (or conflates) commodity fetishism with a scene of seeing, returning the question of value to the aesthetics of the everyday, thus making a muck of Marx. He quotes Taine in the subsequent sentence: "Europe is off to *view* the merchandise" (my emphasis).[24] Benjamin clearly means to repeat the truth of the first chapter of *Capital:* "World exhibitions glorify the exchange value of the commodity. They create a framework in which its use value recedes into the background" (7). But he does so imagining that the institutional frame, the display strategies of the exhibition, effect this eclipse, rather than the fact of exchange as such.[25] As strenuously as Benjamin invokes Marx, his doing so could be understood as a compensation for having abandoned the theoretical foundation of *Capital*'s first chapter while preserving its dominant trope.

For an analogy to this "enthronement of the commodity," Benjamin turns to Grandville's caricatures, asserting that his "ingenuity in representing inanimate objects corresponds to what Marx called the 'theological niceties' of the commodity" (7). The magic of the commodity object here derives not, as in Marx, from its phantasmatically autonomous value but from its presentation, which Grandville's art shares with the world of advertising. This a world where "commodity fetishism" names an erotic fascination with the material object world, the "sex appeal of the inorganic" (8). It would be fruitless to say that Freud's fetishism displaces Marx's in this description (fruitless because the erotic investment in the object is understood according to no logic of compensation). It is nonetheless crucial to say that, despite the invocation of Marx, fetishism has become here a fascination with objects—the very fascination that is utterly absent from Lukács's account of fetishism, and that lingers in *Capital* only in the surreal supplement of the table-come-to-life. In more general terms, fetishism has ceased to name an economic relation and has come to name a psychological one, or an aesthetic relation, in Santayana's sense.[26] Benjamin's appropriation of Marx, which serves here to mark a long history of such appropriation, misrepresents Marx because it seems to insist on understanding our desire for objects as more primary than understanding the structure through which they become commodities.

Insofar, then, as accounts of commodity fetishism describe an aesthetic fascination with objects—the projection of an aesthetic value considered to be the property of a thing—they depart from Marx's theory. But such a departure has become second nature in literary and cultural studies no doubt because those institutions of a rapidly developing consumer culture (developing rapidly even as Marx wrote) have made the human fascination with objects seem the more pressing object of our historical attention. Indeed, it is hardly possible to think seriously about material objects in the closing decades of the nineteenth century without beginning to think about the department store, where people were meant to circulate through a newly theatricalized world of goods, where anyone was welcome to merely browse, where the management's idea was not simply to sell merchandise but also to inculcate desire. By establishing fixed prices, the department store eliminated the human interaction of bargaining, and restricted the act of consumption to a relation between the consumer and the merchandise.[27] In such theaters, objects assumed lives of their own, magically made animate not because of their status as autonomous and abstract values, but because of their sensuous appeal.[28]

The first novelistic treatment of the department store, Zola's *Au Bonheur des Dames* (1883), makes much of the animation of goods, but only after introducing the reader to the novelty of the drama by narrating the responses of provincial visitors to the new *grands magasins* of Paris. Descriptions of the vast plate-glass display windows, focalized through the eyes of the "captivated" visitor, assume something of the status of narration because we are meant to imagine the onlookers' aesthetic attention intensifying as it moves from object to object. The "enormous place" makes Denise Baudu's "heart swell, and [keeps] her excited, interested, and oblivious of everything else."[29] As Kristin Ross has put it, this is an erotically charged novel where the charge activates the relation between people and what she calls the "fetishes of retailing."[30] Instead of reading for the plot, one reads for the next description; and the plot itself pits one store against others—it is a drama of institutions, the story of the war between the emerging giant conglomerate and small commerce, the *grand magasin* and the shop, between commercial scenes that assume the role of protagonists.

Before the institutions as such seem to assume lives of their own, the goods within them become animate. Sitting by the door of an old-fashioned shop, Denise Baudu remains fascinated by the "great shop" across the street and the crowd gathered there, "groups of women pushing and squeezing, devouring the finery with longing, covetous eyes. And the stuffs became animated in this passionate atmosphere. . . . [T]he cloaks threw out their folds over the dummies, which assumed a soul, and the great velvet mantle, particularly, expanded, supple and warm, as if on real fleshy shoulders, with a heaving of the bosom and a trembling of the hips" (16–17). The "furnace-like glow which the house exhaled," coupled with the roar of "the machine at work" (17), establishes the *grand magasin* as an institution where consumption has become characterized by all the energy once associated with production. In this shopping frenzy, as we would now call it, the mannequins and the merchandise achieve their vitality because of the ardor of the shoppers. Decidedly a scene where commodities come to life, it is neither a scene that illustrates Marx's economic point nor a scene that Marx can help to clarify. Rather, the scene depicts a consumer culture where objects thrive on the passions of the patrons.

Au Bonheur des Dames was the first of Zola's novels to be translated into English, the same year it was serialized in France. In the U.S., the department store emerged in the 1880s as a novelty comparable to the *grand magasin* of the 1850s, allowing reviewers to explain that "the 'Bonheur des Dames' was an immense shop in Paris, like Jordan, Marsh, & Co.'s in Boston, or Macy's in New York, where everything is on sale."[31] The novel was read widely while being criticized with disgust by the literary establishment.[32] Theodore Dreiser had not yet read Zola in 1898, despite the latter's notoriety, but when he sat down to write his novel about Carrie Meeber, the country girl come to the city of Chicago, he in many ways rewrote the story of Denise Baudu's confrontation with the new retail establishment. He made Carrie a more pitifully impoverished character at the outset of the novel and he never indulged in the sort of moralism (unacknowledged by the U.S. critics) that prompted Zola to reward his virtuous heroine. The "victim of the city's hypnotic influence, the subject of the mesmeric operations of super-intelligible forces," Carrie is mesmerized foremost by the retail world of the city, overcome by the merchandise displayed in the department store where she has come not to shop but to look for work: "Carrie passed along the busy aisles, much affected by the remarkable displays of trinkets, dress goods, shoes, stationery, jewelry. . . . She could not help feeling the claim of each trinket and valuable upon her personally. . . . The dainty slippers and stockings, the delicately frilled skirts and petticoats, the laces, ribbons, air-combs, purses, all touched her with individual desire."[33] The power of Dreiser's description lies in the way that "individual desire" can be understood here as the claim that each individuated object has on Carrie, and the way that such claims seem to individuate her.

Despite the absence of the sort of crowd that invigorates the *grand magasin* for Denise Baudu, for Carrie Meeber retail objects are no less animate— precisely because they are the source of her own animation.[34] More so than Benjamin's account of the world exposition, then, these iconic novels highlight the institutional grounds on which (in which) objects assume lives of their own, captivating humans with the mesmeric power of their aesthetic value.[35] In contrast to an existentialism (extending from the early Marx to Arendt) wherein the human subject constitutes itself in an act of externalization that transforms the material world (an act of making things), Dreiser fashions subjects who externalize themselves with the act of buying things.[36] Carrie lives in the world charted by the new American theorists of consumption, most famously Simon Patten. In *The New Basis of Civilization* (1907), he explains that "the working-man's home is crowded with tawdry, unmeaning, and useless objects; each pointless ornament is loved, however, as the mark of superiority and success, and its enjoyment energizes the possessor."[37] It is not the production of objects, but their accumulation and display, that generates the feeling of success and the feel of identity.

However overwhelmed Carrie Meeber may seem to be by her first urban encounter with retail goods, she gains sufficient knowledge of objects, and sufficient energy from them, to give her story the trajectory of success. And indeed, the department store in America presented itself not just as a place to buy objects but also as an educational institution in which to learn about them. This is why Neil Harris can figure the department stores, along with the expositions and the new museums, as a "triptych" meant to teach Americans about "art and style in objects."[38] In Chicago, the organizers of the Columbian Exposition counted almost twenty-seven million visits (many of which were second visits), and Paul Bourget described fairgoers as proceeding through the exhibition halls with "a sort of blank avidity, as if they were walking in the midst of a colossal lesson in things."[39] Exhibitors at the fair, along with curators across the country, thought of themselves as offering "object lessons"—one of the great clichés of the Progressive era. The "object lesson" signaled a new investment in material (as opposed to textual, cerebral, or spiritual) education. It was no less a part of John Dewey's pedagogical philosophy or of Frank Lloyd Wright's aesthetics than it was of the *Ladies' Home Journal*'s effort to inculcate good taste in the home.[40] The idea was to teach more (about the civilizations of the past, about foreign countries, about science, about forms) *through* objects, and also to learn more *about* objects.[41]

This new will-to-knowledge was not simply an effort to exert control over people. It was also an effort to exert some control over the physical world at a moment when that world was decidedly changing in the U.S., changing not least because of the sheer proliferation of things. The typical list of inventions and discoveries that had become practical by the closing decade of the century included not just the telephone, the phonograph, the typewriter, the fountain pen, and electric lights, but also aluminum and magnesium, vulcanized rubber and Bessemer steel, hydraulic elevators and cantilever bridges.[42] By 1880, Singer was producing 500,000 sewing machines a year, and the Census Office published a separate and elaborate volume on manufactures.[43] Although the Weed Sewing Machine Company, by producing 14,000 bicycles annually, completely commanded the field in 1881, by the mid 1890s, after the invention of the electric welder and the introduction of the safety bicycle, the industry as a whole enjoyed yearly sales of more than a million bicycles.[44] Moreover, a new visual culture, precipitated by new reduplication techniques, enabled advertisers to turn such media as magazines, art posters, and billboards into a mode of overwhelming people with the latest consumer goods. Stephen Crane reported in 1896 that New York's Western Boulevard had been subjugated not just by bicyclers but also by the billboards advertising "wheels and lamps and tires and patent saddles with all

FIGURE 4
"The Giant Glass Industry." *Scientific American*, April 1909.

the flaming vehemence of circus art."[45] In 1909, illustrating "The Giant
Glass Industry," the cover of *Scientific American* unwittingly offered a comparable image of the surreal enormity of quotidian objects (see fig. 4). Milk
bottles and canisters have become monumental—to the point of containing
the monuments and skyscrapers of the city itself.[46] The "object lessons"
might thus be thought of as efforts to treat the "hyperaesthesia" that Simmel
understood as the pathological condition of modernity—"the fear of coming into too close a contact with objects."[47]

Even as the rhetoric of "object lessons" helped museums and expositions to understand and portray their role as one of offering the right kind of education "for a society in transition from a spiritual to a material age and from a producer to a consumer society," as Simon Bronner has put it,[48] so too the display of objects physically and conceptually organized, just as it distanced, a world of things that was becoming oppressively omnipresent, chaotic, and proximate. But if such a culturalist account of objects in America serves to extend the "surreal supplement" to Marx's account of commodity fetishism, it falls short of apprehending a politics of the object that Twain intimates when he turns his attention to a different historical moment in *The Prince and the Pauper.* Whereas Zola and Dreiser enable us to historicize the longing for objects within consumer cultures, Twain encourages us to imagine a longing that returns as the same in various scenes of history. Whether you wish to argue, on the one hand, that the problem with American culture was "not materialism, but the spread of indifference toward a material world where things were reduced to disposable commodities," or, on the other, that things changed "from objects of possession and envy into vehicles of community" because "communities" were produced and sustained "by their common use of objects so similar that they could not be distinguished even by their owners,"[49] you cannot in either case begin to explain the overwhelming power of things in America, or the sort of passion and repulsion that Twain had for the house that Twain built. *The Prince and the Pauper,* though (unlike *Au Bonheur des Dames* and *Sister Carrie,* and curiously like *Capital*), abandons aesthetics to focus on the structure of the "trivial thing," a structure that helps to account for the tyranny of everyday life in America, and the tyranny of life as such—that helps to explain why things become tyrannical.

A Trivial Thing

Just after exchanging his royal attire for the rags worn by his new acquaintance, Prince Edward "snatche[s] up and put[s] away an article of national importance," the identity of which the text does not disclose. The subsequent plot of *The Prince and the Pauper* hinges on the disappearance and reappearance of this article, a physical object—the monarch's Great Seal— that is no mere object: an implement that authorizes declaration to become action, and that stamps legislation into law. Irritable, sick, and soon to die, Henry VIII has sent the invaluable seal to the Prince of Wales, who sequesters it just before running out through the palace gates, momentarily freed from the shackles of royal life, imagining himself free to "revel in the mud once, just once," yet soon condemned to weeks of a pauper's degradation.[50] He has unwittingly left the urchin Tom in his place as prince, and left the court to face "the puzzle of the Great Seal," the article of national importance that no one in the palace can find (174).

For the court, the solution to this puzzle ultimately solves the more peculiar puzzle of the "marvelously twinned" boys, one of whom must be crowned the new king, Edward VI. As the novel comes to a close, Tom Candy, the "mock-king" splendidly dressed for his coronation, reunites with Edward, who has burst upon the coronation scene in Westminster Abbey "ill shod, and clothed in coarse plebian garments" (369). Together they struggle to convince the court of their true identities, but no amount of assertion will do, given that the court has long ago understood the false prince to be the true prince gone slightly mad. Even after listening to the genuine Prince Edward describe the public and private rooms of the palace as only the genuine prince could do, the Lord Protector nonetheless insists that the boy produce the object: "Where lieth the Great Seal? Answer me this truly, and the riddle is unriddled; for only he that was Prince of Wales *can* so answer! On so trivial a thing hang a throne and a dynasty" (372). Mark Twain prolongs the suspense of the inevitable resolution. For when the "trivial thing" is not in the secret compartment Edward describes, it is clear that the authentic Prince simply cannot recall what he has done with the seal, and indeed only the false Prince recollects the true hiding place for him: the arm-piece of a set of Milanese armor. Coaxing Edward to remember, Tom Candy plays something of the hypnotist, if not the modern psychoanalyst: "List to what I say—follow every word—I am going to bring that morning back again, every hap just as it happened . . . . Follow me still, you shall recall every thing" (377). As Twain put it in a letter to William Dean Howells, the "bogus King" must prove the "genuineness" of the true king "*for* him."[51]

The illogic of the riddle's proper solution—that is, of Edward's recollection not of "every thing," but of the crucial, trivial thing—is lost on the court. And only after the court has granted him his true identity does the Prince of Wales, soon to be crowned King of England, ask his companion the obvious question: "How was it you could remember where I hid the Seal when I could not remember it myself?" (380) How has the wrong boy had the right memory?[52] Unriddling this new riddle is far simpler. For the pauper in prince's clothing has always known *where* the seal is, without knowing *what* it is, having in fact used it to crack nuts. As the narrator earlier explains when the boy, unhappily passing as prince, faces questions about the seal's location, "a Great Seal was a something which he was totally unacquainted with" (174–75). The Great Seal has thus been both absent and present all along, present as a physical object to Tom, but absent to him as the culture's embodiment of monarchical authority.

Read as a moral allegory, "the stubborn mystery of the vanished Great Seal" (372) might seem to confirm the novel's lesson about identity: just as Tom doesn't recognize the identity of the object by its appearance, so too none of us can recognize the true identity of a person by their clothes and behavior. Rank appears as a social effect in the way that race appears as a social effect in *Pudd'nhead Wilson*. Thus Twain's point in this "tale for young people of all ages" may be, rather, that identity depends less on authorized value and function, more on recognition and use. Just as a book being used as a coaster becomes for that time more coaster than book (the physical thing is materialized as a coaster), so too the seal has become a kind of nutcracker. Different subjects materialize the physical object world differently. And thus the appropriate analogy may be that the human subject must produce the material object no less than subjects must produce their king; at the very least, it makes sense to say that just as a pauper understood by the court to be a prince becomes every inch a prince, so too a seal understood by a boy to be a nutcracker becomes every inch a nutcracker, and no more than that. Moreover, though Tom's admission about his misuse of the seal (call it his reproduction of the thing as some other object) provokes peals of laughter from the court, it is he who has discovered some use for an object that has in fact become obsolete: "its term of service," as Lord Hertford explains in the middle of the novel, "ended with our late lord's life" (174). Indeed it is Tom—unmoved because unaware of the object's extraordinary sign value, a sign of the monarchy and the monarch's very sign—who has managed to interact with the physical thing so as to determine its more immediate (that is, less mediated) value.

I don't mean to suppose that these observations and analogies pose, let alone answer, all the questions that *The Prince and the Pauper* raises about the status of this "trivial thing." I do suppose that these questions begin to dislodge the novel from the place it has occupied in Twain criticism, recognized foremost as a transitional text that marks Twain's effort to appeal to the more genteel Eastern establishment—his effort to change identities, as it were, from Western humorist to Eastern novelist, from irreverent rogue to polite romanticist. (The effort, as one reviewer put it, "to prove that the humorous story-teller and ingenious homely philosopher, Mark Twain, can be a literary purist" paid off: the book delighted readers and convinced them that Twain could in fact write "literature.")[53] Written between the publication of *The Adventures of Tom Sawyer* (1876) and *The Adventures of Huckleberry Finn* (1885), during the eight-year hiatus in the latter's composition, the novel relocates boyhood adventure outside the American nineteenth century (wherein Twain could not figure out what to do with Huck and Jim once they drifted past Cairo, Illinois). To write what he called his "historical tale," by which he meant a romance in the manner of Scott's *Ivanhoe,* Twain read both those texts that he ostentatiously cites in the footnotes (Hume's *History of England* and Timb's *Curiosities of London*), and he scoured Pepys's diaries, Scott's romances, and Shakespeare's plays for suitably archaic diction. This fascination with English history, already evident in *1601; or Conversation as It Was by the Social Fireside in the Time of the Tudors* (privately circulated in the summer of 1876), would find further outlet in the antics of the Duke and the Dauphin, and most extensively (and with the further help of Malory) in *Connecticut Yankee in King Arthur's Court* (1889). The charade of impersonation, which structures Twain's own character and career, would complicate the plot of *An American Claimant* (1891) and once again constitute a plot in *Pudd'nhead Wilson* (1894), where the passing narratives of "mysteriously twinned" characters are remapped onto the landscape of U.S. racial ideology.[54] However coherent a piece of the Twain canon *The Prince and the Pauper* thus seems to be, its perennial popularity has been matched by its critical marginality.[55] And yet, though Twain's recourse to historical fiction obviously allowed him to please the genteel readers of the East, it also allowed him to think about "things" beyond the general cultural milieu and the particular decorating farce in which he lived. Twain was so obsessed by objects—by the way their possession and display seemed to confer and sustain his identity as a rich and famous writer—that it is hardly surprising that *The Prince and the Pauper* addresses not only the subject's production of the object (seal or nutcracker), but also the object's production of the subject (prince or pauper). What seems surprising, though, is the extent to which this latter production has nothing to do with the aesthetic phenomenality of the object.

Twain understood himself to be inspired to complete the novel because he recognized the opportunity to expose the severity of Tudor punishments (witnessed by a horrified Edward, during his tenure as Tom, and thus inspiring the leniency of his subsequent reign as king). Despite the infatuation that Twain and England shared for one another during the 1870s, *The Prince and Pauper,* like *Joan of Arc* and *Connecticut Yankee,* was meant to document the dangers, disease, and drudgery of Medieval culture.[56] It was meant as a realist revision of the American Medievalism—expressed in the architecture of H. H. Richardson and Ralph Adams Cram, in books like Henry Adams's *Mont-Saint-Michel and Chartres* and Charles Eliot Norton's *Historical Studies of Church-Building in the Middle Ages*—for which feudal culture offered a spiritual antidote to the materialism of industrial America.[57] But beside this effort to write "a manual of republicanism," as Howells insightfully put it,

Twain was investigating a material antidote to materialism, one which exposed the contingency of monarchical power and the arbitrariness of hierarchy.

During the coronation crisis, the two boys and the court are locked in a moment of ritual without content (no identifiable future king), or, say, structure with too much substance (two future kings where there should be only one), an excess that threatens the coherence of the structure as such. The fact that the throne hangs on "so trivial a thing," as the Lord Protector puts it, suggests how arbitrary, how irrational if unconditional, is the differentiation of the doubles, one from another. As the Prince of Wales explains to his new acquaintance, "Thou hast the same hair, the same eyes, the same voice and manner, the same form and stature, the same form and countenance, that I bear. Fared we forth naked, there is none could say which was you, and which the Prince of Wales" (45). The "trivial thing" that differentiates the boys—that transforms their physical equality back into hierarchy—might thus be said to materialize the immaterial excess that differentiates a royal body from its brute physicality, the aura that is at once absent yet present: the royalty, phantasmatically transmitted by blood, that is in fact metaphysical, neither blood nor bone. That differentiation in turn guarantees the social order, the difference between plebian and lord, the difference not just between the "Prince of Poverty" and the "Prince of Limitless Plenty," but also between the awful court and the "Offal Court" (40, 43).

Plotting his novel, Twain had little room to maneuver: his book had to confirm the outcome of history, the reign of Edward VI. And yet, in the story he tells, the coronation crisis, which is a crisis of the very ritual and spectacle meant to secure and stage the monarch's charismatic power, appears as the moment when history might have taken a different turn, the moment before the absolute symmetry resolves itself into asymmetry, the moment when the members of the court become a crowd, when an instance of anarchy reveals the king to be subject to his subjects, his sovereignty an effect of the people's willingness (however unconscious) to grant him power:[58] "The whole assemblage was on its feet, now, and well nigh out of its mind with uneasiness, apprehension, and consuming excitement. On the floor and on the platform a deafening buzz of frantic conversation burst forth, and for some time nobody knew any thing or heard any thing or was interested in any thing but what his neighbor was shouting into his ear, or he was shouting into his neighbor's ear" (378). Of course what they are hearing about or talking about is not "any thing" (as Twain writes it), but a very specific thing, or let us say a specific cultural object that their vertiginous desire has turned into kind of a totem, into the Thing that transforms chaos into cosmos: it marks the difference between the two identical bodies and in that moment grants the king his double body, both secular and sacred, mortal and immortal, physical and symbolic, individual and collective.[59] Readers have hardly thought of Twain's novel as an engagement with Early Modern Thought. Nonetheless, his twins should be recognized, first off, as the literalization of the double body of the king, the status of the king as "Twin-born," as Shakespeare's Henry V puts it, as Richard II suffers it from first to last, unable to embody the doubleness of kingship.[60] (Formally comparable to the commodity, the king is both a thing and not a thing at all.) The great seal is the "trivial thing," the materialized surplus or supplement that eradicates one doubleness to guarantee the other, that resolves the literal into the figurative, and that thus preserves the symbolic and social order of the kingdom.

The plot of *The Prince and the Pauper*, coupled with its lexicon—the all but incantatory "every thing" and "any thing" that appear in the absence of the "trivial thing"—both prefigures and complicates more recent accounts of the social psychology of power, where, as in Jacques Lacan's reading of Hamlet or Slavoj Žižek's reading of Stalin, the "thing" becomes the "evasive body which is a 'thing of nothing,' a pure semblance without substance"—the thing that is in excess of the king's or the totalitarian's body, "the sublime object, the Thing within a body" that augments the empirical into the auratic.[61] But of course in *The Prince and the Pauper* this "evasive body" assumes substantial form as the Great Seal. And the seal itself might be said to exhibit the very doubleness that it marks and manages in the monarchy. For the "trivial thing" is in fact a sublime thing, irreducible to the physical object: it is at once physical and metaphysical, sensible and suprasensible, both object and thing. And though the king's death has rendered the seal impotent as his seal, the court's desire has in fact rendered it more powerful: no longer that which serves and represents the king, it now has the capacity to identify the king, to legitimate the king before his people.[62] Although the boys themselves could care less about the seal, and though both are completely comfortable with their sameness and their difference, the court submits to the object in its capacity to identify the subject (to whom they are subject). The object's unquestioned importance stabilizes the structure of meaning through which life is lived at court. And in this sense—a sense confirmed by the illogic of the riddle's solution—the seal is the "thing" whose substance is really beside the point, an evasive excess that is irreducible to any body. Indeed, it is not really fair to say that the seal materializes the "semblance without substance" because it remains so immaterial in the text—named but perpetually underdescribed (almost undescribed) in a novel where Twain devotes considerable attention to recreating historical scenes: the details of the court's splendor, the details of the squalor amid London's crooked streets. In fact, the seal is described only once, by Tom—described as a "massy golden disk" (376), as though unrepresentable in any particularity.

Although the novel was lavishly engraved with illustrations, which Twain considered crucial to the marketing of all his books sold through subscription, he hoped that this seal would remain unrepresented: it "wasn't to be engraved—old Brer Osgood [James R. Osgood, the publisher] forgot about that, I reckon. I'm afraid to put it in."[63] This wish to have the Great Seal remain out of sight is a recognition that the object's physical existence, its existence as a physical object, is really beside the point, both for his plot and the structure of authority that the seal guarantees. And yet there is a final irony to this story I'm trying to tell: the Great Seal of Henry VIII was not just engraved, against Twain's wishes; it also served as the frontispiece for the novel (fig. 5). Indeed, by simply reproducing an engraving from the *Pictorial History of England*, his illustrators made the object, so crucially absent or utterly blurred throughout the text, vividly present before the story ever begins, and present as though material history itself, the Great Seal itself, had insisted on stamping its authority, its physicality, on Twain's romance—had insisted on the power of the physical object, and that object's august indexicality, over and against the Thing. We could call this the return of the repressed material object. A more gothic (or appropriately romantic) way to make the point would be to suspect that it is precisely the sixteenth-century object, as Thing, that impressed its presence in the foreground of a book where it was not meant to appear at all.

How can this reading of the "trivial thing" in *The Prince and the Pauper* serve as a parable that helps us re-engage the "object matter" of literature and the cultural logic disclosed there? As in the case of Marx's commodity, the aesthetic perception of the "trivial thing" is utterly beside the point. The "mystery of the Great Seal" clearly dramatizes how an object that is neither a "primitive" fetish nor a modern commodity can have "metaphysical subtleties" that exceed its physical form—how it can become "something transcendent."[64] Which is not to repeat my point that Marx cannot account for all the ways that things come to life in consumer culture, but rather to suppose that Marx describes a doubleness that characterizes not just the commodity object, but inalienable objects as well. The aggression of capitalism lies not least in its ability to appropriate the doubleness of objects: to convert the thingness of the object (the Thing in excess of the object) into value.

FIGURE 5

The Great Seal of Henry VIII. Frontispiece for *The Prince and the Pauper: A Tale for Young People of All Ages* (Boston: James R. Osgood and Company, 1882). The image is a reproduction from George L. Craik, *The Pictorial History of England: Being a History of the People, as well as a History of the Kingdom* (1841–51).

Democratic Objects

Even though Twain helps us to perceive the doubled structure of an object beyond the historical bounds of Marx's analysis, the seal was not just an object of Twain's archaizing fancy. It was also a topic that continued to interest American law in the postbellum era, as it slowly determined that the *sigillum* need not be made in "wax" (generally resin).[65] By the 1890s, when signing had replaced sealing as the generalized mode of authentication, there was considerable discussion about how the "seal was looked upon with some such veneration as the heathen looked upon their idols."[66] An analysis of this institution of the state seemed to show, let us say, that it abounds in theological niceties. As the English press continued to describe it in 1882, the seal is "in effect an embodiment in a tangible form of very much of the regal power," so much so that it had enabled the chancellor under George III, Lord Eldon, to proclaim that, despite the king's personal insanity, "the legal and political sovereign was perfectly *compos mentis*, being the Great Seal."[67]

If in Twain's novel the seal differentiates one human from another, in English history the seal could not be differentiated from the king himself; if the king was a thing, he was a seal; in the absence of this thing, as Twain writes the story, the man is nothing. *This* "personification of things" exemplifies the inalienability of certain possessions, "imbued with the intrinsic and ineffable identities of their owners," that must not circulate and are not subject to exchange.[68] The substitutability of seal for sovereign, object for human, intensified the care with which the seal and signet were protected, for their fugitive circulation or unauthorized use (forgery) could (of course) upend affairs of state.[69] During Henry VIII's reign, in fact, the authority of the signet, which had become "the *primum mobile* of government," authorizing the use of the great seal, was replaced by the sign manual (the royal signature); but even the king's signature became alienable: always aggravated by the task of signing, in his infirm old age Henry deployed a dry stamp (which left an impression that was traced in ink) and the stamp was entrusted to the keeper.[70] Hamlet can forge a commission by using his dead father's signet, and thus, as he explains to Horatio: "the Changeling [was] never known."[71] In Twain's counter-case, no apparatus has been falsely deployed to produce the changeling; rather, the changeling has misplaced the apparatus. And in its absence there can be neither authentic nor forged document, true or false monarch. Without a seal, the court can attain no satisfactory *impression* of just who the new king should be.

I put the matter this way to invoke something of the history of how the physical world has been figured as impressing itself on the human mind. Plato figures the mind as a wax tablet in the *Theaetetus,* and in *De Anima* Aristotle explains that the senses receive the form of matter without its substance in the same way that "wax receives the imprint of the signet-ring apart from the iron or gold of which it is made."[72] In *Rules for the Direction of Mind* (1628), Descartes insisted that his readers take such an analogy literally, for "sense-perception occurs in the same way in which wax takes on an impression from a seal."[73] Less literally, he imagines the transition from *res extensae* to *res cogitans,* the process whereby things become things of thought, as operating in accord with that metaphor. All this is to say only that "the mystery of the Great Seal" in *The Prince and the Pauper* should be read not just as a story about the Thing that confers identity and authority, but also as a story about a particular apparatus that came to metaphorize the human access to the physical world as such. Insofar as this apparatus is no more than a "massy gold disk," it is indeed missing.

It is already missing, of course, in Descartes's *Meditations,* which retains one object, the wax, while giving up on the other and where the wax serves merely as an (unstable) object of perception (resting close to the fire). As Neil Hertz has put it, the wax has been demoted from being "a figure for knowing" to becoming a mere "occasion for knowing"; its epistemological and semiological authority has disappeared.[74] (It seems inevitable that Descartes, to reach his conclusion, would have posited as the exemplary external object the tablet of wax that Plato had used to figure the mind; palimpsestically, that is, he renders a scene by the fire where, at its outset, the mind contemplates the mind.) This is not just the story of the Mind's triumph over the Body; it is also the story of the triumph of the Subject at the expense of objects, a story still manifest in literary criticism and cultural theory.

In contrast, Twain writes his novel with no mention of the wax to be sealed—no figure of the subject, say—and with an elevation of the object, but on sociological not epistemological grounds: the boys know their difference from one another, but only the object can certify that knowledge for others. Twain's great story of the missing object—a story of the object missed—is a story that discloses a power of material objects (in their presence and in their absence) that commodification both banalizes and universalizes. In the story Twain tells about English monarchy, the missing Thing—the object that represents the unrepresentable foreignness that secures the function of the social—is finally found. In the story he doesn't tell about American democracy, some thing is always missing. As Claude Lefort tells this story, the prince within monarchy serves as the embodiment of power, but within democracy "the locus of power becomes *an empty place.*"[75] Democracy promises a world of undifferentiable subjects, a world in which everyone is "marvelously twinned," even as Capital promises a world of fungible objects (where seals, say, would be exchangeable for nut crackers). Thomas Paine, in response to Burke's reactionary account of the French Revolution, argued that a sign of monarchical authority like the Great Seal wasn't a thing, but a "*metaphor*"; in contrast, he argued that a "constitution is not a thing in name only, but in fact. It has not an ideal, but a real existence," a real existence because it could be infinitely reproduced and disseminated.[76] And yet the real existence of this thing hardly functioned to stabilize identities.

However vertiginous this world of shape-shifting may seem, it could also be understood, of course, as liberating. In an early essay on "The Scholastic and the Speculator" (1891), John Dewey, who never fell for American Medievalism, berates the Scholastic of the Middle Ages as the "miser of philosophy" who wished to keep Aristotle to himself. He then expands his "comparison of thinking with commerce," advocates the productivity of speculation over and against Medieval hoarding, and demonstrates how useful economic thought had become to thought itself. "Commerce" assumes the status of a master metaphor: "there is only one economy in the universe; and of this logic, political economy, and the movements of molecules are equally phases. All contact involves two parties; all contact means exchange, and all exchange is governed by the law of reciprocity, is commercial, whether it be exchange of thought with fact, or of cotton with shoes . . . . The due proportion of outgo and income is the problem of intelligence as of business life."[77] Dewey's essay has become a pivotal text for James Livingston in his effort to demonstrate the pragmatist reconceptualization of the subject. In alignment with a burgeoning corporate capitalism, a "credit economy," and the new marginalist economics (all forced to embrace contingent notions of value and to abandon traditional notions of signification), pragmatism imagined a post-Lockean subjectivity released from the confines of possessive individualism and the republican self.[78] Livingston abandons the lapsarian narratives of modernity that extend from Lewis Mumford to Leo Marx and Jackson Lears; he emphasizes the progressive creativity precipitated by corporate capitalism and its new consumer culture.[79]

When it comes to commodities themselves, and to the generalization of the commodity form, Livingston "think[s] John Dewey was correct to say that 'because we are such materialists,' we tend to focus our attention 'upon the rigid thing instead of upon the moving act.' We tend, in other words, to treat commodities as if they were external objects, not moments in a circuit of thoughts as well as things, of language as well as labor" (64). Livingston's other words, here, somewhat misconstrue Dewey's point, which is really that by attending to the act of trade rather than to the objects of trade we can perceive the way that "the comparison of thinking with commerce is no forced analogy" (151). In Livingston's argument, as in Dewey's, all objects become commodities—the specificity of shoes and cotton is beside the point—and all commodity objects are reduced to the commodity form. As in the subsequent history of advertising—where the actual object for sale disappears behind the style, the identity, being sold—concern for the subject all but eliminates the object.[80] Moreover, the distinction between "rigid thing" (or the "external object") and the "moving act" seems to entify or ossify the thing or object into an unproblematic materiality, as though its rigidity or thingness were not already the result of perceptual and cognitive acts, as though physical objects don't have metaphysical properties that have nothing to do with exchange, as though they were not already characterized by a doubleness granting them value in multiple registers, and as though the rigid thing had not long ago been discovered (by physics and chemistry, after all) to be anything but rigid. Both Dewey and Livingston thus describe and symptomatize a culture in which all things seem to have become (or must become) alienable, abstract, and homogenous: that is, a culture in which no physical object (a German gothic house, say) can grant its owner some sense of stable identity—a culture in which inalienable possessions, unexchangeable objects, have been discarded without a trace.[81]

The whole point of this "cultural revolution" is that it destabilizes the subject. Yet political scientists of the day understood this instability as a political fact, not an economic one. A champion of democracy, Daniel Thompson nonetheless recognized that "the abolition of monarchy" turned "humanity . . . into a mobile ocean of rolling and tumultuous waves."[82] Without the "stability" of "recognized status" and the "certainty" of the past's connection to the future, democratic subjects face "eternal contention [as] the price of security": "Nothing is attained, but one is always seeking."[83] More recently, Lefort, reading the original theorist of the democratic *form of society*, has underscored how the individualism described by Tocqueville perpetually fails to produce individuals. "The new assertion of singularity," writes Lefort, "fades in the face of the rule of anonymity; the assertion of difference (of belief, opinion, or morals) fades in the face of the rule of uniformity."[84]

What Tocqueville understood as the Cartesianism of democracy—its production of an aggressive will-to-autonomy—has now become understood as the abstract subject of democracy (which psychoanalysis also recognizes as its own).[85] What Twain's psychology helps us to recognize is how the accumulation of objects might be considered the (futile) effort to materialize that abstraction—to fill up that abstraction, as it were, with particular contents. "The House Beautiful" chapter of *Life on the Mississippi* registers that effort with a five-page catalogue of objects: "ingrain carpet; mahogany centre-table; lamp on it, with green-paper shade. . . . Other bric-a-brac . . . quartz, with gold wart adhering; old Guinea-gold locket, with circlet of ancestral hair in it; Indian arrow-heads of flint." Despite the hyperspecificity of the catalogue, these are simply the generic contents of the generic "residence of the principal citizen, all the way from the suburbs of New Orleans to the edge of St. Louis."[86] However passionate the particularity, it has no particularizing point. It is in fact Poe, writing in Tocqueville's era, who proclaimed in his "Philosophy of Furniture" that American taste alone is "preposterous" (in contrast to English, Dutch, Chinese, or Spanish taste) because we "have no aristocracy of blood," and substitute for it coarse efforts to mark "distinction."[87] Those efforts became more widespread when Americans began to concern themselves with "the democratization of desire," granting everyone (despite age, gender, or race) the right, if the not the means, to "wish for whatever they pleased."[88] This democratization of access (however unrealized), coupled with universal exchangeability, effects a democracy of objects. If everyone has the right (though not the means) to possess the things I possess—if my things are not inherited and exclusively heritable rather than exchangeable—then how can my possessions genuinely distinguish me? The triumph and trial of capitalism in America, the virulence of consumerism in America, amounts to the fact that in the midst of proliferating things, the Thing is always missed.

The abstraction of the subject of democracy and the fungibility (hence the abstraction) of objects in its consumer culture help to explain the persistent credibility of Veblen's account of "pecuniary emulation."[89] What readers of *The Theory of the Leisure Class* too often fail to acknowledge is the absence of any leisure class in the U.S., despite the presence of wealth, leisure, and inequity. It is the absence of such a class that provokes the mimetic rivalry Veblen describes. That is, the absence of stable class markers (the absence of rank) compels the subject to mark. Veblen recognized that pecuniary emulation permeates all "classes" (241–42) and points to the metaphysical accomplishments of a material display meant to confer "spiritual well-being" (103), the physical effort to overcome a metaphysical problem. And in this way he updates and expands Tocqueville's own conclusions regarding "Why the Americans Are Often So Restless in the Midst of Their Prosperity" (his title for chapter 13), which boils down to the point that "when men are more or less equal" it is all but impossible to "get out beyond the uniform crowd."[90]

Twain's first biographer explained that it was hard to persuade the author to "regard himself as anything more than an accident, a news-writer to whom distinction had come as a matter of good fortune."[91] The effort to make and remake his house—literally health-threatening to both him and Olivia—might thus be considered a futile effort to certify distinction within a form of society where such distinction could not be stabilized, a fetishization of the sign-value of things in a society with no stable code of significance.[92] You might say that all the objects on the library mantel, like the general clutter of the so-called Victorian era in America, were amassed in a hopeless effort to give substance to the abstract subject, to fill the void of democratic society—call it the place of the missing body of the prince. This would be a way of saying that the production of consumer desire (in the department store, for instance) succeeds because consumption, possession, accumulation, and display appear as modes through which one might solve the ontological dilemma posed by the structural fact of inhabiting a democratic state. And yet *The Prince and the Pauper* should be read as a manifesto that exposes the difference between monarchy and democracy as an illusion, and writes absolute contingency back into the court, showing that "democracy," as Marx himself was willing to put it, "is the truth of monarchy."[93] It should be read as a lesson in how objects always mediate identity, and always fail to.

M ore casually than Henry James, Twain was given to deploying architectural metaphors, describing the work of writing, for instance, as the "building brick by brick . . . of the eventual edifice we call style."[94] In Twain's case, this can begin to feel like an effort to render fiction more substantial, if not a suspicion that one's house, more than one's writing, might remain as the more enduring record of style. When he referred to his Hartford house as "not unsentient matter," he really meant that he and his family had transformed the building into a living thing; when he was forced to abandon the house, and eventually to sell it, he clearly felt the loss as a loss of self. No doubt this is why the loss of a house becomes his most elaborate figure in the midst of his most moving account of death, dictated for his *Autobiography*. This figure might also be said to compensate—rhetorically—for the fact that Twain's Hartford house failed to serve as heritable property.

While Twain and Olivia lived in England, their daughter Suzy returned to America, living there in the family home, and suddenly dying there, of meningitis, in 1896. Receiving cablegrams with news of her illness but also of her expected recovery, Olivia and her other daughter, Clara, sailed for America while Twain remained in Guildford, Surrey. Before Olivia had ever landed in the U.S. he received a subsequent cable: "Suzy was peacefully released to-day":

> It is one of the mysteries of our nature that a man, all unprepared, can receive a thunder-stroke like that and live. There is but one reasonable explanation of it. The intellect is stunned by the shock and but gropingly gathers the meaning of the words. The power to realize their full import is mercifully wanting. The mind has a dumb sense of vast loss—that is all. It will take mind and memory months, and possibly years, to gather together the details and thus learn and know the whole extent of the loss. A man's house burns down. The smoking wreckage represents only a ruined home that was dear through the years of use and pleasant associations. By and by, as the days and weeks go on, first he misses this, then that, then the other thing. And when he casts about for it he finds that it was in that house. Always it is an *essential*—there was but one of its kind. . . . It will be years before the tale of lost essentials is complete, and not till then can he truly know the magnitude of his disaster.[95]

Written almost ten years after Suzy's death, and after he had finally lost the Hartford house (not to fire, but to debt), this passage reads like a symptom and a theorization of melancholia in a technical sense. (Freud explains that the melancholic "knows *whom* he has lost but not *what* he has lost in him.")[96] Twain—rendered as the abstract "man"—continues to identify with his daughter as the lost object, unwilling to detach himself, and he becomes increasingly aware of what *within* the object he has lost. For Twain, the melancholic life is a life of perpetually learning, incrementally, that one has lost more, even more, than one thought. The absence of any introduction to, any transition into, his effort to metaphorize metaphysical longing with physical form ("A man's house burns down . . .") bespeaks an ongoing, desperate effort to seek relief from the loss of his daughter, and an effort to find rhetorical (though not psychological) compensation in physical objects, to find things, desperately, to think with. It also becomes the occasion when Twain, thinking about material loss, helps to dramatize what Tocqueville called "the strange *melancholy* often haunting inhabitants of democracies in the midst of abundance."[97] And it is a textual occasion wherein, rather than bequeathing his house to his daughter, Twain grieves her loss through its loss.

Whereas *The Prince and the Pauper* intimates how, in democracy and monarchy, the trivial, essential thing will always be missing, here Twain expresses the anguish of lives lived learning that the missing things are what's essential and that only the missing thing is utterly distinct. The fact of loss provokes an unending tale of lost essentials. Still, he seems to write as a consummate materialist—in apparent contrast, that is, to a figure like Emerson, who proclaimed that "Grief too will make us idealists. In the death of my son, now more than two years ago, I seem to have lost a beautiful estate,—no more. I cannot get it nearer to me. . . . This calamity . . . does not touch me." Emerson uses the loss of his son to illustrate the way "souls never touch their objects."[98] Twain uses the loss of his house to illustrate the way objects touch souls, to illustrate the all but palpable proximity, and the intensifying specificity, of loss. Still, given the fact that both the idealist and the materialist, facing human loss, point to the loss of inanimate objects, we might say that both are tyrannized by the way that material possession comes to substitute for human relation. This is hardly to say that any object sublimates Twain's grief, for the object does not exist; or, rather, it exists only as absence, registering each and every thing that he has lost.

TWO

The Nature of Things

Four years after Frank Norris's death, Doubleday, Page and Company re-published "The Joyous Miracle" as a separate volume, printed on heavy paper, a *petit objet* with art nouveau detail. Appearing originally as "Miracle Joyeux" in *The Wave* (1897), then in *McClure's Magazine* (1898) and *Windsor Magazine* (1901), the Christmas story became, in its posthumous republication, a rather different and rather wonderful thing. The plot, though, still amounts to a pallid, extra-biblical tale of Christ's work, awash in the sort of sentiment that made the social gospel novel a best-selling genre in the 1890s.[1] Yet the story begins with a curious account of literature, history, and writing—of textual transmission and circulation in an age of manual reproduction:[2]

> Old Jerome had received a certain letter, which was a copy of another letter, which in turn was a copy of another letter, and so on and so on, nobody could tell how far. Mervius would copy this letter and take it back to his village, where it would be copied again and again and yet again, and copies would be made of these copies, till the whole countryside would know the contents of that letter pretty well by heart. It was in this way, indeed, that these people made their literature. They would hand down the precious documents to their children, and that letter's contents would become folk-lore, become so well known that it would be repeated orally. It would be a legend, a mythos; perhaps by and by, after a long time, it might gain credence and become even history.

Within this ethnographic overture, Norris is clearly captivated by his own counter-intuition: folklore appears *after* the appearance of literature, and recitation *succeeds* transcription; legend and myth emerge out of a public sphere of letters; and it is the sheer habit of repeating the letter that finally yields what we might call the "miracle of history."

Charles Sanders Peirce had argued that habit is the "essence of belief," by which he meant that we should understand the resolution of doubt as the emergence of a rule of action.[3] But for Norris, as for Pascal, say, this logic runs in reverse: belief doesn't change habit; new habits change belief. And yet, as an account of faith—"credence"—Norris's paragraph considerably revises the Pascalian conviction. For in "The Joyous Miracle" only proliferating acts of textual reproduction habituate the collective to a textually constituted truth. This is Norris's way of showing not how history occurs as a set of events *in* time, but how "history" occurs *through* time as the becoming-historical of designated events—as the evolving legitimization of an account of history.

The passage, then, anticipates recent lessons about the priority of Writing, about the reiterative practice whereby discourse effects what it seems to describe, about the scriptural and citational character of history.[4] But it does so casting "history" within an evolutionary paradigm where what gets repeatedly circulated becomes culturally internalized as the known. The degree to which this story prefigures more recent stories about the materializing power of iteration marks the degree to which those accounts may well repeat, however unconsciously, prior formulations about the materializing power of repeated actions.[5]

Of course, "history," "materiality," and "reality" do not name the same phenomena. But for Norris, each seems to be an effect of repeated actions, the recognition of each a *re*-cognition. It was W. D. Howells, reviewing *The Octopus* (1901), who caught on to the force of this dynamic within Norris's philosophy of composition. The characters, he argued, "are each most intimately and personally real, *physically real* . . . [and] their *material presence* is enforced by the recognition of some distinctive and characteristic trait, which is repeated again and again in the very same terms till it is wrought into the reader's consciousness."[6] Although Howells went on to "think it would be well for Mr. Norris to ask himself if it is not a trick," he seemed to believe that the trick worked well enough at fostering a materiality-effect, like the historicity-effect described in "The Joyous Miracle." Norris's bad habit, he suggests, was meant, consciously or unconsciously, to elicit a kind of "credence," to effect the transition (within the evolution of reading rather than in the course of culture) from writing to literature, and from legend to history. In the phenomenon of reading as Howells understands it, repetition tricks the reader into granting words their referentiality, referents their reality.

Such a phenomenology of reading has everything to do with things in Frank Norris's fiction because its logic underwrites the *quality* of material thingness that both he and his characters struggle to achieve *quantitatively*, through repeated action. And this phenomenology prompts a question that readers of Norris have yet to formulate: What is the relation between his representation of habits (both the "little things" people do routinely and unconsciously and the things they do consciously but uncontrollably) and his own habits of representation? Above all, what is to be made—in the face of his narration of compulsively repetitive behavior—of his own compulsion to repeat himself as a writer? It may well be, as J. Hillis Miller has said, that "any novel is a complex tissue of repetitions and of repetitions within repetitions, or of repetitions linked in chain fashion to other repetitions."[7] But no other American novelist has struck readers as so simply, aggressively, and egregiously repetitive, which is why Norris has always seemed a cumbersome and excessive writer, even among the American naturalists. One reviewer of *McTeague* lamented that Norris had used the "cheaper" realist "method of iteration": "We see again and again Trina's narrow milk-blue eyes. . . . Again and again we are reminded of McTeague's enormous red hands. . . . Again and again, too, we hear the story of the gold service from Maria Miranda Macapa. . . . Mr. Norris seems positively to court weariness on the part of his readers by this droning repetition of details."[8] What another called "the trick of repetition of certain adjectives, phrases and descriptions" in *The Octopus* seemed to demonstrate how Norris "undoubtedly copied some of the mannerisms of Zola."[9] His repetitions, that is, comprised a kind of repetition.

Asking about Norris's habits of representation in relation to his representation of habit ought to arrive at a more complex question about naturalism: How do we understand the relation between the most basic question that formal analysis poses—a question about repetition and deviation—and those questions about biological preservation and change established by Lamarck and Darwin?[10]

McTeague became the fulcral text for a shift from reading Norris's naturalism as, on the one hand, an examination of human behavior, to reading it as, on the other, a dramatization of the conflict between material presence and representation—a transition, that is, from concerns that are biological, psychological, and social to those that are semiological and ontological.[11] As this chapter goes on to demonstrate, though, both characterological and ontological questions (among others) are for Norris all questions in what William James generalized as "the philosophy of habit." From the pragmatist point of view, it is in the nature of things to develop habits, and the habits they develop constitute their nature, which humans acknowledge through their habits. Such circularity provoked Josiah Royce to complain (in 1895) about the ubiquity of habit as an explanatory concept in American philosophy, a concept accounting for almost everything and therefore almost nothing.[12] In *McTeague*, which poses both an epistemological understanding of how habit constitutes the material world for the perceiving subject, and a psychological understanding of how habit constitutes the self, Norris might be said to narrate the ramifications of that ubiquity, which amount foremost to an unnerving conflation of culture and nature, subject and object, human behavior and natural law: what we call persons and what we call things. The novel also helps to locate Norris in the overlap between nineteenth-century (Lamarckian) convictions and the experimental writing and thinking of the twentieth century: for the bad habits of one generation, the "droning repetition" of a Norris or a Zola, resurface as the avant-garde technique of the next, the repetitions without which, after all, neither Stein nor Faulkner, neither Proust nor Beckett, would be recognizable.

Iteration

Norris's own "philosophy of habit" could be aligned with many contemporaneous events: the institutionalization of an anthropology that understood cultures to be knowable from their customs; the recognition and theorization of habit and its vicissitudes in education; the intensification of the discourse on addiction, especially drinking and gambling; the emergence of a rigorous managerial rethinking of workplace routine; the increasing importance of technological reproducibility in mass-mediated culture. I want to forego any inquiry into such a broad cultural and material context, though, in the effort not to foreclose the question of how repetition might be said to substantiate history, culture, and what we call materiality to begin with. I want to ask why Norris, given his extensive use of *iterative narration* to represent habitual action, also repeats himself, why the novel relentlessly cites itself, in the mode of *descriptive repetition*.

Different as they are as writers, thinkers, and sensibilities, the Norris of *McTeague* shares with Proust one narratological disposition: the extensive use of iterative narration. Iterative narration substitutes, for an account of discrete events, the account of events that recur in an iterative series; it replaces synthesizing summary with an exemplary abstraction, what amounts to the condensation of events into one narrative statement. *On Mondays I walked to work. She used to drink coffee in the mornings. In the summer we would go to the mountains.* These statements, despite the differences in tense, denote repetition and regularity; they suggest that within the specified time frame, the action habitually and invariably takes place: *On Mondays I (always) walked to work.* Iterative narration has the obvious advantage of being discursively economical (saying once what happened many times); it has the somewhat less obvious liability of substituting generalization for repetition, and thus of eliding all differences within the process of reenactment. The best-known instance of this technique is the celebrated opening of *À la recerche de temps perdu:* "Longtemps, je me suis couché de bonne heure."[13] Throughout the novel, and most adamantly in its "Overture," Marcel represents repeated, all but ritualized events in the iterative mode: "J'appuyais tendrement mes joues contre les belles joues de l'oreiller. . . . Je frottais une allumette pour regarder ma montre. . . . Je me rendormais . . . " ("I *would lay* my cheeks gently against the comfortable cheeks of my pillow. . . . I *would strike* a match to look at my watch. . . . I *would fall asleep*, again, . . . ").[14] He recounts his life, he discursively remembers his life, as a sequence of customary actions.

In *McTeague*, which recounts the tribulations of a "young giant" of a dentist who murders his wife because she won't share her lottery winnings, Norris deploys iterative narration to accomplish two goals—most memorably to convey a general yet highly particularized scene of everyday life in San Francisco. What Howells described as Norris's "miracle of observation" in *McTeague* might be described instead as a miracle of habituation, insofar as the memorable details of Polk Street appear through the lens, as it were, produced by McTeague's habitual action.[15] "Day after day, McTeague saw the same panorama unroll itself": "There were corner drug stores with huge jars of red, yellow, and green liquids in their windows, very brave and gay; stationers' stores, where illustrated weeklies were tacked upon bulletin boards; barber shops with cigar stands in their vestibules."[16] The panorama is at once a single impression and an indelible inscription. The scene fundamentally fuses the descriptive and narrative registers: "On week days the street was very lively. . . . Between seven and eight the street breakfasted. . . . Towards eleven o'clock the ladies from the great avenue a block above Polk Street made their appearance, promenading the sidewalks leisurely, deliberately" (5–7). The iterative technique is no less prominent, though, in Norris's portrayal of McTeague himself as a creature governed by, and thus knowable from, routine. If at times Norris doesn't quite achieve the most satisfying grammatical construction, he generally manages to cast habitual action in the appropriate iterative mode: "McTeague *would walk out* to the end of the Union Street car line, . . . then he *would work* down to the shore of the bay. . . . He *would sit* all day nearly motionless upon a point of rocks" (333). Both character and urban context depend on iterative narration, which can render character indistinguishable from context.

This formal strategy seems to have been integral to Norris's initial efforts to write the novel. The surviving weekly composition themes that he wrote at Harvard in 1894–95 are generally said to exhibit a photographic attention to the everyday details of contemporaneous life that his professor, Lewis Gates, promoted, and that Norris learned from reading Dickens and Zola. More remarkable, though, when the figure of McTeague enters those themes (on January 7, 1895), Norris for the first time begins to deploy the iterative mode: "The other teachers at the kindergarten often noticed that Bessie's fingers were swollen. . . . McTeague her husband *used to bite* her fingertips when he came home after drinking whiskey."[17] For the rest of the year, in his subsequent efforts to work on passages from the project (a mere glimmer of a project at the time—not to be completed until 1897, and not published until 1899), Norris settles into the iterative. Though these exercises were revised if not discarded, he had stumbled upon (or worked toward) the essential means of narrating his "Story of San Francisco."

Gérard Genette, who has done more than anyone to develop our understanding of iterative narration, draws attention to its baroque deployment in the *Recherche,* emphasizing that Proust's characteristic use of the mode is irreducible to any effort to render, as realism often does, the provincial routinization of petit-bourgeois life. Rather, his veritable *"intoxication with the iterative"* both intimates how a human subject (voluntarily and involuntarily) synthesizes events of the past into a single memory, and generates a temporality into which other times can erupt, defying chronology, rendering time, all told, "bewitched, surreptitiously subverted, or better: *perverted.*"[18] These effects obviously depend on the novel's homodiegetic narration, a first person point of view that allows rhetorical vicissitudes to be understood as the vicissitudes of memory. In the case of *McTeague* (written in third person), intoxication and perversion are not so much characteristics of the novel's compositional cognition as human conditions that Norris works to narrate: Trina McTeague's obsessive hoarding, McTeague's drunken fits, his sadism, her masochism—all in the context of Polk Street's "monotonous routine" (322). And the iterative mode helps to stage the confrontation between the habits that constitute our daily lives and the habits that threaten to destroy them, between the routinization that characterizes the life of an "accommodation street," on the one hand, and, on the other, the bad habits that defy any happy habituation to modern life, epitomized by Trina's insistence on hoarding her money as gold.[19]

The rhythm of the plot amounts to the serial alternation between custom and its violation, routine and event, monotony and novelty. This rhythm is clearest in the middle chapters of the novel. Chapter 7 details the signal event of the novel, Trina's winning $5,000 in the lottery, the chance event that disrupts the habits of all the characters ("[t]hey drank and feasted in impromptu fashion" [115]). Chapter 8 then proceeds to recount the "delightful" premarital courtship between Trina and Mac, who see one another "regularly, three times a week" (130) in a quickly established routine: "Trina *would arrive* breathless from her raids upon the bargain counters. . . . She *would drop* into her chair with a little groan. . . . At other times they *would talk* at length over their plans, while Trina sipped her chocolate and McTeague devoured huge chunks of butterless bread" (130–31). Chapter 9 is devoted to the event of the wedding: "When all their glasses had been filled, Marcus proposed the health of the bride, 'standing up'" (168). Chapter 10 then returns to the iterative to describe narratively (to narrate descriptively) the first months of the McTeagues' married life, as their "new life jostled itself into its grooves" and a "routine began": "But very often during that rainy winter after her marriage Trina *would pause* in her work, her hands falling idly into her lap" (192, 183). This is hardly to say that any one chapter of the novel is exclusively iterative or exclusively singulative; indeed, with further attention you could track this rhythm *within* any one chapter. It is to say that these kinds of striking alternations (which could be called the novel's own narratological habit) provide the formal structure by which the novel stages the question of habit, of how lives change (or fail to), of how events intrude on the routine of everyday life.

What we might call the "wouldness" that saturates the novel—"Trina would arrive breathless from her raids upon the bargain counters" (130)—can be transposed into the conditional: *If Trina had been raiding the bargain counters, she would arrive breathless.* And indeed, Norris's overwhelming deployment of the iterative makes much of the plot seem predictable, allowing a reader to imagine future conditionals that the novel readily confirms: *If Trina should refuse Mac money, he would kill her.* If such predictability seems to derive from little more than our familiarity with the characters, that familiarity derives its force from the formal elements of the novel—the way in which the iterative mode portrays characters as creatures of habit. And this predictability does instantiate the role of habit in signification as Peirce understood it. In his unpublished survey of pragmatism ("pragmaticism"), what had been the mise-en-abyme of signification in his early work (the endless deferral of meaning) finally comes to rest in "habit." Though it had been his conviction that the interpretant of any sign is itself another sign—requiring further interpretation, the production of yet another interpretant, ad infinitum—he eventually posits an "ultimate logical interpretant" that is not a sign but a "readiness to act in a certain way under given circumstances and when actuated by a given motive" (5:476, 480).[20] Peirce means not repeated action, but a disposition, or an instinct, a "rule of action." Grammatically, then, he speaks of this as a certain kind of predication: "habitual behaviour" amounts to what he calls the "would acts" or "would dos" of the future conditional (5:467): *If I were to see (what appeared to be) a tree falling I would run.* My instinct here reveals multiple convictions (about the physicality of the tree, the law of cause and effect, &c.) that seem to transcend—or, in Peirce's understanding, to end—the complexity of signification. His grammatical formulation helps to suggest how the grammar of *McTeague* fosters the feel of overdetermination—call it the absence of play and particularity within the field of iterative synthesis. Such synthesis particularizes the scene (Polk Street) at the expense of generalizing the act (McTeague's routine, rendered invariable).

Of course, only play, variation, a disturbance in meaning, a break in habit, the intrusion of event—only these can initiate and sustain a narratable state of affairs. Such intrusion catalyzes and structures the overarching plot of the historical drama in *The Octopus,* the rail monopoly destroying the routines of the California cattle industry, just as it structures the drama of the classic historical novel, Scott's *Waverly,* say, or Cooper's *Pioneers.* Indeed, the orchestrated alternation of the iterative and singulative modes allows Norris to condense historical drama into an excerpt from modern life. And yet, *McTeague* insists on being read as a characterological, and not a historical, novel, precisely by incorporating some of the great technological novelties of the era—the kinetoscope at the Orpheum—in such a way that they exert no pressure on the plot. The introduction of electric lights on Polk Street may prompt a three-day festival, but that festival remains unrecorded, and the lights are hastily woven into the fabric of "the little life of Polk Street" that runs "on monotonously in its accustomed grooves" (198).

More to the point, perhaps, when the realism of *McTeague* transforms into melodrama, the monotony of routine or the homogenizing force of the iterative might be said to remain at work—displaced onto the image of the desert landscape. Once McTeague murders Trina, flees San Francisco, and desperately moves from the Big Dipper mine to the floor of Death Valley, pursued by a posse and his rival, Marcus, the plot unfolds like a Western adventure, with events rapidly succeeding one another. But repetition expresses itself there in a different register, in the profound and grotesque monotony of the land: "There was no change in the character of the desert. Always the same measureless leagues of white-hot alkali stretched away toward the horizon on every hand. . . . Not a rock, not a stone broke the monotony of the ground" (429). Just as spatial monotony has come to replace temporal monotony (the "monotonous routine" of Polk Street) so too the changelessness of the desert seems to ask whether there has been "no change in the character" of the characters. If the desert provides any relief from the city, it is only the relief of a timeless repetition: repetition not as that which both marks and evades time, but repetition spatialized, repetition without time. And thus, this image of the desert might be said to figure the homogenizing potency of the iterative mode itself, further conflating the narrative and descriptive dimensions of the novel, just as it figures the stasis and inertia to which McTeague's compulsion to repeat, represented in that mode, inevitably drives him.

Creatures of Habit

In a complex formulation, Peirce was willing to maintain that "it is clear that nothing but a principle of habit, itself due to the growth by habit of an infinitesimal chance tendency toward habit-taking, is the only bridge that can span the chasm between the chance-medley of chaos and the cosmos of order and law."[21] He means to emphasize not just how habit alone keeps chaos at bay, but also how fortuitous it was that humans chanced upon this mode of taming chance. He casts this claim—about humans assuming the habit of assuming habits—in profoundly evolutionist terms, combining Darwin's emphasis on the accidental with Lamarck's basic presumption about the force of habit.[22] What Peirce called "evolution by the force of habit" Norris learned at Berkeley, in the lectures of Joseph Le Conte, who presented a story of evolution wherein acquired habits become inherited instincts, which is a way of describing how repetition becomes internalized, how culture becomes nature, how recurrent action effects physical transformation.[23] The favorite Lamarckian example is provided by the giraffe: forced by an arid climate to graze only on the foliage of tree tops, the giraffe, "from this habit long maintained," develops its long forelegs and neck.[24] For Peirce, the evolutionary function of habit explained far more than animal behavior—it explained not just creatures and plants, but also things and the order of things. His Tychism—the conviction that the universe is ultimately governed by chance, not by law—had to explain the laws of the natural world, and it did so with an evolutionist cosmology. As Josiah Royce explained, despairingly, "nature's observable Laws might even be interpreted, from an evolutionary point of view, as nature's gradually acquired Habits, originating in a primal condition of a relatively capricious irregularity" (452). Three years later, in a lecture on "Habit" from his series on "Reasoning and the Logic of Things," Peirce himself asserted the point: "We may suppose that laws of nature are results of an evolutionary process." He imagines that light moved faster and faster until attaining its current speed, and that other apparent invariables, such as gravity, in fact achieved their stability over time. The very regularity of the physical world, then, must be explained by "a universal tendency of all things toward . . . habit-taking."[25] In other words, things are as they are because they have settled into a particular mode of being, achieved through a long history of becoming.

Whereas Peirce thus used biology to explain physics, James kept using physics and biology to explain one another. In his chapter on "Habit," widely read both as an article in *Popular Science Monthly* and as a separate pamphlet, he suggests that the very attempt to define the term immediately prompts a discussion of physics—of "the fundamental properties of matter." He understands primary elements as entities that possess habits that cannot be changed, and he understands compounds as having habits that yield because of "outward forces" or "inward tensions."[26] If it is true, as the essay explains at the very outset, that "creatures" are "bundles of habits" (109), then creatures ought to resemble compounds. And of course, among American novelists it is Norris who portrays characterological compounds—most notably and schematically "man" and "brute"—and these are best understood as competing habits that constitute competing selves. In *Blix* (1899), Condy explains that "when it comes to gambling, there seems to be another *me* that does precisely as he chooses, whether *I* will or not."[27] It makes no sense to say that Condy's gambling threatens his work routine as a writer, for it is more clearly the case that he is a writer, and then a gambler; there may be a single body that contains the gambler and the writer, but there is no individuated will or psychological subject who transcends them.[28] The transformation of character in *McTeague*, such as it is, seems to unfold according to James's physics: "When the structure has yielded, the same inertia becomes a condition of its comparative permanence in the new form," James writes of the compound; "[e]ach relatively stable phase of equilibrium in such a structure is marked by what we might call a new set of habits" (110). In *McTeague*, the orchestration of the iterative and singulative modes mediates such characterological physics.

In James's *Psychology* habit is explained in terms of the "mechanical facts" of the nervous system. Habitual association and action result from a worn path of nervous energy, a path in the brain where one impulse continually excites another. The woman can knit as she talks because one impulse triggers the next in the absence of signification, and this means that we need to imagine the process without recourse to semiology. He approvingly cites Maudsley's image of the spinal cord with a memory (118). Like Pascal before him and Proust after him, James dissociates habit from cognition, but then imagines habit and thought in the process of perpetual negotiation. In Pascal's scheme, the automaton "can lead[ ] the mind unconsciously along with it,"[29] but the mind can likewise lead the automaton. In Proust's narrative, their relation regulates experience.[30] In the case of *McTeague*, however, no such negotiation between habit and thought can take place. You can't really say, in pragmatist terms, that McTeague's ideas manifest themselves in actions, for there seems to be only action in the absence of ideas, only habit in the absence of thought, which is why as a character he seems so thoroughly unpsychological and so utterly physiological—why, in other words, his psychology seems reducible to physiology:

> It was Sunday, and according to his custom on that day, McTeague took his dinner at two in the afternoon at the car conductors' coffee-joint on Polk Street. He had a thick gray soup; heavy, underdone meat, very hot, on a cold plate; two kinds of vegetables; and a sort of suet pudding, full of strong butter and sugar. On his way back to his office, one block above, he stopped at Joe Frenna's saloon and bought a pitcher of steam beer. It was his habit to leave the pitcher there on his way to dinner. (1)

Between the "custom" with which this first paragraph of the novel opens, and the "habit" with which it ends, not a thought intrudes.[31] Norris depicts a routine that, exacerbated by the heaviness of the meal, turns process into stasis, activity into a kind of inactivity. He certainly succeeds in discarding (as James and Dewey sought to) an idealist concept of "self" distinct from experience, but this novelistic realization acutely reifies the human, rendering it as mindless matter. One of the effects of the iterative narration is to transform action, even action meant to cure inaction, into a kind of inertia: "Then, wearied at his inaction and feeling the need of movement and exercise, McTeague *would light* his pipe and take a turn upon the great avenue one block above Polk Street" (304).[32] Given Lamarck's argument that "the power of habits over actions is inversely proportional to the intelligence of the individual,"[33] and given that McTeague is repeatedly described as "stupid," he is an obvious candidate for exhibiting the potency of habit over humans. Indeed, although he is not a brute in *Vandover's* sense of the term— not suffering from lycanthropy, not seized by the impulse to howl—he remains a brute nonetheless.

Still, it is habit, designated as *habit*, that identifies the more human characters in the novel. The one successful relationship, the "affair" between the veterinarian, Old Grannis, and Miss Baker, an "ancient little dressmaker," evolves because, living across from one another in the rooming house, the excruciatingly refined individuals "had come to know each other's habits" in an all but biblical sense (18, 16). Miss Baker takes her tea at the precise time each day that Old Grannis works on his hobby of bookbinding—"a little habit, you know; a diversion, a—a—it occupies one, you know. I don't smoke; it takes the place of a pipe, perhaps" (35). Their intimacy with their things, the repetition through which they take intimate possession of them, gets transposed into a human relationship, and their intimacy with one another as creatures of habit fosters their affection. As with McTeague, Norris stages the very violations of routinized life as emerging out of routine (27, 53, 28).

The novel, all told, is legible as the story of McTeague's stasis, his incapacity to slip out of his "old habits," to overcome his former life as a "carboy" in Placer County.[34] After escaping San Francisco, returning to the Big Dipper mine, and thinking about the Burly drill used in the mines there, he has some recognition of mining as a "queer counterpart" to dentistry, the "same work . . . only magnified, made monstrous, distorted" (386–87). Yet the profession of dentistry as practiced by McTeague has always resembled a miniaturized mode of mining. The novel demonstrates the extent to which McTeague has never escaped from being a miner (from the habit of mining) when he returns "[s]traight as a homing pigeon, and following a blind and unreasoned instinct" to Placer County, where the "colossal mountains [take] him back again like a returning prodigal" (385, 387). There is a tragic structure here—a protagonist unable to evade his origins—but there is no tragedy because the protagonist more simply *is* his origins; he is what he is in the same way that a physical element is what it is.

Yet this story that tracks (and formally registers) the reducibility of the human to habit is no more stark than James's own socio-economic account of habit as the "most precious conservative agent." "It alone," James writes, "keeps us all within the bounds of ordinance, and saves the children of fortune from the envious uprisings of the poor" (125):

> It alone prevents the hardest and most repulsive walks of life from being deserted by those brought up to tread therein. It keeps the fisherman and the deck-hand at sea through winter; it holds the miner in his darkness, and nails the countryman to his log-cabin and his lonely farm through all the months of snow; it protects us from invasion by the natives of the desert and the frozen zone. . . . *An invisible law, as strong as gravitation, keeps him within his orbit, arrayed this year as he was the last.* (125–26, my emphasis)

Having described physical laws as habits, James is able to describe social relations as though their maintenance were a matter of physical law—in short, as a matter of second nature. "'Habit a second nature! Habit is ten times na-ture,' the Duke of Wellington is said to have exclaimed" (124). Having ar-gued that "the philosophy of habit is . . . in the first instance, a chapter in physics rather than in physiology or psychology" (110), James produces a physiological psychology that fully underwrites this account of an invari-able social world. This is the uncanny moment in American philosophy where the organic and inorganic, the animate and inanimate, are not mis-taken for one another, but conceptualized as one another. Lamarck himself, in his *Zoological Philosophy,* had been careful to qualify his discussion of the "power of habit—a power from which even man can only escape with great difficulty by the help of his highly developed intellect."[35] Extending his de-fense of habit, James suggests that the more "details of our daily life we can hand over to the effortless custody of automatism, the more our higher pow-ers of mind will be set free for their own proper work" (126). But only such freedom to think can prompt us to resist the power of habit to begin with. If, in its absence, the "automaton" simply supplants the mind, then James ends up peopling the world with two classes, laboring automata (controlled by the sort of habit that "holds the miner in his darkness") and working minds (re-leased, thanks to habit, from quotidian details). The class distinction achieves ontological force as the difference between people who are people, on the one hand, and, on the other, people that are things.

Possession

From the pragmatist point of view, Frank Norris reads as the American nov-elist who most scientifically depicts humans as things, the human thingified as a result of habit. But human habit in his fiction can also have the effect of animating an otherwise inanimate world of objects. In *Vandover and the Brute* (completed in 1895, not published until 1914), the eponymous dilet-tante, a bohemian dandy, grows increasingly idle, dedicating his days of "idleness" to "doing little things," winding the clock, mixing tobacco, twist-ing paper, and elaborately fussing with his stove:[36]

> But the stove, the famous tiled stove with flamboyant ornaments, was the chiefist joy of Vandover's new life. He was delighted with it; it was so artistic, so curious, it kept the fire so well, it looked so cheerful and inviting; a stove that was the life and soul of the whole room, a stove to draw up to and talk to; no, never was there such a stove! There was hardly a minute of the day he was not fussing with it, raking it down, turning the damper off and on, opening and shutting the door, filling it with coal, putting the blower on and then tak-

ing it off again, sweeping away the ashes with a little brass-handled broom, or studying the pictures upon the tiles: the "Punishment of Caliban and his Associates," "Romeo and Juliet," the "Fall of Phaeton." He even pretended to the chambermaid that he alone understood how to manage the stove, forbidding her to touch it, assuring her that it had to be coaxed and humoured. Often late in the evening as he was going to bed he would find the fire in it drowsing; then he would hustle it sharply to arouse it, punching it with the poker, talking to it, saying: "Wake up there, you!" And then when the fire was snapping he would sit before it in his bathrobe, absorbing its heat luxuriously and scratching himself, as was his custom, for over an hour. (182)

Norris both aggrandizes and belittles the way this protagonist spends his time cherishing the things that surround him in his San Francisco flat. Not only does the fame of "the famous tiled stove" depend only on Vandover's assessment, of course; it also ends sullied by the image of the young man's habit of scratching. The passage concludes by deflating all the quotidian grandiosity, banalizing the rich detail, and disclosing the burgeoning beast within Vandover even while exhibiting his most refined accouterments.

Yet the novel here describes what is unquestionably the happiest relationship that Vandover has, the one intimacy he really enjoys. Indeed, this is a persuasive account of how human beings achieve an intimate relation with their possessions—how, rather, they transform the merely owned into the genuinely possessed—and how, within the dynamics of projection and cathexis, we turn these "good objects" into personalities that must be subsequently managed, satisfying not least our will-to-management. Our habitual interactions with objects both bring them to life and impose order on that life; our habits both mark time and allow us to escape from time, as we perform the present in concert with the future and the past. By doing the same thing with the same things you create the illusion of sameness and continuity over and against the facts of disorder and change. In the image of Vandover's great intimacy with his stove, Norris depicts an animation of things that is utterly familiar, *heimisch,* making us feel at home in the homes we create.

This canniness—call it quotidian animism, the utter ordinariness of the life of things—depends on the subject retaining control of the material object's vitality. And in Norris's novel, Vandover never exactly loses *control* of his things. But he does in fact lose his things—because he loses control of himself. Unable to suppress his addiction to gambling, just as he is unable to suppress his lycanthropy, Vandover sells his precious possessions to pay his mounting debts. "Above all," of course, he mourns the loss of his stove, a possession so inalienable it seemed more friend than possession, "a stove that had its moods, caprices, like any living person, a stove that had to be coaxed and humoured, a stove that he alone could understand" (279). He quickly finds himself living in an unpeopled, empty flat. To allay his hunger for "harmonious colours, pictures, ornaments," he pins placards to the walls—"'Pipe-rack Here.' 'Mona Lisa Here.' 'Stove Here'"—signs that demonstrate the irrevocable fate of objects, the insubstantiality of objects, once they're released from inalienability (280).

Soon Vandover regards the missing things, like most of his old quotidian pleasures, as "things of habit" that could no longer arouse his interest. Gambling alone can generate the "fresh violent excitement" that will "rouse his jaded nerves" (287).[37] Gambling not for the money but only for this "excitement of the moment" (289), Vandover propels himself into an affective economy where money no longer functions as a medium for purchasing goods. And he inhabits a flat where his representation of the missing things—"the little placards, scrawled with ink, that read 'Stove here'; 'Mona Lisa here'" (311)—signify less and less. Without its objects, the flat is now without a recognizably human subject. If, as William James would have it, "*a man's self is the sum total of all that he CAN call his*" (279), then the "bare, white wall" of Vandover's flat specifies his erasure.[38] If the apprehensible self is an effect of doing the same thing with the same things (hence preserving continuity over time), then the loss of things spells not a physical but an existential crisis. In Vandover's case, the crisis is critical on all counts: in the empty flat, he runs naked, "four-footed," "back and forth the length of the room" (311).

However one wishes to understand the etiology of Vandover's condition, it is clear that his new habit has destroyed all his former habits, and with those have gone the once cherished possessions with which he lived his life. Rather than writing the traditional cautionary tale, wherein a drinker or a gambler ruins the life of his family, Norris writes a novel where the gambler ruins the life of his things, pursuing his passion at the expense of the physical object world.[39] That world has its revenge, however, when Vandover, sick and penniless, can only find work cleaning out a filthy workman's cottage, a cottage built across from the vast boot and shoe factory that occupies the land he has lost to a friend. In the shadow of that monument to the world of production, he faces the detritus of the world of consumption, caught by and between the end points of an economy he once, as a gambler, seemed to elude. He now finds himself crawling under a sink "in the sour water, the grease, the refuse," to dig out "an old hambone covered with a greenish fuzz . . . a rusty pan half full of some kind of congealed gravy that exhaled a choking, acrid odour; next it was an old stocking, and then an ink bottle, a broken rat-trap, a battered teapot lacking a nozzle, a piece of rubber hose, an old comb choked with a great handful of hair, a torn overshoe, newspapers, and a great quantity of other débris" (351). The excessiveness with which Norris catalogs the waste overwhelms the image of the thin and weary man who seems to shrink, now, deep within a scorial cavern—back into the magic hat from which the novelist keeps pulling things out, one thing after another.

Norris's first completed novel shows how committed he was to charting the life of a human subject as the relation to inanimate objects, a relation threatened by a habit that effectively (if temporarily) dematerializes the physical object world. But in *McTeague* (begun in 1895, published in 1899), which seems to have begun as a subplot of *Vandover*, Norris commits himself to a different project, one where the very habits that threaten to tear down that world also work to build it. McTeague himself shares Vandover's kind of pleasure with his possessions: a stone pug dog, his concertina, his canary. But Trina, once she has won the lottery, is willing to sell their possessions and to commit the couple to squalor on behalf of turning money itself into a possession—in order to possess gold in a way that prohibits it from serving as money. She doesn't use gold to acquire things; she sells things to acquire gold. What seems perverse about her "avarice" is less her "love of money for the money's sake" than her dismissal of the "machine-like regularity" of the interest she receives from her money invested for the machine-like regularity of counting her gold (354, 353). "She counted it and recounted it and made little piles of it, and rubbed the gold pieces between the folds of her apron until they shone" (209). Trina isn't interested in gold as a medium of exchange; she is interested in gold as substance and form; like a collector, she wants to preserve her coins from the fate of exchange. Her mode of possession—her habitual interaction with the coins—preserves the gold from being a function and maintains its status as a thing. Wealth isn't expressed, as Marx would have it, by commodities, but by gold in its distinction from commodities. Thinking of her money invested, she imagines not a numerical figure but an image of "her wonderful five thousand dollars piled in columns, shining and gleaming" (355–56). But the image alone is hardly sufficient. When she has the gold pieces again, she counts and recounts them: "She laid them out in a row on the ledge of the table, or arranged them in patterns—triangles, circles, squares—or built them all up into a pyramid" (357). Here it is not so much that the miser counts as that the counter becomes a miser: the practice intensifies "all her intuitive desire of saving, her instinct of hoarding, her love of money for the money's sake" (209). Her inherited parsimony becomes an addiction because she seems unable to maintain any faith that the gold is there, is hers, is gold, without making repeated physical contact, without achieving a kind of possession more erotic than economic.

Trina's habits seem to respond to an epistemological problem customarily solved by what James called the *internalization* of habit. He understood the perception of the thingness of things to be precipitated by a combination of "sensational and reproductive brain processes" (724); that is, the coalescence of our sensations in and as a "thing" depends on habit. Biologizing Hume, as it were, he pressed for a fully physiological explanation of our experience of physicality as such: "the forms of habitual and probable things," because of their "incessantly repeated presence and reproduction," have "plough[ed] deep grooves in the nervous system" (891), so that even fragmentary glimpses will be transformed into an apperception of the material whole.[40] Real form (what Edmund Husserl would come to call the inauthentic image as opposed to the authentic image we actually see) is *habitually* conjured up. In Trina's case, though, only a thorough interaction with her gold can convince her of its presence.

She counts for the sake of touching. "Next she laid herself upon the bed and gathered the gleaming heaps of gold pieces to her with both arms, burying her face in them with long sighs of unspeakable delight" (359). Her pleasure derives from the fully physical contact with gold's physicality. According to the Jamesian paradigm, then, you could say that something has gone wrong not just psychologically, but physiologically: there are no worn paths in her nervous system that prompt her to accept the gold for what it is. Habit remains *externalized* as a pathological compulsion to repeat (as though you had to grasp the same coffee mug over and over to certify its three-dimensionality). This compulsion, then, is a symptomatic effort to stabilize and possess the physical world, a compulsion that unfolds as, say, a phenomenological version of the Freudian logic whereby repetition marks the effort both to exert control and to achieve stability or stasis. From one point of view, the pervasiveness of habit in the novel seems to count solely as the naturalist denial of agency and the psychological subject (the mode through which socio-economic or biological determinants are realized); from another, though, it shows how the "tendency toward habit-taking" can generate not cosmos but chaos.

That chaos results, in both *Vandover* and *McTeague*, from an individual's refusal to inhabit the economy-as-usual. Vandover's irrational expenditure (in the form of gambling) and Trina's irrational thrift (in the form of hoarding) violate the system of exchange on which economy as such depends. The fluid and flourishing economies in Norris's (uncompleted) Trilogy of Wheat

(*The Octopus* [1900] and *The Pit* [1901]) effectively normalize the perverse economies of *Vandover* (excessive spending) and *McTeague* (excessive saving) with the machinery of corporate and finance capitalism. In both *Vandover* and *McTeague*, money has lost its relation to goods: Vandover gambles for the sake of gambling, and Trina hoards for the sake of hoarding, not circulating money to circulate things, but bringing circulation to a stop.

Trina protects her gold from an economy in which exchangeable goods are fungible (the wheat you sell becoming the coat you buy). However unchangeable people seem to be in this novel, inanimate objects enjoy no such stability. The enormous gilded tooth, which she buys for McTeague as a shop sign, suffers, once he has lost his practice, a typically transformative fate. The "gigantic golden molar of French gilt, enormous and ungainly, sprawled its branching prongs in one corner of the room, by the footboard of the bed. The McTeagues had come to use it as a sort of substitute for a table. After breakfast and supper Trina piled the plates and greasy dishes upon it to have them out of the way" (337). When you use a tooth as a table, it becomes a table. Trina fights to preserve the quiddity of her gold, unable to fathom spending it, and unable, really, to fathom consumption as such. Whittling Noah's Ark animals ten hours a day for her uncle's toy business, her fingers flying, she is utterly bemused by consumer desire. "'Where *do* all the toys go to?' she murmured. 'The thousands and thousands of these Noah's arks that I have made—horses and chickens and elephants—and always there never seems to be enough'" (342). The point is not just that she doesn't know how seriously children had become a marketing focus for department stores and mail-order catalogues, but also that consumer desire simply makes no sense to her.[41] Gold is the only physical thing she cares about as a thing, which is why she works, whittling and painting with "non-poisonous paint" to the point of destroying her body, which hardly prevents her from continuing to work: "One can hold a scrubbing brush with two good fingers and the stumps of two others even if both joints of the thumb are gone" (352).

The Miracle of History

Trina's eagerness to dispossess herself and Mac on behalf of possessing gold stands in obvious contrast to the novel's own effort to render a world replete with things. And the habits of seeing that generate the catalogues of objects extend the iterative mode. When it comes to habits of saying, though, Norris represents them more mimetically: repeated acts are repeated in the text. Maria, the Latin American "maid of all work," always names herself with the same inexplicable tag: "'Name is Maria—Miranda—Macapa.' Then, as if struck with an afterthought, 'Had a flying squirrel an' let him go'" (21). This verbal tick (repeated in—or by—the text) is the inconsequential version of what more elaborately manifests itself in the fantastic story she tells about her family's gold service: "There were more than a hundred pieces, and every one of them gold. You should have seen the sight when the leather trunk was opened. . . . There was dinner dishes and soup tureens and pitchers; and great, big platters as long as that, and wide too . . . and then a great, big punch-bowl with a ladle, and the bowl was all carved out with figures and bunches of grapes. Why, just only that punch-bowl was worth a fortune, I guess" (46). Though residents of the flat are simply amused by the story, the local dealer in junk, the Polish Jew, Zerkow, finds the story mesmerizing. He becomes her best audience, willing and eager to listen: "There were more than a hundred pieces, and every one of them gold—just that punch-bowl was worth a fortune—thick, fat, red gold" (63). Norris keeps the description in fully legible circulation: "Every piece was just like a mirror, smooth and bright; oh, bright as a little sun. Such a service as that was—platters and soup tureens and an immense big punch-bowl" (122). Zerkow is not simply "ravished . . . with delight" by the story; he comes "to believe in this story infallibly" (47, 240). He himself soon knows the tale and, like a child, insists on hearing it over and over in precisely the same words: "Begin now with 'There were more than a hundred pieces, and every one of them gold.' Go on, begin, begin, begin!" (127). Zerkow finally suffers the inverse of Trina's dilemma: in the absence of the actual gold, he is fully convinced of its presence. His credence—based on the habit of hearing the story repeated again and again—becomes something like a tactile embrace of description. The dealer in junk, perpetually conferring value on detritus, transforming one thing into another, has turned words into things.

The reproduction of the story has the effect of substantively producing the plates for Zerkow. But after their marriage, itself fostered by their collaborative retelling and retelling of the story, Maria's biological capacity to reproduce (to produce an actual thing), arrests her capacity to reproduce the story. After she gives birth to "a wretched, sickly child, with not even strength enough nor wits enough to cry" (239), the baby dies, Maria suffers ten days of "dementia," and she no longer has any story to tell. Still, in Zerkow's "perverted mind the hallucination had developed still further" (240); "it existed now, entire, intact" (240); he pries up floor boards and tears down walls looking for the treasure (247, 295). To claim that Zerkow's desire for the gold and for the story are comparable is to overstate the case,[42] but it is true that only when the description ceases does his need to find the actual

gold become overwhelming. Maria's life thus ends as what we might call a realist tragedy: Zerkow murders her, convinced that she has hidden the treasure from him, convinced of the reality of her representation. In other
words, this tragedy can be cast as a lesson in the dangers of the reality-effect
of the word, the dangers of iterative materialization.

But if Maria's impulse to repeat herself again and yet again seems pathological and ultimately self-endangering, it is a pathology shared by the novel
itself, which recites her recitations as though refusing the efficiency and generality of its own iterative narration, as though succumbing to the mimetic
fallacy. Moreover, in the mode I wish to call simply descriptive repetition,
the novel keeps recirculating the same adjectives and the same descriptive
catalogues. In the opening pages of the novel McTeague himself undergoes
a gratuitously repetitive characterization: he "altogether suggest[s] the
draught horse, immensely strong, stupid, docile, obedient," he gazes "stu-
pidly," he seems "absolutely stupid" in response to a speech of his friend,
Marcus, and he is defined yet again as "[t]his poor crude dentist of Polk
Street, stupid, ignorant, vulgar" (3, 12, 13, 28). Similarly, the long list of
Trina's defining features—"royal black hair," "narrow half-open eyes,"
"pale ears, suggestive of anemia"—recur with the regularity of a heroic tag
(78). The objects in McTeague's parlors—the steel engraving of the court
of Lorenzo de' Medici, the stone pug dog, his concertina—are re-catalogued,
object by object, when a character sees them for the first time, just as they are
re-catalogued when they are sold at auction. But even in the absence of such
motivation, Norris seems unable to resist repeating what he's already written. In the closing desert scene we're told that McTeague "at times, with a
vague, nearly automatic gesture . . . reached his hand forward, the fingers
prehensile, and directed toward the horizon, as if he would clutch it and
draw it nearer" (416). Then, as though inscribing the automaticity of the
gesture within the text, Norris recirculates the salient details: we're told that
McTeague goes "straight on . . . at times reaching his hand forward, the
fingers prehensile, grasping, as it were, toward the horizon" (428). Though
not an exact restatement, the congruence of the lines certainly creates a rep-
etition-effect, an effect sufficient to elicit the reviewers' sense that "Mr. Norris seems positively to court weariness on the part of his readers by this
droning repetition of details."[43] If we understand Trina to suffer from a disorder that provokes her to make compulsive contact with her gold to insure
its presence, then we might understand Norris as a writer who projects
something like the same disorder onto his reader. That is: it is as though he
has no faith in a phenomenology of reading wherein an image can be re-
trieved through association, where readers possess the capacity of object

conservation. As readers, we seem meant, like Zerkow, to learn a description by heart and thus to have full faith in the existence of the referent.

Repetition in Norris's fiction, of course, characterizes more than the "droning repetition of details." For just as the awkward repetition of the fact that Trina uses "'nonpoisonous paint'" to paint the Noah's Ark animals makes her toxic reaction seem wholly predictable, so too the fact that her relationship with McTeague seems to repeat the relationship between Maria and Zerkow makes her murder seem inevitable. The novel produces the effect of fate—or of fatedness—by lodging its protagonists within the already written. Moreover, *Blix* and *A Man's Woman* (1900) are novels that repeat Norris's more experimental tales, however seriously they revise them, exorcising the Zolaesque passions, depathologizing the characters, turning stories of degeneration into stories of regeneration, transposing relationships into more publishable and potentially popular plots. Thus in *Blix* it is not the brutishness of the brute, but the manliness of man that stirs and takes hold of Condy Rivers: "A sudden male force had begun to develop in Condy. A master-emotion had shaken him, and he had commenced to see and to feel the serious, more abiding, and perhaps the sterner side of life" (263). Whereas Vandover loses everything because of his gambling, Blix saves Condy from gambling; whereas Vandover loses touch with his artistic talents, Blix inspires Condy to dedicate himself to the hard work of successful writing. Even as *Blix* thus "normalizes" *Vandover*, *A Man's Woman* "normalizes" *McTeague:* it is the story of an Arctic explorer, Ward Bennett—a "colossal" man, with a "a great brutal jaw, with its aggressive, bullying, forward thrust," "a brute"—and the woman he loves, Lloyd Searight, who dedicates her life to him.[44] Though Blix is called "a *man's* woman" (279) who "made a man" of Condy (313), that relation becomes more literal in *A Man's Woman*, where Lloyd becomes her man's amanuensis, and the relationship is built upon her desire and power to prosthetically rejuvenate the man. The plot remains devolutionary, only here the man must devolve into the real man that he was.[45]

Within *A Man's Woman*, the question of habit and of repetition are staged as questions of writing: Lloyd and Bennett gradually develop the routine of writing together, and what they write gradually comes to repeat what Bennett has already written.[46] In the opening chapters, the account of Bennett's grueling, unsuccessful Antarctic expedition includes excerpts from his journal: "December 1st—Wednesday—Everybody getting weaker. Metz breaking down. Sent Adler down to the shore to gather shrimps. We had about a mouthful apiece for lunch. Supper, a spoonful of glycerin and hot water" (35). In the closing chapters, as Bennett dictates the draft of a book

about his adventure, he finally begins to "read simply and with grim direct-
ness from the entries in his journal precisely as they had been written," unable as he is to find new words for the horror of the experience: "December
1st, Wednesday—Everybody getting weaker. . . . Metz breaking down. . . .
Sent Adler to the shore to gather shrimps; . . . we had about a mouthful
apiece at noon; . . . supper, a spoonful of glycerin and hot water" (256–57;
Norris's ellipses). During these lengthy quotations, which amount to the
novel's autocitation, the woman who serves as Bennett's "amanuensis" (251)
begins to see and to feel the desperate scenes described, shaking with com-
passion for the tormented men. Norris finds here a diegetic justification for
the repetition without which, it seems, he felt unable to convince his readers
of the reality of what he represents. For though this dramatic, cooperative
reproduction of Bennett's adventure in writing has an erotic charge (one
might call it, indeed, the novel's substitute for sex), this scene of writing
seems rather to motivate the act of repeating, to legitimize the autocitation,
as though the reader of the novel—a novel that implicitly transcribes much
of Bennett's book, much of which transcribes Lloyd's transcription, which
itself turns out to be, in large measure, a transcription of his journal—might
thus, finally, share Lloyd Searight's empathy, or indeed might thus develop
sufficient faith in the story to feel its force as history.

Just as this "trick" recalls Mrs. Obermann's comment on the kinetoscope
in *McTeague*—"it's all a drick"—so too the repetition in Norris's fiction
might be said to instantiate discursively the kind of reproduction taking
place in other media, most obviously photography and film. But even as those
media may seem to be at work in the material unconscious of *McTeague,*
both "The Joyous Miracle" and *A Man's Woman* clarify how insistently Norris focused on the medium of writing.[47] A writer like Gertrude Stein would
go on to say that she "was doing what the cinema was doing" (even if she had
yet to see a movie) because "each of us in our own way are bound to express
what the world in which we are living is doing," and "our period was undoubtedly the period of the cinema and series production."[48] But if Norris
was thus "bound" to express other media, his compulsion to repeat looks like
a rival effort to materialize the referent through his own reproductive technique. If his fiction nonetheless offers a moral for modernity, it is that reproduction and representation, however much they may reduce objects and
events to abstractions, are also the means—or one means—by which they
can fully confront us as things.

Which is to say that, confronted by the very reproduction of an object,
we may recognize its thingness—may recognize some "thing" about the object.[49] For Stein, one of William James's most famous students, the relation

between the representation of habit and the habits of representation came to vitalize her experiment in the novel form. Her use of repetition in *The Making of Americans* (completed in 1911, published in 1925) risks nonsense, but chiefly because it so thoroughly literalizes the conviction—a Jamesian conviction—that sense results from habit. About the "men who knew" David Hersland, she writes that "they would leave him to his strong fighting to his brushing of people away from him to his going another way away from the man in front of him in his blustering fashion that was to himself a brushing away of the people around him."[50] She also claims that "they left him to his fighting, to his brushing people away from around him, to his going away from them in a blustering fashion which was to himself brushing them away from before him" (146). Repetitive as Stein's book is, the repetition, of course, is never exact, and the proximity and intensity of the repetition foregrounds that inexactness the way that Norris's fiction does not.[51] Easy as it is to consider Stein's novel a merely linguistic experiment—one in which, as William Carlos Williams argued, language becomes opaque, and thus an object itself rather than a transparency disclosing other objects—she was clearly interested in the epistemological role of habit, and, no less than Norris, in preservation and change.[52] She said of everyone that there is "repeating coming out of them [that] makes a history of each one of them," that "repeating slowly comes to make in each one a completed history of them" (292–93). In a clause: repetition is the mode of becoming historical; alternatively, we know people through their repetitions.

But Stein also argued that "there is no such thing as repetition"; the phrase of music, as Proust would have it, returns "the same and yet other, as things return in life."[53] This is to suppose that she shares the conviction, more explicitly formulated in a tradition running from Nietzsche to Gilles Deleuze, that repetition is irreducible to replication, and that, above all, it must be radically distinguished from habits, those "passive syntheses of which we are organically composed." Repetition, Deleuze goes on, must be differentiated from abstraction, and thus from modes of iterative narration; the reenactment of "non-substitutable singularities" is irreducible *"to all forms of generality,"* which always obscure the play of differences in the return of the same.[54] If no event (given its uniqueness in time) is reducible to another, then "repetition" must name a difference.

Still, if repetition can be differentiated from habit, it may seem harder to imagine differentiating habit from repetition, on which our common sense understanding of "habit" depends. Human habit, we might say, is simply repetition that has become unconscious. And yet, even as Deleuze makes much of preserving repetition from habit, Dewey makes much of preserving habit from repetition. "Repetition," he came to argue, "is in no sense the essence of habit": "habit means special sensitiveness or accessibility to certain classes of stimuli, standing predilections and aversions, rather than bare recurrence of specific acts."[55] Extending the Peircian understanding of habit, Dewey draws attention away from the specificity of discrete yet repeated acts and toward the generality of disposition or character, toward habit understood as a mode of organization and not as a set of actions. The perpetual nonconvergence of that specificity (those specificities) and that generality goes far toward explaining the coexistence of iterative narration and descriptive repetition in *McTeague,* and it goes far toward explaining the sheer length of *The Making of Americans.* In Stein's case, the repetitive, noniterative mode of disclosing habit (in Dewey's sense of the word) amounts to the originating impulse to write. The impossibility of accomplishing that disclosure through repetition means that the project could never end. Although she abandoned the novel, she never finished it.

Misuse Value

Gertrude Stein shows scant interest in physical objects, as opposed to the human "history" of everyone, and she never threatens to conflate the organic and inorganic worlds. Nonetheless, *A Long Gay Book* (1933) written just after Stein abandoned *The Making of Americans* in 1911 and dedicated to the depiction not of individual types but of pairs (and "sometimes threes and fours and fives"), moves toward an engagement with the sensuous world. That move, though, hardly settles for the figurative, in the pictorial sense. Whereas "things" appear subjective and abstract throughout much of the book—"If there is a thin thing some are denying that it is a thin thing. . . . In all men . . . there is always something in them of being certain of seeing the thing at which they are looking"—they eventually achieve specificity and matter-of-factness: "A tree which is thick is a tree which is thick."[56] But such an apparent recognition of the physical object world (which is no conviction about its unalterable objectivity) transforms into linguistic experiment— "Lecture, lecture a hat and say it is a cat, say it is a lively description, say that there is collusion" (249–50). The book concludes with the sort of aural riffs that comprise the "Objects" section of *Tender Buttons* (1913), leaving the matter at hand far behind: "Beef yet, beef and beef and beef. Beef yet, beef yet" (252).

In contrast, Leo Stein, after his aesthetic break with his sister over (in part) the formalist, non-figurative impulse of cubism, remained committed to approaching art through the aesthetic recognition of objects. On his way toward elaborating the "thingness" of art (its "capacity to have objective character"), Stein discusses in his *A-B-C of Aesthetics* (1927) how those instrumental, everyday objects of which we are not "vividly aware" can become objects of our attention: "It is when an instrument ceases to work as an instrument," he argues, "that it gets to be an object," something that demands "our most particular attention."[57] He thus describes how the interruption of habit, the failure of repetition, can call our attention to what we might call the thingness of the object.

Recognizably modernist as such a description is, versions of it certainly surface before the century's turn.[58] Whereas pragmatism established habit as the governing dynamic to explain human behavior, physical law, and the human apprehension of the physical, Josiah Royce wanted instead to focus on the potency of habit's interruption. For Royce, "reality" made sense only as the product of social consciousness, a literal or imagined collective authentication. As for individual consciousness, he understood it as diminishing in inverse proportion to the intensification of habit; we become conscious of consciousness, as it were, only as "an incident of an interrupted adjustment to our environment" (454).[59] "Not routine," he insists, "but irregularity, gives the physically interpretable sign of mind" (454), which is to say that the sign requires both repetition and its interruption. Humans may be bundles of habits, as James would have it, but when those habits shift we recognize mental capacity.

Even as Royce pointed to "phenomenal irregularities" as that which disclose the mind at work, so James, despite his conviction that habit grounds our apperception of objects, pointed to other irregularities that disclose a different sense of things, the sensation of their properties. There is a disjuncture in the *Psychology* that in fact allows us to differentiate between objects and things precisely because it temporalizes, it narrates, an interaction between the somatic and the cognitive. In his chapter on the "perception of things," he tells the story of what happens when our habits are broken, when for instance you look at a landscape with your head upside down or when you turn a painting bottom upward: "the colors grow richer and more varied, we don't understand the meaning of the painting, but, to compensate for the loss, we feel more freshly the value of the mere tints and shadings" (727). James understands perception and "naked sensation" as different acts that cannot take place at the same time, since sensations in themselves do not add up. We might say, rather, that we need to understand two distinct, dynamic, intertwined materializations: one where we seem to begin with sensations, which precipitate perception; and one where the proximate sensuous engagement lies between one and another perceptual horizon. The viewer's perceptual failure prompts a different kind of attention; but, in the routine of daily life, perception perpetually forecloses sensuous experience in order to render the physical world phenomenal (which means rendering it habitable). The difference between the apperceptive constitution of the thing, in what we might call its objecthood, and the experience of the thing, in what we might call its thinghood, emerges in the moment (and no doubt only as a moment) of re-objectification that results from a kind of misuse—turning the picture bottom up, standing on one's head. We might materialize the world around us through habit, but only the interruption of habit will call our attention to brute physicality. The point may be less that "sensation is one thing and perception another," and more that the experience of sensation depends on disorientation or dislocation—which is to say, on both habit and its disruption.

However unintentional, it hardly seems surprising here that James's examples—the landscape, the painting upside down—locate us squarely in the realm of the aesthetic. And in American aesthetics—the Santayana not of *The Sense of Beauty* (1896), with its Humean epistemology, but of *Interpretations of Poetry and Religion* (1900)—the power of art (if not, admittedly, its beauty) is explicitly claimed to lie in its capacity to break through our habitual modes of interacting with the world. Poetry forces us to "plunge for a moment into that torrent of sensation and imagery over which the bridge of prosaic association habitually carries us safe and dry to some conventional act. How slight that bridge commonly is, how much an affair of trestles and wire, we can hardly conceive."[60] The Romantic effort to derange the senses, the modernist effort to defamiliarize the world—these work to pitch us off the very bridge that Peirce understood to be "span[ning] the chasm between the chance-medley of chaos and the cosmos of order and law." Santayana's "torrent of sensation" amounts to the undisclosed sublimity that lurks within and threatens the everyday.

All this is to say that both a modernist aesthetic fixated on repetition (marked by Gertrude Stein) and a modernist aesthetic fixated on the interruption of habit (Leo Stein) can be seen, in nascent form, competing within pragmatism, and indeed within James himself—as mere descriptions of our access to the physical object world. And just as James's *Psychology* at times belies its faith in habit, so within the prosaic world of *McTeague*, we can be plunged into a "torrent of sensation."

I have been reading Norris as a writer for whom habit elides time while repetition marks it, and I have been reading *McTeague* as a novel where, both diegetically and formally, the compulsion to repeat persists where habit has failed to evolve into instinct. Instead, the failure of repetition, in the novel's most comic scene, provides "poetic" access to the physical object world. At an early stage in the novel, McTeague and his friend Marcus play a game of pool, after which Marcus bets his companion that he cannot repeat his parlor trick of mouthing a billiard ball. Marcus himself performs the feat efficiently, poising a billiard ball "in front of his face, then with a sudden, horrifying distension of his jaws cramm[ing] it into his mouth, and shut[ting] his lips over it." Amazed, McTeague is quickly alarmed at the task he faces:

> McTeague fell suddenly grave. The matter was serious. He parted his thick mustaches and opened his enormous jaws like an anaconda. The ball disappeared inside his mouth. Marcus applauded. . . . Then suddenly [McTeague's] face grew purple, his jaws moved convulsively, he pawed at his cheeks with both hands. . . . It was terrible. The dentist rose to his feet, stumbling about among the dogs, his face working, his eyes starting. Try as he would, he could not stretch his jaws wide enough to slip the ball out. (57–58)

The scene (finally resolved when the ball suddenly slips free) establishes the competitive nature of this friendship, foreshadowing the physical struggles the men will have over Trina and over her gold. The scene marks the homo-erotic aggression that characterizes those struggles, and it marks McTeague's oral-sadistic stage of development, his irrepressible habit of putting things— like Trina's fingers—in his mouth, and of putting things in the mouths of others. The episode also anticipates the extent to which the novel will concentrate on aberrant modes of possessing physical objects. Further, the oral blockage can be read as an emblem of the nonfunctioning economy of this novel, the hoarding (of both junk and of gold) that brings circulation to a stop. I want to emphasize, though, how this blockage results from McTeague's failed—or barely successful—attempt to repeat Marcus's exhibit, which itself fails to comply with the rules of the game, dislodging the billiard ball from its customary scene of circulation just as Trina dislodges her gold from circulation. I want to imagine that the difficulty of replication here provokes a reader to concentrate on the size, shape, substance, and taste of a billiard ball the way that no narrative account of a game of billiards could.

The moral of the scene boils down to the admonition against putting things where they don't belong, which can re-thematize the novel spatially (as opposed to temporally) as a story less about habit than about the dimensional effects of dislocation. For just as the ball is really too big for McTeague's mouth, so McTeague is simply too big for his environment until he leaves the city for the hills and the desert. He fits San Francisco no better than his dentist's hands—"enormous, red, and covered with a fell of stiff

yellow hair"—fit his patients' mouths (3). And just as it is the original dislocation of McTeague from the mines that makes his size matter, so too when
his famous gold tooth must be removed from its position as a shop-sign, it asserts its physicality: "in one corner of the room, next to the window, monstrous, distorted, brilliant, shining with a light of its own, stood the dentist's
sign, the enormous golden tooth, the tooth of a Brobdingnag" (288). Once
both a sign and a thing, the tooth (like Trina's gold) has simply become a
thing.

These scenes of misuse and dislocation all result in the magnification of
physical properties. Indeed, although Marx imagined that "use value" foregrounds the "sensuous characteristics" of an object that are "extinguished"
in the abstracting medium of commodity exchange, in fact the medium of
habitual use, from an experiential point of view, can similarly conceal the
"character of things as things."[61] This is why Adorno insists that the human
contact with "things" is severely limited "under the law of pure functional-
ity."[62] "Unnatural" use, uncustomary use, is what, in contrast, discloses the
composition of objects. Forced to use a knife as a screwdriver, you achieve
a new recognition of its thinness, its hardness, the shape and size of the
handle.

My point about all this is that, within a novel whose own aesthetic depends so much on habituating the reader to its referents, there is a diegetic
account of an altogether different aesthetic that will come to energize the
modernist capacity to call our attention to objects—be it the urinal that becomes Duchamp's *Fountain*, or the bicycle seat that becomes Picasso's *Bull*,
or the refuse that attains formal brilliance in a Walker Evans photograph, or
"the broken / pieces of a green / bottle" that assume luminosity in William
Carlos Williams's "Between Walls."[63] Part of the point of such dislocations
(which can be coded as misappropriations) is to interrupt the habits with
which we view the world, the habits that prevent us from seeing the world—
to call us to a particular and particularizing attention. Such writers and artists
become the new dealers in junk, descendants not of Norris but of Maria and
Zerkow, who confer new value with an act of relocation. The objects that
Vandover finds under the sink—"a battered teapot lacking a nozzle, a piece
of rubber"—could be resituated (in two or three decades) within an exhibition and could attain there the status and value of art. Which is in part to argue that, just as Mary Douglas has taught us to think of dirt as "matter out of
place," so too modernism teaches us that finding a new place for detritus, re-
cycling it into some new scene, confers new value on it.[64]

Such generalizations, though, may well detract from apprehending the particular conceptual stakes raised by Norris's billiard scene. In his discussion of objects and objectness outside the realm of art, Leo Stein calls his readers' attention to the "objectification" that "comes about from games," his point being that "a multitude of objects have been created by and for games, and few things awaken more acute attention, or lead to more perceptive discrimination" (61). If Stein is right, then such acute attention (which results from the interruption of daily routine) may well have prompted Norris to isolate the billiard ball as the object that provokes questions about repeatability, on the one hand, and physical discrimination, on the other—a scene intensifying our attention by being staged beyond the bounds of the game (the game's prescribed routine). Moreover, if Stein is right, then such "acute attention" may have determined the central place that billiard balls have assumed in Western epistemology.

When Hume turned to the question of how human understanding develops the impression of necessary connection, of cause and effect, he turned to the billiard table. Knowledge of this relation is not attained by "reasonings *a priori*," he argues, "but arises entirely from experience."[65] Since there can be no impression of "necessary connexion" between objects, it must be "custom" that convinces us that "a billiard-ball moving in a straight line towards another" will force the second ball to move in the same line. Our "feeling," our "sentiment," our "belief" in the inevitability of the result derives from repeated experiences: "after a repetition of similar instances, the mind is carried by habit, upon the appearances of one event, to expect its usual attendant, and to believe, that it will exist" (125, 145).

Just as the very formalism of the game of billiards may have made the case of the two billiard-balls an "obvious illustration" (147) in a philosophical text, so too these objects, created for a game and thus, by Stein's light, enjoying particular objectification, may have helped Hume elide the question of objective physicality (and to deal only with impressions and experience). Kant, though, raised a particular question about the philosophical efficacy of the example, revising Hume with a formulation that might be said to return the matter to the ludic: for just as one does not derive the rules from the game, but, rather, the game is made possible by the existence of the rules, so, with causality and the other pure concepts of understanding, "they are not derived from experience, but experience is derived from them."[66] Habit thus loses its pedagogical potency, which is one reason why pragmatism found Kant so antipathetic. In the first *Critique*, the image of the billiard balls famously gives way to the image of the glowing stove, warming a room while lurking, hidden, behind a screen in the corner (not disclosing itself as the source of an effect). A pragmatist might well argue, though, that only our knowledge of stoves (a synthesis of our experience that could go by the name of habit) makes the Kantian scene make sense.

This gestural reference to Western philosophy intimates how overdetermined Norris's attention to billiard balls and stoves might be. Foremost, though, the image of McTeague, outside his routine, struggling desperately to dislodge a billiard ball from his mouth, dramatizes the threat of the physical object world engaged beyond "some conventional act." In a novel saturated by the explanatory power of habit, Norris might be said to have dislocated the billiard ball not just from the scene of the game, but also from the familiar scene where habit first attained its epistemological force. Outside such scenes, the physical object, the physical world, confronts us with its alterity, not as a thing come-to-life but as an utterly familiar thing that can suddenly feel life-threatening.

THREE

Regional Artifacts

The true history of our race is written in things.
—Otis T. Mason, Bureau of Ethnology,
U.S. National Museum

"I thank you very much for your kind note and your beautiful piece of quartz which I shall treasure very much."[1] In 1897 Sarah Orne Jewett wrote this expression of thanks to Irving Mower, curator of Maine's geological exhibit at the World's Columbian Exposition four years before. Much as she admired the quartz, she was apprehensive about accepting the gift: "I cannot quite bear to rob your collection of such a fine thing or to rob you of your pleasant associations with it. A collector has a peculiar affection for such treasures, as I very well know." Yet this knowledge hardly quelled her own attraction to the quartz. She resolved the ambivalence by considering the "robbery" a long-term loan: "This shall live on my desk as long as my conscience will let it and perhaps a little longer, and I shall never see it without remembering the kind thought that sent it there" (108). The successive dislocations of the quartz—wrested from the ground and into the international exhibition site, into Mower's private hands, then on to Jewett's desk—these obviously produce and complicate the object's value and meaning. The quartz may have once represented the geological state of Maine (if not that childhood that precedes the existence of all nations, as Cuvier would put it), but it comes to represent, by way of new "associations," the generosity of Mower, and the history of a friendship. Not geology, then, but anthropology, history, and biography become the relevant modes of explanation for the memento: not the natural, but the social and humanistic, sciences.

Were I to re-exhibit the quartz today, contextualized with some such knowledge of its provenance, but situated as a bit of *realia* to round off an exhibit of Jewett's study—her study reconstructed as a period room—what sense would you make of this rock? You might say that it represents Jewett's habit of collecting (restrained for the era, really, for someone of her class—think of Twain's House in Hartford, or of Freud's study); perhaps her fetishization of certain objects, especially gifts; perhaps her sense of touch; perhaps—"living" there on her desk, along with a silver dish of old-fashioned peppermints, a box of matches, and a glass lamp, but there right beside the inkwell—her commitment to incorporating material objects into her sketches of coastal Maine.

But has my mise-en-scène thus mortified the quartz, drained it of any material vitality, its very shimmer dulled by being subjected to an archeological epistemology where its role, within this too harmonious scene we call history, is never to be itself but always, always to represent something else? And if the remaining relic can be thought to suffer such a fate, the fate of *dislocation,* what of the absent author herself and her *location* within this materialized scene of writing? Here Jewett is metonymically conjured up by these things that she consciously and unconsciously touched. And here she is incarcerated in the material sediments of her occupation, into the scene of writing.

But a desire to so situate this writer would seem to respond to the converging impact of history and anthropology on the field of literary studies. One of the outcomes for the study of Jewett, the American regionalist most celebrated as a regionalist (as opposed to Twain, hypercanonized as a nationalist), has been how profoundly regionalized her work has become. "Like the countryfolk she describes," Richard Brodhead writes, Jewett's "literary identity bears an inescapable mark of local derivation"—the mark, that is, of the Boston literary milieu in which Jewett thrived, centered by Annie Fields's famous home in Beacon Hill, 148 Charles Street.[2] In this scene of Boston's most significant salon, and the home of Jewett's most intimate friend, she spent hours talking and reading, and hours writing. In what Willa Cather called this "sanctuary," and what Henry James understood as a "waterside museum" (with its display of "votive objects"), Jewett assumed a celebrated place.[3]

And yet, compelling as this presentation of Jewett may be as "a single historical exhibit,"[4] she herself would certainly have objected to being placed in Boston, and thus displaced from her home town of Berwick, Maine: "I count myself entirely a Maine person and not a transplanted Boston citizen even though I may spend many weeks of the winter within the limits of Ward Nine!"[5] Moreover, of course, regionalism was perceived in the 1890s as providing relief from the urban scene, as the antidote to "the same cosmopolitan monotony which is everywhere effacing the last vestiges of local color and local feeling."[6] More ironically, the Boston milieu was precisely where the artistic possibilities of transcending the specificities of time, place, and milieu (anthropology's culture) were being thought and felt as a new American devotion to Culture (in Mathew Arnold's sense). As Cather reported of the Fields salon, "The ugliness of the world, all possibility of wrenches and jars and wounding contacts, seemed securely shut out. . . . [T]he tawdry and cheap have been eliminated and the enduring things have taken their proper, happy places."[7] The enduring things, not quotidian things. Just as the genre of regionalism provided new access to the literary scene for a demographically diverse generation of American writers, so too for Jewett regionalist writing was meant to promote access to more than merely regionalist thinking—and access to something like a transcultural and transhistorical "human condition."

In the following pages, then, rather than "reading nineteenth-century regionalism back into its original scene of operation,"[8] understood as the literary scenes of writing and reading, I read *The Country of the Pointed Firs* (1896), Jewett's best-known book, into a more expansive scene of anthropological and historical thought—which is to say precisely back into those scenes from which the legitimization of such scenic thinking originally derives. I do so in part to suggest how ambivalent Jewett came to be about the "scene-agent ratio," to borrow Kenneth Burke's phrase, the ratio that establishes a "synecdochic relation" between place and person, that equates the quality of character with the quality of the context by which that character is contained.[9] This is the ratio through which we can understand a convergence of American naturalism and regionalism, and the compatibility of these genres with the historicist, culturalist turn in literary criticism, which has been particularly successful with the closing decades of the American nineteenth-century (as it has been with the English Renaissance and the English eighteenth-century). If, as Burke says, "variants of the scene-agent ratio abound in typical nineteenth-century thought, so strongly given to the study of motives by the dialectic pairing of people and things" (9), then we might say that a new variant—the scene-text ratio—abounds in recent historicist thought, governing the demonstration of consistency between text and culture. In Burke's illustration: it is as though you've stepped too close to a Seurat painting and lost the foreground figures, which have dissolved into the background.

The "pairing of people and things" has played a persistent role in accounts of *The Country of The Pointed Firs*, from the description of how the narrator's "empathic style" turns physical details into evocative signs, to the claim that the inhabitants of Dunnet Landing live "their passions into their objective world to such an extent that every object bespeaks a history of human association."[10] In this chapter, then, I take up something of a critical commonplace about *The Country of the Pointed Firs* in the effort to make it seem both a little more common and a little less. More common by showing how extensive such a materialist epistemology became in the 1890s, as evident in professional anthropology and history as it was in museology and retailing. Less common by working out some of the preconditions of this epistemology. But I also want to show how, even as Jewett participates in the logic of a new "object-based epistemology" where physical things attach people to place, she dramatizes the limits of any such materialism.[11] As a conclusion to the chapter, I begin to sketch an underground genealogy of modernism, which both traces William Carlos Williams's concern for things in the 1920s to the local colorists of a previous generation, and recasts Cather's modernism as the effort to rethink the "dialectic pairing of people and things." Whereas in the previous chapter I tried to determine, for pragmatist and naturalist thinking, how a physical thing is experienced materially, I now want to draw attention to *object culture* and to address the problematic of the significant thing—the set of questions raised by the effort to turn matter into meaning. Jewett's novel about a summer spent in Dunnet Landing, Maine, is an account comprised of sketches that relate, foremost, the narrator's developing intimacy with her proprietor, Mrs. Todd, and their visits to various local villagers. It is an account comprised, no less, of scenes where people are "paired" with things in ways that prompt several questions. What ideas are embedded in things? How does the narrator gain access to them? What sort of staging is involved in this object-based epistemology? How does Jewett's fiction dramatize the work involved in determining the value of material objects not *in* culture but *for* culture, for an apprehension of culture? How does the pairing of people and things connect those people to place, or how does the pairing of people and place foreground the role of things? And what, finally, are the limits and liabilities of such pairing for the culturalist thinking of the 1890s as for our own?

Natural Histories

"Not Things, but Men." These words serve as a motto on the title page of the *Memoirs of the International Congress of Anthropology*, held during the 1893 World's Columbian Exposition, the Chicago World's Fair. But at the fair it was really things more than men—"numerous detached collections of objects"—that offered the fairgoer, let alone the professional, an "abundant supply of material for Anthropological study."[12] That supply included knives and arrow heads, board games and dice, pots and mortars, masks and boats, chisels, adzes, drums, looms, mush-sticks, and mummies—more stuff than you can find in a novel by Dickens or Balzac. Some experts, notably Francis Ward Putnam (of Harvard's Peabody Museum), believed that the living exhibits along the Midway Plaisance (the so-called ethnological villages) provided the fairgoer with "instruction" as well as "joy."[13] The Midway, after all, had come under the auspices of the Exposition's Ethnological Department. But few members of the anthropological profession, neither the folklorist nor the ethnologist, doubted that the genuine anthropological achievement was to be found not in the fair's exhibit of "men" but in its vast accumulation of "things." The anthropologist of the day, after all, had to devote a professional life to things: to the business of securing artifacts from amateur archeologists, of curating exhibits, of funding fieldwork through the sale of sundry relics to both individuals and institutions, of sustaining the traffic in ethnological artifacts by certifying their value. In retrospect, Chicago's Exposition, no less than the Paris exposition of 1889, appears as a culminating manifestation of anthropology's museal era, that era when an anthropologist's place was in a museum, not in a university.[14]

"Don't try to write *about* things: write the things themselves just as they are." Sarah Orne Jewett considered this advice from her father (a doctor) to have been career-defining, and it was advice she repeated in private and in public.[15] But of course "things," things just as they are, can disclose only the heterogeneity of the world. Writing things to make them meaningful—to make them legible—requires rhetorical work no less impressive than the curatorial work that took place at the fair. This is why the valorization of things, and its concomitant and inseparable valorization of regions, provides a point of access for reading the epistemological endeavor that goes by the name of regionalism. For though Jewett hardly shared Otis Mason's "ruling thought"—that people leave their "history most fully recorded in the works of their hands,"[16] and not, that is, in their language, rituals, or social systems—she nonetheless shared something of his fixation on the artifactual record of human history. It is simple enough to sense how the collection of underplotted sketches that comprise *The Country of the Pointed Firs,* as they work synecdochically to represent a self-contained culture, may be said to depend on those "poetics of detachment" that Barbara Kirshenblatt-Gimblett describes as the requisite work for producing the "ethnographic object": the act of excising a fragment that, reappearing as part of a collection, comes to express the culture as a whole.[17] But though readers have often described regionalism as an ethnographic or anthropological pursuit (as the study of particular people in particular places), American anthropology itself was just being *regionalized* in the closing decade of the century. And though other readers routinely call attention to the important function of objects and their interpretation in Jewett's work, they've done so with no sense of how such materialism was also bound up with (or bound by) a regionalist temper that precipitated a significant shift in anthropology: away from the diachronic, evolutionist narration of technology that considers "the whole human race in space and time as a single group,"[18] and toward the synchronic description of cultures that are symbolically and physically self-contained.

Indeed, the analogy between regionalist writing and anthropology has been underwritten by a sense not of epistemology but of genre: the ethnographic narrative of the participant observer's fieldwork, where the "rapport" with the native population provides access to the "webs of significance" that constitute culture.[19] But this genre of ethnographic writing, so familiar from a tradition that extends from Malinowski to Geertz, had little place in the profession (not yet a discipline) of the 1880s and 1890s. Fieldworkers like Frank Hamilton Cushing, who published celebrated accounts of his four-year interaction with the Zuñi in *Century Magazine*, published very different work for his colleagues: in his contribution to the *Memoirs* of the Anthropology Congress in 1893, for instance, he provides a detailed story of how he recreated the process of using clay-lined sand pits for shaping the kind of pottery he'd found in the Erie shore middens.[20] He appears less the ethnographer, more the archeologist and technological historian.

Jewett's original work in the 1870s, like a great deal of the local-color writing that commanded the U.S. literary market after the Civil War, can be said to anticipate the ethnographic narrative we've become familiar with.[21] During the months when *The Country of the Pointed Firs* was being serialized, the *Atlantic* also published articles on "The Spirit of a Illinois Town," Japanese folk songs, "Some Yorkshire Good Cheer," "A Night and a Day in Spain," "The German and the German-American," among many other accounts of local cultures. A wave of globalization in the U.S. (a result of immigration, middle-class travel, and international trade) provoked a romance of the local and an insatiable desire to know about innumerable locales. Most every region of the nation was reproduced *as knowledge* that could be incorporated, no matter how eccentric, into the nation's knowledge of itself—the eccentricity being an effect of the knowledge itself. But marking "the anthropological dimension" of regionalism, understanding local-color fiction as a kind of "anthropological fieldwork," translating regionalism into "nineteenth-century ethnography"—this has meant overlooking more literal connections between literary figures and anthropological institutions (for instance, the fact that Twain was an inaugural member of the American Folklore Society in 1888), and it has meant effectively foreclosing any inquiry into the way that Jewett's particular attention to objects more provocatively situates her within the anthropological matrix—the museal matrix—of the day.[22]

Yet the narratorial investment in objects in *The Country of the Pointed Firs* is not ubiquitous. Indeed, differentiating between objects that are named and noticed, but hardly dwelt upon, on the one hand, and, on the other, objects that are affectionately singled out and lingered over, establishes the foundation for constructing significant objects. When Captain Litttlepage and the narrator leave one another, he asks her "to stop at his house some day," so he can show her "some outlandish things that he had brought home from sea."[23] And Mrs. Todd has decorated her house "with West Indian curiosities, specimens of conch shells and fine coral which [three sea-faring husbands] had brought home from their voyages in lumber-laden ships" (384). Such objects, which could well come from Melville's Spouter-Inn, are the remnants of the mercantile economy by which coastal villages like Dunnet Landing thrived before the Civil War. But just as that economy has disappeared, providing the overarching economic pathos of the novel, so these remnants never become fully present in the text. Unexamined and undescribed, the "curiosities" seem dismissed as mere curiosities. The novel thus differs from *Deephaven* (1877), Jewett's first collection of sketches, where the first-person narrator seems to relish any accumulation of things, from the "treasure" of a kitchen cupboard to that of a "large cabinet holding all the small curiosities and knick-knacks . . . old china figures and cups and vases, unaccountable Chinese carvings and exquisite corals and sea-shells, minerals and Swiss wood-work, and articles of *vertu* from the South Seas."[24] Such catalogues bespeak an indiscriminate fascination.

The discrimination in *The Country of the Pointed Firs* enacts the kind of effort advanced by the nation's foremost curators to shift the museum-goer's experience from mere sensation to education, an effort repeatedly voiced as a need to abandon the *cabinet des curiosités* on behalf of a new pedagogical practice. The Smithsonian, once called the National Cabinet of Curiosities, was originally responsible only for exhibiting the interesting objects accumulated by government-sponsored exploring expeditions. Renamed the U.S. National Museum in 1876, it became responsible for representing natural and technological history.[25] The transformation of American museums meant eradicating the "chance assemblage of curiosities," discarding the "cemetery of bric-à-brac," and replacing it with a "nursery of living thoughts."[26] As Curtis Hinsley has summarized this transformation, "the everyday, the mundane . . . rather than the exceptional," had become recognized as a historical resource.[27]

Curiosities were abandoned in the effort to produce genuine object lessons, the "object lesson" being one of the great clichés of the day. The imperative of the object lesson, as G. Brown Goode understood it in "The Museums of the Future," shared in a generalizable trajectory of the senses, the eye "used more and more," the ear "less and less." He aligned the museum project with a new visual culture where "the public lecturer uses the stereopticon, . . . the editor illustrates his journals and magazines with engravings, . . . and the merchant and manufacturer recommend their wares by means of vivid photographs." But the case of the museum provokes a somewhat different conclusion, with "descriptive writing set aside for pictures," and pictures "replaced by actual objects."[28] Indeed, Goode seems to voice a counternarrative to the story of modernity in which the subject endures an increasing estrangement from the material object world.[29] For from his point of view in 1893, "actual objects" had finally begun to appear, asserting themselves above and beyond verbal and visual representation.

Of course, though the dismissal of mere curiosities might be said to contribute to the anthropology-effect in *The Country of the Pointed Firs*, Jewett draws explicit attention not to anthropology at all, but to botany. If there is one occupation and preoccupation that makes the sketches cohere as a novel, just as it solidifies the relationship between the narrator and Mrs. Todd, it is the gathering of plants. The opening chapters establish the first months of summer as "herb-gathering season," a season the narrator spends not just letting a room from Mrs. Todd, but also sharing her life, caught up in the "slow herb-gathering progresses through woods and pastures" (380). Mrs. Todd's "slender business" enacts an appropriation and commodification of nature that renders it far more concrete than any appropriation of it on behalf of knowledge. For anthropologists like Goode, human artifacts bespoke as secure a system as did natural specimens. For writers like Emerson, Natural History had exquisitely "marrie[d] the visible to the Invisible."[30] But Jewett describes instead a culture of nature—the preparation and medicinal deployment of natural specimens, in the form of syrups, elixirs, and teas. Their value derives from their human use, not their natural form—their function, not their place in the taxonomic table, evolutionary time line, or divine system. All of which is to say that the explicitly botanical in Jewett's fiction has been transposed into the cultural.

It was such a transposition, *within* the field of anthropology, that accounts for a fundamental shift in its object of knowledge. In the 1880s, provoked by the question of how to organize objects in a meaningful exhibition, Boas worked to "regionalize" anthropology, and to *displace* artifacts from their traditional place within a taxonomic and evolutionary scheme. A curatorial question prompted his first theoretical claims in the field, his first published conceptualization of culture, where cultures are understood as nonsynchronous, and as nonsynchronizeable within some overarching human Culture.[31] His attack on Otis Mason's curatorial principles in the National

Museum (1887) was an attack on the absence of the geographical specificity with which to make sense of the ethnological collections, typologically arranged there according to basic form (the kind of object) rather than to specific function within a historically, geographically, and tribally specific milieu: "From a collection of . . . drums of 'savage' tribes and the modern orchestra, we cannot derive any conclusion but that similar means have been applied by all peoples to make music. The character of their music, the only object worth studying, which determines the form of the instruments . . . requires a complete collection of a single tribe."[32] By the time of the Columbian Exposition, Mason had taken much of the point. Convinced though he was that the American Indian constituted a single race, he wished to emphasize distinct cultural regions—cultures regionally bounded and defined both linguistically and materially, by words and by things.[33] He had come to believe that objects achieve significance not by being fit along a time line but by being placed within a particular chronotope—historically embedded in a particular place, where they embed people in place. The "acts of life," as opposed to language, "are in each culture area indigenous. They are materialized under the patronage and directorship of the region." Whereas language could be transported easily, there was considerable difficulty in mobilizing what he called "impediments."[34] His neglect of trade (and thus the very idea that goods might circulate beyond the reach of any one language) symptomatically demonstrates how thinking about things—thinking about things as embodied thoughts—meant fetishizing place, just as thinking about place meant fetishizing things.

By denigrating the "attempt to classify human inventions and other ethnological phenomena in light of biological specimens" (61), Boas had challenged the very idea that ethnological artifacts belonged in natural history museums, and thus challenged the ground rules for making sense of human technology. Mason had previously joined Goode in asserting scientific authority by analogizing ethnology to botany or zoology; artifacts were grouped to show the sequence of technological developments, invariable among disparate peoples and regions; typological classification was both the impetus and telos of anthropology. Mason, as Boas quoted, believed that ethnological artifacts "may be divided into families, genera, and species" and "regarded as products of specific evolution out of natural objects serving human wants and up to the most delicate machine serving the same function" (61). In his report on "The Progress of Anthropology 1890," Mason had insisted that only phenomena "arranged, classified, and studied after the manner of the naturalists . . . should be admitted into the laboratory of the anthropologist."[35] Goode, who praised Mason for "treating each savage art as the anatomist or embryologist treats his subject," wanted to dramatize the scientist's power, the capacity to transform "great accumulations of material objects" into the order of things, with such an emphasis on order that the objects themselves, in these "object lessons," seem to disappear from view.[36] As Foucault said of the natural history collections of another era, the importance of the ethnological exhibits lay in what they made visible—as a classificatory scheme, a taxonomic chart—at the expense of rendering specimens invisible, screening off the question of function.[37]

For Jewett, natural history has no such force; there is nothing of Emerson's sense that the naturalist's "study of things leads us back to Truth";[38] and her most popular story, "A White Heron," quietly condemns the naturalist's search for specimens. Natural history depends on privileging the sight of visible form, on attaining a "visibility freed from all other sensory burdens," on suppressing the other senses that threaten the whole domain of the orderable.[39] The naturalism of *The Country of the Pointed Firs*, in contrast, generally suppresses the visible on behalf of the tactile, the gustatory, and above all, the olfactory. To spend the summer with Mrs. Todd is to luxuriate in the "fragrant presence" of herbs: "the sea-breezes blew into the low end-window of the house laden with not only sweet-brier and sweet-mary, but balm and sage and borage and mint, wormwood and southernwood"— all visually homogenized into nothing but a "bushy bit of green garden" (378). The small house is similarly suffused by the aroma from Mrs. Todd's kitchen stove, where she brews an "old-fashioned spruce beer" in a small cauldron, if not "compounds" of herbs and molasses and vinegar (379, 378). This is how Jewett establishes an overwhelming intimacy between natural and human matter: whereas the *sight* of objects always depends on sufficient distance, the *smell* of things depends on proximity, on chemical contact, on physical infiltration. The culture of nature, as she describes it, is one where nature comes to saturate bodily life.

Which is why the metaphorization of the Dunnet villagers themselves as both flora and fauna seems so artless: it simply reads like the rhetorical effect of the narrated fact of the intimacy between people and place. Captain Littlepage, the narrator writes, "looked like an aged grasshopper of some strange human variety"; wearing "a narrow, long-tailed coat and walk[ing] with a stick," he "had the same 'cant to leeward' as the wind-bent trees on the height above" (385, 383). We might conclude that Jewett simply participates, here, in the kind of environmental determinism familiarly expressed by other New England writers. (Lucy Larcom begins *A New England Girlhood* [1889] by remarking that "people as well as plants have their *habitat*," and by proclaiming that "these gray ledges hold me by the roots, as they do the bayberry bushes.")[40] Yet attention to geo-environmental determination plays a secondary role in *The Country of the Pointed Firs* to those curious acts of classification where Mrs. Todd ("she seemed to class him") comprehends the human world according to her own natural history (385). "There's a great many such strayaway folk, just as there is plants" (462), she says, explaining the correspondence between a displaced laurel she knows and a displaced member of the Bowden clan, both of which thrive despite their unaccommodating environment. No less, she comprehends natural history in terms of human behavior: "grown trees act that way sometimes, same's folks" (454).

Whereas Otis Mason thought of the phenomena of "all mankind as natural objects,"[41] Mrs. Todd simply regards social behavior as a kind of natural behavior, which has the effect of naturalizing any "strange and unrelated person" (384), incorporating any anomaly into her scheme by explaining it in the analogical relays between local culture and local nature. But when the narrator herself contemplates the many Bowdens she's met during the Bowden reunion, she at once shares something of Mrs. Todd's metaphoric impulse and considers herself a botanist, sharing something of Darwin's wonder at the natural economy. "It was not the first time that I was full of wonder at the waste of human ability in this world, as a botanist wonders at the wastefulness of nature, the thousand seeds that die, the unused provision of every sort. . . . One sees exactly the same types in a country gathering as in the most brilliant city company" (466). Such a comment helps to accomplish what Jewett described as her literary "mission," the effort to "teach the world that country people were not the awkward, ignorant set those [city] people seemed to think."[42] But it also cuts against the grain of the novel's objective to document the "elaborate conventionalities" of the quaint village (377). And if the narrator's recognition of types allows her to see characterological congruities between city and country (with the sort of characterological typology classically deployed by realism and naturalism), those congruities challenge the role of local determinants; they must arrest the relay between culture and nature just as they release her characters from their physical environment.[43] The reference to general human types may be said to expose the limits and liabilities of the naturalization of culture: the fact that human history can begin to seem something less than human.

As I understand the achievement of the culture-effect in *The Country of the Pointed Firs* and in the changing field of anthropology itself, this depends both on differentiating the meaningful object from the mere curiosity and on overcoming the explanatory paradigm provided by the natural sciences. The narrator's abrupt deployment of typological thinking—to characterize not inanimate objects, but humans—appears as a recognition that the culture-region, in turn, has insufficient explanatory force. At this moment in the text Jewett may be said to struggle against the logic of the scene-agent ratio in the way that Burke suggested that the naturalist must struggle. For if character is explicable too narrowly in terms of indigenous scene, then the humanitarian concern for the waste of ability makes little sense. The difference between materialist anthropology and the materialism at work in Jewett's fiction amounts foremost to the difference between describing a culture and narrating the lives that compose a culture, for narrative—even naturalist narrative, even regionalist narrative—can hardly proceed without imagining alternative fates for its characters.

Life-Groups and the Cultural Thing

And yet by the 1890s, and extensively in the 1893 exposition, anthropology had begun to rely on a narrative exhibitionary genre—the environmental reconstruction, the so-called life-group exhibit that became increasingly popular with curators despite their expense. These marked the contingencies of time and place the way previous displays could not. They constellated person, place, and thing into an absorbing drama, supposedly bringing a local culture to life. These were the exhibits that wrested anthropology away from natural history and insisted that the meaning of things is disclosed by their function within a specific environment, not by their place within a history of technology. They replaced the serial display—fifty jugs lined up on a shelf—with the recreation of a scene of use: a woman holding a single jug to bring water to her child. They supplemented a "poetics of detachment" with a poetics of attachment, establishing contact between the singularized material object and a materialized human body (a mannequin made of plaster and wax), itself attached to a materialized milieu, composed of other objects. In *The Country of the Pointed Firs,* Jewett's sketches attain, in their tableaux of the everyday, something of the uncanny arrangement of these life-group exhibits, and together the sketches and the exhibits help disclose the logic—or the synecdochal magic—whereby an object emanates an aura of culture, whereby an everyday object becomes a cultural thing. The tableau is an especially simple and thus powerful mode for producing such magic, and it shows how much the cultural thing depends on our willingness to accede to what political economy would call the labor theory of value—to believe that what is "cultural" about a human artifact is what it tells us about the history of human work.[44]

The act of differentiating between the merely curious and the meaningful recurs on Green Island, in the home of Mrs. Todd's mother, Mrs. Blackett. But in this case, the shift of focus from the exceptional to the mundane appears as the narrator's departure from the "little old-fashioned best room," with its "few pieces of good furniture and pictures of national interest" and its "green paper curtains . . . stamped with conventional landscapes of a foreign order" (408–9). Rather than in these signs of the national and the international, it is in Mrs. Blackett's bedroom where the narrator finds "the real home, the heart of the old house on Green Island" (420). Here the woman has spent years sitting by the window, sewing. "There was a worn red Bible on the light-stand, and Mrs. Blackett's heavy silver-bowed glasses. Her thimble was on the narrow window-ledge, and folded carefully on the table was a thick striped-cotton shirt that she was making for her son. Those dear old fingers and their loving stitches, that heart which had the most of everything that needed love!" (420). Sentimental to a fault, this description suggests how the value of the objects depends on a history of human touch, on the metonymic trace that reveals a life of devotion, but also a daily life of production.[45] When Mrs. Blackett encourages the narrator to sit in her "old quilted rockin'-chair" (420), she asks her to occupy her occupation, her productive place in her universe.

The effectiveness of the scene depends on physical intimacy, an evocation of the intimate relation between the human body and the artifact. Such "sentimental materialism" had been dramatized by the famous Scandinavian folk exhibits of the late nineteenth century, which captivated their American spectators and became a curatorial standard.[46] In the exhibits, as Mark Sandberg describes them, small objects were arranged in a scene to suggest the recent presence of the human hand: "A Bible would be left open, a bedspread turned back, a costume left draped over a chair . . . anything that could have been in direct contact with a human body or hand."[47] For the Philadelphia Centennial, Artur Hazelius added scenery behind his Nordic life-groups and arranged them in narrative form to mimic popular genre paintings. Though Jewett left no record of having seen the exhibit, she could hardly have missed it, a hit with American fair-goers, who were entranced by the realistic effect.[48] "Within these courts," as one commentator reported, "there is always a throng gathered about the life-size groups of Scandinavian peasants, which are executed with such a sturdy realism as respects ungainly pose and actual costume, and the swart color of their faces, that children who come upon them suddenly, shy away, at first, as if they were intruding upon uncouth visitors."[49] Hazelius was hardly alone in exhibiting mannequin tableaux: not only were "specimens of the arts and manufactures" of Native Americans on display, but also both "famous and obscure braves" were shown "in all their glory of life-size papier-maché and stuffing, streaked on the face with red paint, and wearing the head-dress of feathers."[50] Still, it was the specificity of the scene and the narrative force of the grouping that established the Scandinavian contribution as the ideal to be achieved, and that established the life-group as the mode of localizing culture while bringing artifacts to life.

For the Atlanta exhibit of 1895, and working for the Smithsonian, Boas himself created a display to supplement the "scientific" exhibits celebrated by Goode. He exhibited life-size Indian figures, "clothed in their native costumes, and engaged in their customary occupations," arranged in small groups, the mise-en-scène meant to dramatize how particular instruments were used.[51] Just as the challenge to natural history lay in the revelation of the function of the organism within the specimen, the challenge to typological ethnology lay in the dramatization of the function of the artifact within a human organization. Although the National Museum still exhibited isolated figures, the new tendency was to portray the figures in "occupational groups," "engaged in some characteristic work or art illustrative of their life and particular art or industry," as Boas put it.[52] This means, of course, that as artifacts were disengaged from one typology, the human figures were represented within another: as weavers or soldiers, hunters or bakers. They mediated the relation between spectating subject and material object with the presence of an occupational type. Moreover, they demonstrated that the cultural aura of an object amounts to some point of contact, however ghostly, between one human and another.

This emphasis on occupation helps to answer the question of why the narrator of *The Country of the Pointed Firs* so painstakingly writes herself into the novel, from its very outset, as the figure of the writer—the question of why, after describing, in the second chapter, the way her "literary employments" required her to withdraw from "seein' folks," she goes on, in the third chapter, "The Schoolhouse," to detail the scene of her retirement, the scene of her "industries" (382–83). For though the drama of her writing gives her an identity she doesn't otherwise have, moreover, within this novel, the fact of having an occupation (the condition of being, despite the failed economy, occupied or preoccupied) might be called the condition of representability. The narrator, moreover, occupies the occupations of others in the novel: she sails, she fishes, she assumes Mrs. Todd's task of both gathering and selling herbs; on Green Island she digs potatoes, she sits in Mrs. Blackett's sewing chair. These re-enactments constitute her mode of learning about the people of this place; by taking their place, and touching the things that they touch, she achieves bodily insight into their daily lives. She seems to literalize the mode of learning prompted by the new life-group exhibits. For to represent the tribe in its occupations, Boas, Cushing, and others would mime the occupations of the figures they wanted the plaster artists to represent.[53] We might say that the anthropologists established a logic of substitution—the mannequin substituting for the anthropologist who had substituted for the tribal member—that invites the spectator to inhabit the occupation, to phantasmatically enter the scene. The difference between the isolated mannequin, such as the National Museum's Xivaro Indian, and the museum's life-group exhibits, such as the Zuñi Bread-Makers and the Indian Women Dressing Hides, is not just that the latter portray arrested action and orchestrate a host of implements within a scene of the everyday (see figs. 6, 7, 8). For whereas the isolated figure theatrically addresses the museum-goer—establishing eye contact, and thus insisting on a kind of mutual objectification—instead the groups are utterly absorbed. And that absorption invites the onlooker to participate in the occupation, to imaginatively inhabit the local scene. This logic is clearest perhaps in the case of the Indian who stands dressing a hide with her back to the museum-goer, in a posture that the museum-goer might easily adopt, stepping into the scene, into the act, into the interaction with objects.[54]

Just as the genre of the life-group thrived beyond the walls of the ethnology museum—in the 1880s the first wax mannequins (still headless) were used in display windows, which became inseparable from the success of the ready-to-wear garment industry—so too the genealogy of the life-group in America can be traced to various forms of representation: tableaux vivants, photographs, habitat groups, the Scandinavian folk museums, and the wax museum and its progeny in circuses and dime museums.[55] Such a diverse genealogy no doubt contributed to Goode's sense that the environmental groups necessarily interrupted the "dignified and systematic order, which should be characteristic of every museum," as well as to Boas's anxiety about the "ghastly impression such as we notice in wax-figures" that could be made by "too close an approach to nature."[56] It was of course a "ghastly impression" that Mme Tussaud had both sought and deployed, her impressions of the severed heads of the French Revolution making her Chamber of Horrors the most famous waxworks display in Europe.[57] Indeed, if the Revolution in fact prompted the essential literary genre for recording change, the historical novel, it also prompted the exhibitionary genre that dramatized stasis, intensely indexical and iconic signs meant to arrest and spectacularize history. Despite his cautions, the plaster life casts used by the artists working for Boas could result in the same effect, of an uncannily lifelike body in motion but out of time. Such uncanniness remains in the record of the exhibits

FIGURE 6

"Xivaro Indian in Feather Costume." *Report of the U.S. National Museum for 1893*, plate 49.

FIGURE 7

"Zuni Bread-makers" (prepared by Frank H. Cushing). *Report of the U.S. National Museum for 1893*, plate 51.

at fairs, where the life-group displays competed with the exhibits of living natives: when Rebecca Harding Davis describes an Eskimo exhibit at the Centennial Exposition, it's impossible to tell whether the family is a family of mannequins or a family that lives.[58]

The use of the life-group to vitalize material objects thus brings the human into a kind of crisis, into an unstable ontological status between the animate and the inanimate. The cultural thing that fosters a cultural apprehension of objects always threatens to transform the human into no more than an object. As much as the anthropologists wanted to exhibit "not things, but men," they did so in part by representing men as things. Jewett's penultimate chapter intimates the presence of such a risk within her own culturalist project. For when the narrator concludes her account of the taciturn seamen she's studying, she slowly denaturalizes their resemblance to natural things.

97

FIGURE 8

"Indian Women Dressing Hides" (prepared by William H. Holmes). *Report of the U.S. National Museum for 1893*, plate 52.

Arguments and opinions were unknown to the conversation of these ancient friends; you would as soon have expected to hear small talk in the company of elephants as to hear old Mr. Bowden or Elijah Tilley and their two mates waste breath upon any form of trivial gossip. . . . Speech seemed to be a light and elegant accomplishment, and their unexpected acquaintance with its arts made them of new value to the listener. You felt almost as if a landmark pine should suddenly address you in regard to the weather, or a lofty-minded old camel make a remark as you stood respectfully near him under the circus tent. (473)

The analogical relay between local inhabitant and local nature breaks down here, for if the "landmark pine" still seems to be a part of the world of Dunnet Landing, the circus animals certainly do not. And yet, given that the point of the story is precisely that Mr. Elijah Tilley *does* talk to the narrator, the account is meant to confer "new value" on the intimate conversation she manages to have with him at his house that evening. But though Elijah Tilley first enters the scene coming softly "out of his dark fish house, as if it were a burrow," he keeps "the afternoon watch" together with the narrator more as a human statue, silent as he knits and forgets his visitor (472). However much the scene is meant to suggest that she too now participates in the kind of "silent alliance" he enjoys with his aged companions, it also sentences them both to a kind of sclerosis.

This image of the two figures sitting silently together for an afternoon simply magnifies the standard resolution of the sketches into tableaux, which Jewett herself understood as her "narrative" predilection. In an early response to Horace Scudder's interest in having her develop her sketches further (an interest Jewett would hear throughout her career), she explained that if the story were longer it "would have no plot. I should have to fill it out with descriptions of character and meditations. It seems to me clear I can furnish the theatre, and show you the actors, and the scenery, and the audience, but there never is any play."[59] Drama without a play amounts to a life-group exhibit, a tableau, where humans remain as inanimate as the things around them, and where time has come to a stop. Indeed, the remarkable absence of young children from *The Country of the Pointed Firs*, coupled with the absence of Christian faith, does not simply mark Jewett's difference from the sentimental tradition.[60] It also manages to erase both secular and spiritual futurity; it helps to arrest time on behalf of apprehending an autonomous and self-contained culture. The cultural thing summons us to inhabit only a perpetual present, or only a perpetual present as the manifestation of its past. Wrested from the diachrony of technological progress, the material object is now frozen in the synchrony of cultural coherence. If Jewett's fiction helps us to understand the narrative force of the life-group exhibits, then those exhibits help to show how her fiction can feel like narrative standing still—less like a tableau, even, than a still-life.

Material History

And yet, when it comes to the genre of still-life, you can, afer all, emphasize not the stillness of the scene but the human vitality that the depicted objects seem to express. Although Norman Bryson, among others, has argued that "still life is the world minus its narratives or, better, the world minus its capacity for generating narrative interest," the trompe l'oeil still-lifes of William Harnett and John Peto clearly depend on investing objects with a narrative dimension that energizes their intensely formal compositions, as in

Harnett's *After the Hunt* (fig. 9).[61] In Peto's *Things to Adore: My Studio Door* (1890s), the traditional objects of the still-life (the fruit and flowers, the half-eaten meal) have been displaced by relics (a powder horn, an ammunition pouch, a knife and pistol), as though the genre itself wished to cite its inverse, the genre of history painting. In Peto's work of the 1890s, national narrative assumes material form in (and *as*) the remnants of the Civil War. Compressing national history into the sparest of compositions, Peto offers an allegorical miniature in *Reminiscences of 1865* (1897), where a relic from the war, the bowie knife, hovers just above the Lincoln engraving even as it obscures the "Head" of the house.[62] If these paintings captivate attention, they do so because of the dialectic by which the ephemeral object, extracted out of time, nonetheless seems imbued with time. This is the dialectic that activates and animates material history.

Once dismissed by the art-critical establishment as popular tricks, now perceived as integral to an American tradition that begins with the Peale family and extends to Walker Evans, Joseph Cornell, and Roy Lichtenstein, the still-lifes of Harnett and Peto distinguish themselves not just by their evocation of a quotidian temporal dimension. Their rack pictures, containing letters, postcards, and newspapers, fold the time of writing and reading into the suspension of time; it is not the sublime calm of objects rightly seen, but the haste of human communication, something of the chaos of modern life, that dominates the canvas (fig. 10). In Harnett's *Still Life—Violin and Music* (1888), the legibility of the sheet of music behind the instrument not only integrates musical time and rhythm into the still image but also registers the life that has been *in* the violin and will come from it, transferred by the bow that hangs beside the scripted notes and the instrument (fig. 11). By infusing time into the still-life, the picture registers the temporality of materiality as such, the way in which (as Marx the existentialist would have it) the interactivity between humans and objects confer and confirm their material existence.[63]

Of course, the success of these paintings, and above all their success in the register of material history, depends on the engagement of the spectator. This is why, during his return to America in 1904, walking through the "documentary chambers" of a museum in Richmond, an unengaged Henry James can regard the "relics of the Confederacy" as "sorry objects," unlovely, uninspiring. The "scrawls of memoranda, old vulgar newspapers, old rude uniforms, old unutterable 'mid-Victorian' odds and ends of furniture"—these all seemed like "ghosts as of things noted at a country fair," which is to say ghosts understood only as a kind of absence. Though the starved spirit of the South might cling to these "things of the heroic age," James himself

FIGURE 9
William Michael Harnett (1848–1892), *After the Hunt*, 1885.
Oil on canvas, 71 1/2 × 48 1/2 in. Fine Arts Museums of San Francisco,
Mildred Anna Williams Collection, 1940.93.

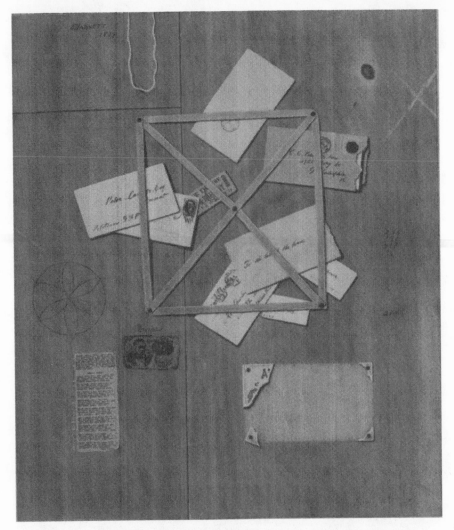

FIGURE 10

William Harnett, *The Artist's Letter Rack,* 1879. Oil on canvas, 30 × 25 in. The Metropolitan Museum of Art, New York, Morris K. Jesup Fund, 1966 (66.13).

finds the cumulative air of the place to be "of some dim, dusty collection of specimens, prehistoric, paleolithic, scientific, and making one grope for some verbal rendering of the grey effect." He nonetheless witnesses how those lifeless ghosts can become a living presence when he encounters a "very handsome, young Virginian," a Southerner "all the world like the hero of a famous novel," who brings the things to life, describing similar

FIGURE 11
William Harnett, *Still Life—Violin and Music*, 1888. Oil on canvas, 40 × 30 in. The
Metropolitan Museum of Art, New York, Catharine Lorillard Wolfe Fund,
Catharine Lorillard Wolfe Collection, 1963 (63.85).

"relics preserved in his own family," and narrating the martial adventures of his father.[64]

During her summer return to Dunnet Landing, the narrator of *The Country of the Pointed Firs* erases any such discrepancy between herself and the villagers she meets, between herself and the objects she sees.[65] Jewett creates a world of legible artifact. Our sense of the narrator's overwhelming intimacy with the people and place of Dunnet derives in large measure from the very casualness with which she herself looks at an object and sees there some record of the past, as though the past remained perpetually present, as though it could be repossessed—through the object—as affective experience. When she published her serialized stories in the form of a novel, Jewett added a penultimate sketch, "Along Shore," that describes a signal scene of preservation. Elijah Tilley has created a kind of museum to preserve the memory of his wife. The narrator is surprised by the neat and modern exterior of his house—surprised because "a man's house is really but his larger body, and expresses in a way his nature and his character" (476) (a claim voiced throughout the century, most romantically by Poe). But she comes to understand that the house is meant to express instead Elijah Tilley's wife. Although Tilley muses "how strange 't is a creatur' like her should be gone an' that chair be here right in its old place" (478), this is a strangeness upon which his own domesticity insists. He insists on keeping things in their place, preserving her metonymic presence, the objects she's touched, from which, even after her death, he continues to learn about her life. Showing the narrator the set of real china he bought his wife when they first married, he describes the broken cup discovered during her funeral. "I knowed in one minute how 't was. We'd got so used to sayin' 't was all there just's I fetched it home, an' so when she broke that cup somehow or 'nother she could n't frame no words to come an' tell me" (480). In moments like this Jewett portrays what we might call the narrativity of material objects, a capacity to evoke the history of their possession, and thus to transform artifact into history.

The narrator herself has no less access to this narrativity than does Tilley. For eight years he has kept the "best room" just as it was, enabling the narrator to imagine there the "patient saving," the ambition, the "great day of certain purchases, the bewildering shops of the next large town," the anxious spending of "hoarded money" (479). "I looked at the unworn carpet," the narrator writes, "the glass vases on the mantelpiece with their prim bunches of bleached swamp grass and dusty marsh rosemary, and I could read the history of Mrs. Tilley's best room from its very beginning" (479). The proclaimed legibility of these objects—the capacity to translate them into a kind of memory—extends beyond the more familiar capacity to sense the history of their human production. (Although Tilley tells the narrator that "You can see for yourself what beautiful rugs she could make" [479], these are objects the reader never sees.) And the legibility extends beyond Lucy Larcom's sense that "inanimate objects" are legible because they "gather into themselves something of the character of those who live among them, through association."[66] For Jewett's narrator reads here neither a record of production nor one of intimate possession, but a record of acquisition and, indeed, of alienation.

Above all, though, it is through some dynamic of interiorization that human subjects come to find the world of objects replete with meaning. The broken cup is discovered "pushed way back here, corner o' the shelf" (480). In Mrs. Blackett's house on Green Island, it is not the best room, but the bedroom where the narrator finds "the real home, the heart of the old house on Green Island." We can say of any object resting there what Gaston Bachelard says of "every object invested with intimate space": it "becomes the center of all space."[67] The novel intensifies a dialectic of outside and inside, public and private, superficiality and authenticity, which catalyzes the longing for human interiority (registered as affective space) and the projection of human history. This projection effects a narrativization of still-life.

The emphasis on intimacy and interiority is what distinguishes the American trompe l'oeil paintings from classic Dutch still-life. The latter is a genre devoted to exquisite surfaces. It establishes an aura that depends on distance, achieved by a finish that gives the objects a surface glow, eliciting wonder at the luxurious display. Aside from their designation of class, these objects are magnificently illegible, significant not because of what they mean but because of what they are. American trompe l'oeil invites instead a kind of figurative touch as the requisite interruption of the illusion, and permits an intimacy with the casually abandoned pedestrian objects. In John Peto's *Office Board for Smith Brothers Coal Company* (1879) or *Old Souvenirs* (1885?), the envelope reading "Important Information Inside" is a joke: not only is the letter gone, but there is of course no inside to the painting (no inside to painting), no actual depth despite the intensity of the illusion (figs. 12, 13). But it also seriously represents what we could call the epistemological condition of the image: the surfaces we see—the front of postcards, envelopes, the covers of books—make it clear that what is important lies elsewhere. The objects are not just meant to be read (because they are reading matter); they also establish the structure of presence and absence on which legibility as such depends. Dutch still life portrays objects that, however humble, are utterly ample, conveying a world of abundance; Peto's objects are insufficient and incomplete.

FIGURE 12

John Frederick Peto (1854–1907), *Office Board for Smith Brothers Coal Company*, 1879. Oil on canvas, 28 1/4 × 24 in., 1956.13, museum purchase © Addison Gallery of American Art, Phillips Academy, Andover, Massachusetts. All rights reserved.

This is hardly to say that an art-historical approach to Jewett clarifies her ambitions. Indeed, it is the practice of material history as such that Elizabeth Ammons cites in her effort to specify the importance of objects in Jewett's fiction. She describes *The Country of the Pointed Firs* as the work of a "material culturalist," working in the mode of "material history" as recently de-

FIGURE 13

John Peto, *Old Souvenirs,* falsely inscribed and dated WMH (monogram)
ARNETT/1881. Oil on canvas, 26 3/4 × 22 in. The Metropolitan Museum of Art,
New York, bequest of Oliver Burr Jennings, 1968 (68.205.3).

scribed by Robert Blair St. George: "Things," become "whole texts," as he puts it, "each one an objectification of thought, a concrete enactment of morality, an eloquent essay in the difficult reconciliation of ethics, aesthetics, and economics."[68] But as with Jewett's ethnographic sensibility, Jewett's materialist sensitivity participates in an epistemological mode that becomes fully recognizable in the 1890s (not in the 1980s), the era now recognized as witnessing the origin of American material culture studies.[69] An article on the "reorganization of American history," published in the *Atlantic* during the months of her novel's serialization, describes a shift from accounts of major political and martial events to a "sociological interpretation of history," the "study of economic life and the development of social institutions."[70] By 1912, even Theodore Roosevelt, addressing the American Historical Association as its president, argued that the historian must present the "every-day life" of "the plain people, the ordinary men and women": "The historian must deal with the days of common things, and deal with them so that they interest us in reading of them as our own common things interest us as we live among them."[71]

Though Roosevelt's understanding of everyday life never goes so far as to mention "material history," Edward Eggleston had moved toward that paradigm in the articles he had been publishing since the beginning of the 1890s. Best known for his extraordinarily popular *The Hoosier Schoolmaster* (1871), an all but inaugural text both in the genre of regionalist fiction and in the genre of the boy's book, Eggleston published the first of what was to be a several-volume history of the U.S. in 1896: *The Beginners of a Nation: A History of the Source and Rise of the Earliest English Settlements in America With Special Reference to the Life and Character of the People.*[72] "The distinctive purpose of this work," Eggleston writes, "is to give an insight into the life and character of the people, and there are details that make the reader feel the very spirit and manner of the time. It is better to let the age disclose itself in action; it is only by ingenious eavesdropping and peeps through keyholes that we can win this kind of knowledge from the past" (viii–ix). Eggleston's understanding of the historiographical shift seems inseparable from a vision of passing by a historical or ethnographic display—the organization of the scene of history into what would become the "living history" museum, set in the sort of "period room" inaugurated in 1896 by Charles P. Wilcomb at the Oakland Museum in California.[73] This is a fantasy of unobtrusive intrusion constructed so that we get a chance to see what we're not really permitted to see, a chance to see *inside;* that is, he literalizes *insight* as a seeing *in.* Though it was unquestionably Eggleston's archival research in England that enabled him to thicken his account of the James River experiment, his own archeological work at the site inspired the project and no doubt the museal image. He describes the work at length in a note: as the lone excavator of the area in 1889, he "picked out of the crumbling sand" both human bones and "wrought nails, bits of glass grown iridescent from long burial, and an exploded bombshell of so small a caliber as to mark its antiquity."[74] It is as though the "details that make the reader feel the very spirit" of the time are comprised of these relics, refurbished and rearranged so that the reader encounters them not in the archeological but in the spectatorial field of vision.

Even as curators had come to believe that objects needed to be exhibited within the scene of history, so historians had begun to be attracted to the power of things. As Eggleston's work makes clear, object-based epistemology was hardly confined to the field of anthropology. The object-lesson—a belief that objects (as opposed to words) would speak to more people (young and old, immigrants and natives) in a universal language—was beginning to become a part of daily life, helping to satisfy what Michael Kammen has extensively documented as the "public's new hunger for history." The work of Americanizing memory—which meant both discovering a past to remember and inventing traditions to keep—was performed most assiduously by the scores of historical societies and associations that emerged in the closing three decades of the century, home to innumerable genealogists and antiquarians. These, as Kammen emphasizes, exemplify how a regionalist inflection to the nation's history intensified the engagement.[75] That engagement, during and after Philadelphia's Centennial Exposition of 1876, became a familiar topic in newspapers and journals, where the passion for collecting relics often became an object of fun. As one writer said of "these times," "everybody seems to be furbishing up his ancestors and setting them on end, as it were, in company with all the old tea-kettles, queue-ties, rusty muskets, snuff-boxes, and paduasoys."[76] In "Tools of the Nation Maker" (1897), explaining the importance of a collection that would become the basis of his history museum, Henry Mercer argued that "these castaways" offer "manifold elucidations of nationality" by "leading us by way of an untrodden path, deeper into the lives of people . . . until at last the heart is touched."[77] For him, the objective is to reach not the interior of the object, but human interiority itself.

When Mrs. Fosdick, one of the tea-drinking interlocutors in Dunnet Landing, complains that "new folks nowadays . . . seem to have neither past nor future" (426), she doesn't mean to designate the narrator, but she could. For though readers of the novel have described it as depicting a locale that resides outside history (by which they really mean national history), the village as such is in fact saturated with history, the villagers have memories that span more than a generation, and it is rather the narrator who seems to possess no past. Or, rather, her summer's engagement with Dunnet, the hours she spends listening to stories and looking at things, can be thought of as the effort to "furbish up" and incorporate its past into her memory. Just as she lives in Mrs. Todd's house "as if it were a larger body," she assumes the woman's memories to the point of making them her own; the collection of sketches that comprise the novel reads as an incorporation of recollections that suffuse the narratorial voice with the aura of intimate local knowledge.

Like the title character of "The Queen's Twin," a Dunnet story that Jewett didn't include in *The Country of the Pointed Firs*, the narrator of the novel lives life vicariously. Abby Martin, "born the same day" as Victoria, "and at exactly the same hour, after you allowed for all the difference in time,"[78] devotes her life to accumulating stories and pictures of the Queen—not to make them hers, but (to invoke William James) to make them *her*, translating having into being, so that (to put the matter awkwardly) she can experience the experience of experience. The Twin has transformed her best room into a shrine dedicated to the Queen, decorated with pictures of her in hand-decorated frames; there she can cherish the Queen's book about the Highlands (which one might call the geographical source of the older British "twin" of American regionalism), and "a real china cup" that belonged to her grandmother, a cup she calls the Queen's (510). Idiosyncratic as the Twin seems to be, having collected these things to constitute a self, her act of accumulation and arrangement figures the narrator's own. And the latter's act of incorporation becomes literal in the scene that concludes the Bowden reunion. "Feast's End" describes pies that have "dates and names . . . wrought in lines of pastry and frosting on the tops," and finally a "model of the old Bowden house made of durable gingerbread, with all the windows and doors in the right places," a house which the participants eat "as if it were a pledge and token of loyalty" (467). This is an image of incorporating the particularity of place into the body itself; an image where person, place, and thing converge in the moment of physical consumption; an image not of occupying a material environment but of being occupied by it. It is the narrator's opportunity not to get inside an object or space, but to get objectified space inside her.[79]

"Perhaps," the narrator writes as she concludes her account of the Bowden reunion, to which four successive sketches are devoted, "it is the great national anniversaries which our country has lately kept, and the soldiers' meetings that take place everywhere, which have made reunions of every sort the fashion" (469). In a novel that perpetually elides the nation as it marks the interaction of the local and the global (Dunnet and the South Seas,

FIGURE 14

"Washington Relics." Printed in *Harper's Weekly*, September 23, 1876.

the Mediterranean, London, Bordeaux, the China Sea), this claim appears as a chronotopic rupture. It connects events of the novel with the history Kammen describes, which began in earnest with the Centennial exposition. Though Kammen emphasizes the forward-looking aspects of the Exposition, crystallized in the celebration of the Corliss Engine (135–37), Jewett herself, who went to the Centennial twice, remembered it as a memorializing event. At the time of the Chicago fair, she recalled its Philadelphia predecessor as an antiquarian delight: "The Philadelphia exposition gave a new regard for our antiquities (our 'Centennial' chairs and Plates!)." And she expected much the same from the Columbian exposition: "if I am not mistaken, the Chicago exposition will teach us to be more careful about buildings."[80] Texts like *Early New England Interiors* (1878) had already begun to inspire such care, as had exhibits at the Centennial like the log houses from Massachusetts and Connecticut. The latter functioned as the "New England Kitchen," where eighteenth-century food was prepared and served by women in eighteenth-century costume.[81] But even as this predecessor to the living history museum vitalized the constructed space and its objects, other objects could summon the past back to life on their own.

They did so most compellingly in the display of the so-called Washington Relics, exhibited by the U.S. Patent Office as a camp scene, a scene where the general's spirit seemed all but palpable (fig. 14). A writer for *Harper's*

Weekly, despite the accompanying illustration, detailed the mise-en-scène, with its bed and blankets, sword and leathern scabbard, pistols, a portmanteau, "a pair of andirons, two saucepans, a coffee-pot, and gridiron, and the bellows wherewith he urged the fire and kindled the unwilling wood when snow lay upon the ground and all was sodden and dreary." This metamorphosis from description to a kind of narration—crucial in the subsequent life-group displays—recurs in the account of the camp chest: "this has compartments large and small, deep and shallow. Some of them are for the dishes, plates, knives, and forks seen on the table; others for the square bottles holding vinegar, salad dressing, probably oil, if his Excellency indulged in it, as we may reasonably hope that he did; smaller bottles for red and black pepper, square boxes for his salt, flour for his gravy, butter and what not." The hyperspecificity marks a gaze that explores the crevices and depths of the chest as though to find there the ghost of the general himself. If Bachelard is right to designate chests as "veritable organs of the secret psychological life" (78), the means by which we image and imagine intimacy, then the display as described in *Harper's* might be said to insist on a kind of intimate knowledge one would never have gotten from the general himself. Yet the general was in fact figured into the scene, his "regimentals" propped up "in a somewhat natural position on a chair." The uncanniness inspired the closing celebration: "Which of the worthies in his confidence has not sat at the table and looked at his chief across these plain furnishings? Oh! but it is almost a history to look at and handle them."[82] The history in things here far exceeds expectation, as the writer finally fantasizes contact with the dead.

Jewett describes such contact in "The Foreigner" (another uncollected Dunnet story), where, on the day of the foreign woman's death Mrs. Todd sits beside her and hears her guitar sound "as if somebody begun to play it" (552). Again, on the day of the funeral, she hears "some long notes o' dronin' music from upstairs that chilled me to the bone" (547). Though the supernatural event is eventually naturalized (the guitar's inspiration coming from the wind, from outside the house), nonetheless there is a parallel narrative in which the depths of the house are explored. A friend of the family's, Captain Lorenzo, wanders through the house in search of a chest that the woman's sea-faring husband was supposed to have hidden somewhere in the house. He "rummag[es] in the arches an' under the stairs, an' over in some old closet where he reached out bottles an' stone jugs" (549). The story of the guitar's animation is inseparable from the search through the house, the investigation of all the dark insides of the house. The past seems to reside in objects; historical *insight* seems to be graspable from *inside* the material record, from the way a *genius rei* seems to animate objects with the presence of the past.

This *genius rei* extends to a *genius loci* in Jewett's village, a *genius* that manifests itself most generally in the casual yet ghostly humanization of the natural world.

"A Kind of Fetichism"

When Jewett added "Along Shore" to the book version of *The Country of the Pointed Firs*, she not only returned her narrator from the Bowden reunion to the coast, but also foregrounded her own equation of human subjects and inanimate objects. Spending the early afternoon watching a boat off Burnt Island, she finds herself conversing at last with one of the "old fisherman," one of that "small company of elderly, gaunt-shaped great fisherman," Dunnet Landing's "survivors of an earlier and more vigorous generation" (472– 73). She describes these four "large old men" as an intimate group, working in concert, helping one another dock, tending one another's traps, and cleaning one another's fish. The intimacy extends to an intimacy between the men and their boats: "Abel's boat and Jonathan Bowden's boat were as distinct and experienced personalities as the men themselves, and as inexpressive" (473). On the one hand, to declare that the boats have personalities is simply to perpetuate the casually persistent way Jewett anthropomorphizes inanimate objects. In the opening page of the chapter, for instance, "the very boats seem[ ] to be taking an afternoon nap in the sun" (472). On the other hand, the cumulative effect of such persistence is to license the additional claim that the boats are as inexpressive as the men, rather than the more predictable claim that these old men are as inexpressive as the boats. By its closing chapters, though, *The Country of the Pointed Firs* has depicted a world where it makes complete sense to say that material objects have assumed the inexpressivity of men, because this is a world where the animate and inanimate seem to have exchanged registers, where things behave like humans and humans like things.

When Otis Mason argued that is was "not things, but men" being exhibited at the Chicago Exposition, the conjuring trick of transforming artifacts into human-being required a rhetorical sleight-of-hand. He made one overarching point as he stressed the importance of the "material element" in ethnology: "Languages are not only spoken, but written, and speaking and writing are not the only ways men have of expressing thought. There is a proposition in every work of men's hands. Indeed there are many propositions."[83] While Mason argued against the bias towards the linguistic account of cultures (as exemplified by Franz Boas's contribution to the *Memoir*), he nonetheless had to imagine translating the artifactual into the linguistic; he had to express faith in a kind of prosopopeia wherein the past comes to life again in the inanimate things left behind; he had to believe that things all but speak for themselves. Indeed, at the forefront of what we now call museology, the "thing that talks" had become a prominent trope. Stewart Culin, director of archeology and paleontology at the University of Pennsylvania's University Museum (and winner of the gold medal for his exhibit of games at the fair), came to profess that he had "no other thought than of making things tell me their story, and then," as he added, of "trying to coax and arrange them to tell this story to the world."[84] Though the trope as such obviates the concern for connecting words and things by erasing the gap between them, Culin's account of aggression and persuasion suggests that things could be a bit tight-lipped, recalcitrant in their mute physicality. But my point here is really that when American museum history tells a story where the mundane *supplants* the extraordinary, it neglects the way the curators try to *transform* the mundane *into* the extraordinary. Instead of curiosities, they wanted to exhibit "living thoughts" and talking things. The significance of the everyday, the mundane, and the imperfect is sustained by a kind of animism that effects a metamorphosis from thing to thought, to word, to proposition.

In the story of such a metamorphosis told thirty years earlier, Marx understood "the conversion of things into persons and . . . persons into things" as one of the fundamental "mysteries" of capital, at once part of the antithesis immanent in the commodity, and a formal requirement of the capitalist form of production.[85] His repeated point about the personification of things and reification *(Versachlichung)* of persons is that sensuous things appear social, enjoying a relation to one another irrespective of any human relation; that the products of labor appear to the laborer to live autonomous lives; and that the value of commodity objects seems to inhere in the things themselves. Just as Simmel transposed the point into the mode of materialist phenomenology, so too, as I suggested in chapter 1, scenes from the American 1890s seem to have literalized the object's autonomy and potency: the buildings of south side Manhattan stare down at Maggie in *Maggie, A Girl of the Streets* (1891), for instance, and gloves whisper seductively from a display case to Carrie, in *Sister Carrie* (1900). The display strategists of the new department store windows, like their museum counterparts, understood that things must be brought to life. Culin, who worked not just for the University of Pennsylvania's University Museum (heavily funded by John Wannamaker) but also for Wannamaker's store, believed that museums could teach consumers about design, that department stores could teach museums about display, and that both depended on making "treasures, recently so remote, so dead it seemed, come again to life."[86]

The literary and exhibitionary animation of objects converge most clearly in the wizardry of Frank Baum, who wrote *The Wizard of Oz* (1900) while writing *The Art of Decorating Show Windows and Dry Goods Interiors* (1900), which placed him at the very forefront of the National Association of Window Dressers..Enthralled by the Columbian Exposition (which he continued to cite for its display strategies), Baum moved from South Dakota to Chicago, where he began the publication of the magazine *Show Window* (1897). His message remained the same: the window dresser must develop skills for letting objects "come alive."[87] As Stuart Culver has argued, when, in an episode from *Oz*, Dorothy encounters living porcelain figurines who tell their own story, she witnesses the animate objects of the window dresser's dream.[88] Dorothy visits the "country of the china people" full of anxiety about breaking one of the creatures and full of desire to bring one back to Kansas. But when she asks the beautiful princess whether she wouldn't like to stand on "Aunt Em's mantel-shelf," she learns about the curious fate of the animate object: "You see, here in our country we live contentedly, and can talk and move around as we please. But whenever any of us are taken away our joints at once stiffen, and we can only stand and look pretty."[89] The animate object is hardly a new figure in fiction: the object narratives and object narrators of the eighteenth century, Hoffman's uncanny objects, Dickens's and Stowe's animate furniture—these are part of a well-established if uneven tradition.[90] But in Baum's belated fairytale, by having the figurine address the entranced young girl, he locates the scene squarely within a culture newly devoted to teaching children consumer desire, and devoted to reenchanting the physical object world.

When in *Deephaven* the narrator's friend Kate speculates about the "simple country people" who "have a kind of fetichism" (103), she means that they believe there is a "personality" in "what *we call* inanimate things" (104, my emphasis). Needless to say, this kind of fetishism is not the kind that Baum narrates or Marx describes, but the kind detailed by E. B. Tylor in *Primitive Culture* (1870), where the general topic of animism all but overwhelms the two-volume cornerstone of modern anthropology. More particularly, Kate is trying to describe a "complete sympathy with Nature," a topic she blithely concludes by describing the local villagers as part of nature: "They have much in common, after all, with the plants which grow up out of the ground and the wild creatures which depend upon their instincts wholly" (103–4). In *The Country of the Pointed Firs*, Jewett permits no such simplifying account of the local population, but the rhetoric of the novel achieves much the same point. Not only are people perpetually metaphorized as natural objects, but artifactual objects are thoroughly personified. In the opening chapter, the narrator describes the coastal houses of Dunnet as having "small-paned high windows" which are "like knowing eyes that watched the harbor and the far sea-line beyond" (377). She knows the village itself as though being "acquainted with a single person" (377). The intensity of personification—objects assuming human personality or human form—utterly changes the dynamics of reification in the novel, for becoming a thing hardly means becoming less than human. In "A Strange Sail," where the chapter title itself marks an ontological ambiguity between the animate and inanimate (the noun "sail" designating either an object or an action), a visitor to Mrs. Todd's house appears "like a strange sail on the far horizon"—thoroughly reified. The narrator then extends the metaphoric possibilities close to the point of incoherence. As though to explain some local patois, she writes that "you may speak of a visit's setting in as well as a tide's, and it was impossible, as Mrs. Todd whispered to me, not to be pleased at the way this visit was setting in; a new impulse and refreshing of the social currents and seldom visited bays of memory appeared to have begun" (424). The end result of the initial reification is the coalescence of the social and natural, the material and psychological, orders. And whereas the narrator and her friend Kate in *Deephaven* function as a community of outsiders, who have the capacity to remark and to explain the "fetichism" of the locals, the narrator of *The Country of the Pointed Firs* participates in the fetichism, fetishizing the landscape and villagescape for herself.

Which is hardly to say that fetishism—at least fetishism as it was understood in the era—doesn't have some explanatory power for determining how or why the physical object world of Dunnet Landing seems alive. It was Herbert Spencer's overarching point that in the "fetichistic conception" of the world (or what he called "fetich-theory"), each "person's nature inheres not only in all parts of his body, but in his dress and the things he has used," to the point where such things could assume lives of their own.[91] When the narrator writes that she lived in Mrs. Todd's house "with as much comfort and unconsciousness as if it were a larger body" (421), she quietly erases the division between individual and environment, subject and object, transforming the scenic into the somatic. Jewett has replaced the "pairing of people and things" with their integration. The ghost story in the novel introduces an aura of enchantment while literalizing Spencer's claim that inanimate objects, natural or artifactual, assume life because of the "indwelling ghosts" within them, his logical approach to the question insisting that within the fetish one could typically find the presence of the dead. In "The Waiting Place," Captain Littlepage recounts the story of an English exploring party that discovered a kind of limbo, apparently populated by human spirits, "human-shaped creatures of fog and cobweb" (399). The subsequent chapters devoted to Mrs. Todd's mother, Mrs. Blackett, provide a quotidian version of that confrontation. They begin with the narrator and Mrs. Todd staring at the harbor, the shore "all covered by the great army of the pointed firs, darkly cloaked and standing as if they waited to embark" (400). The personification here, following the account of the spirit world, seems foremost to extend that account. The firs that figuratively people the landscape seem to embody people, which is one reason why Dunnet seems so haunted by its past.

Just as the term "fetishism" initially named a valuation of material objects that Western reason could not comprehend, so "fetishism" has more recently been deployed by critics to name a challenge to Western reason and the logic of capital.[92] Whether this is the "sentimental fetishism" of Stowe, or the devilish fetishism of rural groups in Colombia, or the fetishism of the museum-goer, the fetishism-that-is-not-commodity-fetishism has been fetishized as the power to interrupt hegemonic systems of value.[93] But by tracking the "kind of fetishism" that vitalizes the culture and nature of Dunnet or Deephaven I hardly mean to argue that Jewett offers a critique of capital, however obviously she depicts an alternative value system and a nonindustrial economy. My point is, rather, that multiple institutions—the ethnology museum, the department store, the world's fair, and local-color fiction—each in their own way fostered and depended on a kind of animism. And the animation of material objects makes it seem as though there is something hidden within them.

This hardly means that the "indwelling ghosts" of local-color fiction couldn't explicitly serve to confront the advance of modernity. Charles Chesnutt's "Po' Sandy" tells the story of a slave whose wife, in order to prevent him from being shuttled between plantations, transforms him into a big pine tree. When the tree is chopped down, the milled boards are used to construct a kitchen where the other slaves "hear sump'n moanin' en groanin'. . . . en w'en de win' would blow dey could hear sump'n a-hollerin'en sweekin' lack it wuz in great pain en suffer.'"[94] Rendered useless by being "ha'nted," the kitchen is torn down, the boards used to build a schoolhouse. By telling the story, which evokes and transposes the legal reification endured by slaves, Uncle Julius prevents the new owner from tearing down the schoolhouse to make use of the lumber. Insofar as such a story records the power of animism (actual or fabricated) to interrupt the Northern appropriation of Southern property, it would seem to tell the story of how the spirit world can retard the course of change and "progress." But something like this kind of fetishism could be rechanelled on behalf of expropriation. At Philadelphia's Centennial Exposition, furniture and ornaments made from Charter Oak wood—that is, from the tree in Connecticut where the colonial charter had supposedly been hidden in 1687—were sold to fascinated fair-goers. And similar relics were sold from the Elm under which Washington supposedly assumed command of the Continental forces in Philadelphia in 1775.[95] This objectification and commodification of national history as material history bespeaks a kind of historicist fetishism where possessing a thing comes to feel like possessing history itself.

Waste Matter

By 1905, Franz Boas, who had been so ambitious about altering exhibition practices, began to abandon museal anthropology. He resigned from the American Museum of Natural History because of administrative disputes, but also because he had become increasingly convinced that the most important elements of culture were irreducible to artifacts, that anthropological facts could never become artifactual—that the cultural Thing, let us say, was too intangible to be found in things.[96] Jewett herself, even while writing with such apparent faith in the capacity of objects to disclose meaning, raises considerable doubt about their legibility. Whereas I've concentrated on the dynamics by which objects become replete with meaning, Jewett proceeds to evacuate objects of meaning in the sequence of sketches she devotes to the hermit Joanna. In those sketches, just as the meaning of one set of objects, the Indian relics of Shell-Heap island, is overlooked, so too there seems to be no lingering correspondence between Joanna and her physical world. The sketches show Jewett contesting the premise of any object-based epistemology, suddenly abandoning any thought that "the true history of our race is written in things," as Otis Mason had put it. Along with scenes that express an extraordinary coalescence of person, place, and thing, *The Country of the Pointed Firs* offers episodes when, as it were, things fall apart: when a regionalist materialism provides no access to genuinely ephemeral human-being.

In *Deephaven* (1877), the character Kate recalls her sadness when she used to see her deceased Aunt Katherine's "little trinkets lying about the house," and she laments the limits of human possession. "I can't help wishing that it were possible to keep some of my worldly goods always" (137), she says, meaning to keep some possessions with her beyond the grave. To offer solace, the narrator explains how those worldly goods left behind perpetuate a bond with the living. The house where the two women have spent the summer, once belonging to Aunt Katherine but now belonging to Kate herself, has been slowly transformed by their residence. Thus, what still felt like the house of the aunt now feels like the house of the niece: "now it belongs to you, and if I were ever to come back without you I should find you here" (137). Comforting as this comment is meant to be, its logic ought to convey little solace: for if Aunt Katherine has been so quickly exorcised as the spirit of the house, then one might imagine that, were the narrator to return alone and to settle in for the summer, she would soon "find" there not her absent friend but herself. All but needless to add, Aunt Katherine's worldly goods would have become little more than illegible, meaningless relics. However unwittingly, the narrator's comment proclaims the rapidity with which a prior inhabitant can be displaced, both physically and spiritually.

Evidence of such displacement—or, rather, displacement of a different order—is scattered throughout Jewett's descriptions of Maine, and most concentrated in *The Country of the Pointed Firs*. Indian relics are noticed and named—as "relics"—but they bear no memorializing function; they are incorporated into the everyday landscape, a meaningless reliquary over which a new daily life is lived, and lived with no sense of an Indian presence, present or past.[97] These relics in the novel can thus be read as evidence of Jewett's own effort to validate the Anglo-American past with the aura of Native American cultural authenticity, just as the classical allusions—Mrs. Todd "had mounted a gray rock, and stood there grand and architectural, like a *caryatide*" (401)—can be read as her effort to confer Cultural authority. This is to argue that Jewett works to legitimate the Maine folk, both past and present, as an object of literary and anthropological knowledge: an effort to transpose the writing of New England nature from an account that, in a case like Thoreau's, inevitably finds the Native American, to one that incorporates the contemporary American as an inhabitant worthy of the same fascination; an effort to promote the "curious ways" and "complex conventionalities" of the life of the "clan" in rural Maine to the status of the customs of an Indian tribe. She thus might be said to participate both in an effort to privilege ethnography over archaeology, and in the effort to centralize the anthropological and historical study of Anglo-American heritage. From the Smithsonian, Goode himself authorized the collection of "humble and simple objects" of the American past. Indeed, he came to lament the time and energy lost in excavating and collecting Indian relics "when much that is of equal or greater importance belonging to our own ancestors has been allowed to go to destruction."[98] This is a crude example of the logic of substitution that occurs in Jewett's texts, and that would come to underwrite a nativist modernism.[99]

By entitling one of her sketches, one of the chapters, "On Shell-Heap Island," Jewett invokes the signal source for the recovery of Indian artifacts displayed at institutions like the Smithsonian, New York's American Natural History Museum, and Harvard's Peabody. Though the great deposits of shell had once been "universally considered as natural deposits" by geologists, as F. W. Putnam explained, science had since caught up with the local traditions that understood the mounds to mark ancient Indian campsites; indeed, the artifacts found among the shells were soon thought to be not merely neolithic, but paleolithic, as ancient as the artifacts unearthed in Europe.[100] The excavation of those sites didn't really take off until 1861 (when the Smithsonian published Adolphe von Morlot's paper on archeological discoveries in Europe), but by the 1880s a network of amateur and semi-professional archeologists and collectors passionately explored the middens. To fill out the collections he hoped to display at the 1893 Exposition, Putnam had provided standardized instructions for amateurs to excavate local mounds.[101] As curator of the Peabody, he already had men in the field in New Jersey, Ohio, Tennessee, Florida, and Maine, where he could capitalize on the local hobby of collecting relics.

Thoreau, for one, who collected Indian arrowheads in Maine with the same kind of passion he had for collecting natural specimens, significantly anticipated the scholarly recognition that shell-heaps are cultural, not natural formations. But it is less his particular archeological work—as expressed in the journals, in his "Natural History of Massachusetts" (1842), in *Cape Cod* (1865)—then his sense of sedimented history that distinguishes his work on Maine from Jewett's. In the first chapter of *The Maine Woods* (1864), the Ktaadn excursion will finally lead to an encounter with "matter" itself—"the *solid* earth! the *actual* world! the *common sense! Contact! Contact! Who* are we? *where* are we?"—but it begins as it ends with material signs.[102] Before describing himself searching carefully for Mohawk relics on the banks of the Mattawamkeag (600), he has described the figure of a disheveled Indian whose image captivates "the Indian's history, that is, the history of his extinction" (595), a comment he makes in the midst of telling the story of being guided by a Penobscot. In this trip through the woods, the woods are vitally palimpsestic: he finds an ancient Indian trail, Emerson's pamphlet on West Indian Emancipation, an "aboriginal pattern" in a knife currently used by an Indian, the log-houses of lumbermen; and he gathers anecdotes, legends, and stories of Yankee types, of Catholic missionaries, of Lecarbot's account of the local fish (702). Thoreau's world is sustained by the simple logic of accretion. As though to allay his fear that "the hunter race," along with the "bear and panther," will be "'civilized off the face of the earth'" (712), Thoreau expands his archeological imagination: "Perchance where *our* wild pines stand, and leaves lie on their forest floor, in Concord, there were once reapers, and husbandmen planted grain" (712). Heterogeneous histories, all meriting attention, rest both on and within the earth.

By 1875, S. Weir Mitchell wrote in a popular journal of his "pleasure in raking over an Indian shell-heap," finding bone needles, fragments of pottery, and odds and ends of nameless use, in the company of the naturalist Jeffries Wyman.[103] By 1891, Mary Murfree's *In the "Stranger People's" Country* (1891) showed how the archeological imagination could frame regionalist writing, and how the palimpsest of the land could devolve into a single text. In her novel, the lawyer Shattuck, in the Tennessee mountains to pursue "semi-scientific researches in his idle summer loiterings" spends time (as the mountaineers put it) "a-diggin' fur jugs an' sech ez the Injuns hed—least wise them ez built the mounds."[104] Though his excavations are unsuccessful, and though the secret of the more mysterious "strange burial grounds of the 'pygmy dwellers' of Tennessee" (1) remains undisclosed, what Shattuck learns about, of course, and what Murfree reports, is the customs of the mountaineers themselves. The excavation of a prior culture has been displaced by the recognition of a living one: the stranger people of the mounds are forgotten so that the stranger people of the mountains can be remembered. Jewett said that Berwick, the town where she grew up, was "full of interesting traditions and relics of the early inhabitants, both Indian and Englishmen."[105] But the story she tells about Shell-Heap Island, the story of the hermit Joanna, displaces any account of Indian history or of the relics lodged in Native American mounds, while nonetheless assuming—appropriating—the tragic aura of the Native Americans' fate.

The story of Joanna begins not with a discussion of Joanna but with the mention of Shell-Heap Island. It is one of those locales in regionalist fiction—like the river in *Huckleberry Finn,* or Grand Terre, the island beyond Grand Isle in *The Awakening*—that reassert the center/periphery structure and extend remoteness to another site. The narrator asks her interlocutors, Mrs. Todd and Mrs. Fosdick, about the place, and they begin by recounting the legends of its Indian history. " 'T was 'counted a great place in old Indian times," Mrs. Fosdick says, "you can pick up their stone tools 'most any time if you hunt about" (428). Though the older women exchange competing stories of Indian life there, it is their comments on current life in Dunnet Landing that captivates the narrator's attention. For having lamented the loss of the old days, the days of whaling and trips to the South Sea Islands, they complain of the homogeneity of the current population: "there was certain a good many curiosities of human natur' in this neighborhood years ago. . . . In these days the young folks is all copy-cats, 'fraid to death they won't be all just alike" (429). To the narrator, there seem to be "peculiarities of character in the region of Dunnet Landing yet" (428) as she thinks of characters like Captain Littlepage. But by "peculiar persons" the older women mean someone as peculiar as Joanna (429).

"Crossed in love," jilted, Joanna retired to Shell-Heap Island, "thirty acres, rocks and all," where she lived the rest of her life, and died, a recluse (429–30). The story that Mrs. Todd tells of Joanna is a Robinsonade: the woman raised potatoes and fished; out of swamp rushes she braided mats for the floor of a cabin that had been her father's, and she braided a cushion for the bed, and braided sandals for shoes. The one time Mrs. Todd saw Joanna, on a visit with the village minister, Joanna distracted the man by interesting him in the "old Indian remains." After taking "down some queer stone gouges and hammers off of one of her shelves [to show] them to him same's as if he [were] a boy," she encourages him to walk over to the shell-heap, allowing the two women to talk between themselves (438). At its most significant, then, the shell-heap serves as a distraction.

When the narrator herself finally has the chance to go to the island, the man who sails her there, Captain Bowden, presumes she's interested in gathering Indian relics. But the Indian relics, the shell-heap—these are beside the point. She goes to linger there where Joanna lived her isolated life. As she walks the path leading to her grave, she understands that the path itself marks the presence of other pilgrims. But the specificity of Joanna's tragedy slowly becomes a generality: "Later generations will know less and less of Joanna herself, but there are paths trodden to the shrines of solitude the world over,—the world cannot forget them, try as it may" (444). When she writes of these "paths trodden," she effectively spatializes and universalizes the human condition beyond historical or cultural specificity. The narrator's very capacity to generalize might seem to depend on the absence of remains: the cabin is gone, except for the foundation; there is no sign of the garden "except a single faded sprig of much-enduring French pinks" (444); there is no rug; there are no sandals. There are no relics to be read as signs of a daily occupation. Joanna's is the life lived beyond the archeological capacity to excavate and recover some material remnant of life lived. There are no artifacts that disclose a proposition or several propositions, there are no things that speak. If, as Hannah Arendt famously argued, mankind, understood as *homo faber*, has a will-to-permanence that expresses itself in the making of things that share the durability and thing-character of the world, then Jewett might be said to record the pathos of that will's utter interruption.[106] In one of Harriet Beecher Stowe's eloquent meditations on death, she says to her readers: "You are living your daily life among trifles that one death-stroke may make relics. . . . [T]he pen-knife, the pen, the papers, the trivial articles of dress and clothing, which to-day you toss idly and jestingly from hand to hand, may become dread memorials of that awful tragedy whose deep abyss ever underlies our common life."[107] Jewett extends the threat by pointing out that the trifles, saturated as they may be with your presence, will also disappear.

But it is as though the very absence of artifacts enables the narrator to reconceptualize the issue of time and of place: "In the life of each of us," she goes on, "there is a place remote and islanded, and given to endless regret or secret happiness; we are each the uncompanioned hermit and recluse of an hour or a day; we understand our fellows of the cell to whatever age of history they may belong" (444). The confusion of temporal and spatial registers—an island in life, the hermit of an hour—releases Joanna from both time and place; she really has no place there, she cannot be placed there, because the poetics of attachment have no things, no signs, to work with. Instead, it is only the transcultural and transhistorical isolation of the human individual as such that offers an explanatory "context." On the one hand, the image can be aligned with other self-consciously and exuberantly extra-spatial and extra-temporal moments in the text: atop a hill on Green Island, the narrator records the "sense of liberty in space and time which great prospects always give" (413). But of course, on the other, it is hardly the liberty of timelessness that the story of Joanna evokes; it is rather an immaterial confinement. It is the psyche itself at once materialized and abstracted, spatialized and generalized as the place everyone is destined to share.

Though the Native Americans who lived on Shell-Heap Island remain more materially present than Joanna, and though oral culture rather than object culture seems to be the sole means of preserving the marginalized individual, nonetheless an object remains from Joanna's story. When Mrs. Todd visited the island, her husband Nathan, Joanna's cousin, had sent the hermit "a beautiful coral pin" purchased in a Mediterranean port (434). Refusing to accept the pin, as part of her refusal to re-enter society, Joanna gives it back to Mrs. Todd. When the narrator leaves Dunnet Landing at the end of the summer, Mrs. Todd leaves her some gifts on the kitchen table, including the pin. Among the souvenirs that seem to embody the world of Dunnet Landing, replete with the life lived in this place, there is, within the box, a token of how the life within remains inaccessible. This is a token of the nonalignment of the psychological and the anthropological—a token, then, not just of Joanna's refusal to remain in Dunnet society but also of Jewett's refusal to believe that personhood is reducible to place. The coral pin nonetheless expresses the potency of an object that, circulating as a possession possessed by no one, prompts people to think of one another.

And yet the force of Joanna's story, told within the overarching scene of cultural coherence maintained by the scene-act ratio, by the "pairing of people and things," lies in its attention to the human suffering and endurance that is neither regional nor national, that is neither rural nor cosmopolitan, that is irreducible to being Anglo-American or Native American, and for which there is no concrete evidence. The force of the sketches lies in their intimation of all the peculiarities, islanded beyond the reach of anthropology and history, that are overwhelmingly proximate—anything but remote. To the degree that Jewett uses the story to stage the singularity of the subject (that remains culturally unintelligible) she may be pointing out how, after all, the apprehension of culture seems to depend on recognizing human nature (and thus, of course, on suppressing the extent to which the apprehension of "human nature" is determined by "culture").[108] By reading *The Country of the Pointed Firs* into one epistemological culture (as evident in the popular press as it is in the annals of American anthropology), I have meant not just to elucidate regionalism's own epistemology, and not just to perceive its challenge to that culture. Rather, read as a chapter in what James Chandler has called the "study in the cultural history of our cultural-historical literary practices"—a chapter whose salience resides in tracking professional anthropology's development of a notion of culture to make objects meaningful, and historiography's new regard for the things of everyday life—I mean to exhibit the way the most anthropological of literary genres makes trouble for our own culturalist thinking.[109]

Modernist Archeology

"Not things, but Men."

"Don't try to write *about* things: write the things themselves just as they are."

"No Ideas but in things."

Could it be that William Carlos Williams's great modernist dictum—however clearly it expresses a post-romantic effort to erase (rather than to overcome) the subject / object division—is a relic of the museal and local-colorist imperatives of the 1890s?[110] Though we have come to understand the imbrication of modernism and anthropology within the paradigm of "primitivism" or "ethnographic surrealism"—the *objet sauvage* refracted into *Les Desmoiselles*, or the alterity of Africa or Oceania re-imagined as the unconscious itself—the most domestic of American modernisms may have pursued a materialism adamantly expressed by the curatorial anthropologists of a preceding generation: the faith that thoughts could be found in, and expressed by, things.[111] Indeed, another aspect of Williams's creed, his intense localism, was inseparable from Otis Mason's own understanding of how ideas and things converge. With Robert McAlmon, Williams began to publish the short-lived *Contact* in 1920, which, while borrowing the blast/bless polemics of Lewis and Pound (who had borrowed them from Apollinaire), "insists on that which we have not found insisted upon before": "locality."[112] It hardly seems surprising, then, that Williams should have come to locate his modernist dictum—"Say it, No ideas but in Things"—within his monumentally localist epic, *Paterson* (1946).

But if Williams's materialist localism seems uncannily locatable within a nineteenth-century paradigm, *Contact* itself begins to disclose a more specific genealogy. For to legitimize the aesthetics of the local (over and against modernism's internationalism and its virulent nationalisms), Williams cites an article he recently read in the *Dial*, John Dewey's "Americanism and Localism," which proclaims that "locality is the only universal." Writing from abroad, Dewey notices how "the United States tend to merge into a unit," whereas local interests are what define the country—"the country," he emphasizes, "not the nation, much less the state," "the country" understood as "a spread of localities." Though Dewey addresses local and national print cultures, and impressively proclaims the unintelligibility of Americanization as a project, his affective resource for thinking about locality is New England's local-color fiction: "Mary Wilkins," he writes, is "local with a faithfulness that is beyond admiration."[113] It may be that in local-color fiction, the most recherché and retrospective of American genres, lies a prehistory of modernist materialism. For that faithfulness to locality that Dewey admired has everything to do with the place of material objects in human life, with the "pairing of people and things." Still, the difference that Williams achieves lies in his *unpairing* of people and things, in the fact that the "red wheel barrow" merits attention in and for itself, and not because of its participation as a prop in some human tableau.

Nonetheless, the most recognizable American modernism might be said to unconsciously and ambivalently refunction an American anthropological project of the 1890s. For the modernist fixation on things—Duchamp's *Fountain*, Strand's bowls, O'Keefe's jugs—this takes place just as the historical or anthropological content of artifacts was being evacuated. What Steven Conn calls the "object-based epistemology" that sustained the vitality and centrality of America's museums was being challenged by America's refunded and refurbished universities; "objects could no longer hold the meaning with which they had been invested."[114] The source of knowledge had drifted from the halls of the museum to the university's laboratories and libraries. From objects to books. From things to discourse. On the one hand, the modernist attention to the physical object world can be said to extend museal anthropology's focus on things; on the other, of course, this attention functions according to its own poetics of detachment, dislodging the object from its cultural milieu, from the scene of habitual use, from a scene of historical knowledge to one of aesthetic engagement.

In 1897, Boas had planned to add a historical exhibit to the American Museum that would depict the impact of geography and environment on the whaling culture of New England, dramatizing "the nature of the country, its products, its inhabitants, the manner in which the natives utilized the products of nature and how the immigrants used them."[115] Though the plans were never realized, they point to his willingness, which he shared with regionalist writers, to produce Anglo-American culture as an object of study no less appropriate and important than Native American culture. Indeed, we might think of Jewett as providing the contemporaneous literary version of the Boas exhibit, were it not for the fact that her sketches never depict whaling culture, but are instead haunted by the industry's postbellum demise. The appropriate, if noncontemporaneous, literary exhibit would be *Moby Dick*, although it too casts a backward glance at the genuine heyday of whaling culture. It would be logical to suppose that Jewett meant her backward glance to direct attention at Melville's own, but that would assume that Melville was widely read in the 1890s, which he was not. *Moby Dick* did not become central to the American literary tradition until the famous Melville revival of the 1920s, when regionalist, local-color fiction, which had seemed so vital before the century turned, was quietly excised from that tradition. What we might call Melville's overplotted collage supplants Jewett's underplotted sequence of sketches, and it does so for many reasons.[116]

But what interests me here is the way that Melville's novel produces a world replete with things, but with things that refuse to disclose their meaning. In other words, *Moby Dick* seems to enact precisely the modernist detachment of objects from culture while at the same time casting those objects within an ethnological frame. During his first night at the Spouter Inn, Ishmael discovers in his bedroom, among the "things not properly belonging to the room," Queequeg's hammock and seaman's bag, his hooks and harpoon, but also something wholly in excess of these accouterments: "But what is this on the chest? I took it up, and held it close to the light, and felt it, and smelt it, and tried every way possible to arrive at some satisfactory conclu-

sion concerning it. I can compare it to nothing but a large door mat, orna-
mented at the edges with little tinkling tags something like the stained porcu-
pine quills around an Indian moccasin."[117] Ishmael tries it on, continues to
examine it, and finally abandons it as a mystery. The scene establishes one
part of the novel's nondialectical relay between opacity and legibility, the ex-
tremes of which—from the mystery of the ethnological artifact to the allegorical potency of the doubloon or the whale—never admit shared meaning.
When, carving the lid of the coffin he has come to use as a sea-chest, Queequeg reproduces the hieroglyphic tattoos of his body, he might be said to in-
scribe himself within the physical object, but the object, like the man,
remains a riddle. And the vast cetological and phrenological knowledge that
Melville incorporates into the text never eventuates in explanatory power.[118]
Staging an elaborate will-to-knowledge while elaborating the perpetual failure of knowledge to achieve power, Melville prefigures the modernist epistemological shift *away* from objects as a source of secure meaning that is
nonetheless an aesthetic shift *toward* objects as the source of phenomenological fascination.

But even as the emergence of Melville as a major writer speaks to the fate
of the object within modernity and modernism both, and even as the canon-
ization of *Moby Dick* may help to explain the diminishment of *The Country of
the Pointed Firs*, the regionalist paradigm continued to attract modern writers.[119] For although modernism remains most recognizable as an international, cosmopolitan aesthetic drive, its intensely nationalist and nativist
idioms have more recently become the object of scholarly attention. Within
the American field, an intensely regionalist idiom characterizes the work of
Sherwood Anderson and of William Faulkner, for instance, or that of Zora
Neal Hurston and of Willa Cather. If there is a modern writer who seems to
perpetuate hallmarks of a nineteenth-century regionalist tradition, it is certainly Cather, whose *My Ántonia* (1918), for instance, can be read alongside
Hamlin Garland's *Main-Traveled Roads* (1891) as a more sustained and emo-
tionally complex account of the agrarian Midwest, similarly framed by the
cultured Easterner's return to the prairie town, by the insider's new perspective from without, a new sensitivity to conditions and conventions. But it is
in a novel that hardly occupies this tradition, *The Professor's House* (1925),
where Cather invokes the archeological component of regionalist fiction so
prominent in Murfree's *In the "Stranger People's" Country;* where she evokes
the regionalist passions that led to the first excavations of the American
Southwest; and where she reinvigorates Jewett's questions about the relation
between person, place, and thing. Indeed, the novel's eponymous subject
(which is an object) designates material possession as the mode through

which the modern subject struggles both to resist and to effect change. The novel can be summarized as the story of Godfrey St. Peter trying to retain some stability in his life by preserving his scene of reading and writing, maintaining the third-floor study in the emptied house from which he and his family have moved. He rents the entire house in order to keep the things of his "dark den" in place so that, ostensibly, he can complete the final volume of his *Spanish Adventurers in North America*.[120]

For the most part, this room seems stereotypical, with its "worn and scratchy" matting, its "old walnut table, with one leaf up, holding piles of orderly papers," and its "cane-backed office chair that turned on a screw" (16). But there are also remnants of the life that the space has lived as a sewing room, where the family seamstress has shared quarters with the professor for a few weeks every year. And the professor insists on keeping the two "forms"—"headless, armless, female torso[s]"—despite the seamstress's own objections. "They stay right here in their own place," the professor argues, "You shan't take away my ladies" (17, 21). St. Peter professes that the forms remind him of the time when his daughters "were little girls, and [their] first party frocks used to hang on them at night" (60); they help him to preserve the memory of having "lovely children in his house, fragrant and happy, full of pretty fancies and generous impulses" (126). But despite the capacity of these objects to summon up past pleasures, one of them also—in its very physicality—seems to manifest the problems that the professor currently faces.

> It presented the most unsympathetic surface imaginable. Its hardness was not that of wood, which responds to concussion with living vibration and is stimulating to the hand, nor that of felt, which drinks something from the fingers. It was a dead, opaque, lumpy solidity, like chunks of putty, or tightly packed sawdust—very disappointing to the tactile sense, yet somehow always fooling you again. For no matter how often you had bumped against that torso, you could never believe that contact with it would be as bad as it was. (18)

This is to say that within the novel, this form—or, more precisely, the substance of the form—prefigures the increasingly distant, unperceptive relations St. Peter has with the women in his life, especially his wife and his older daughter Rosamond, whose lack of sympathy and of generosity are always worse than he believes they will be. "Since Rosamond's marriage to Marsellus, both she and her mother had changed bewilderingly in some respects—changed and hardened," increasingly caught up in the conspicuous comforts of Rosamond's married life (161). We might say that, however much the form prompts the professor's fondest images of the past, even within the past its hardness disclosed what the professor's experience of the women in his life would come to be. Which is to say that in Cather's fiction, it is not just history, but also futurity, that objects seem able to express; in this case, the relation between form and substance becomes the relation between image and reality, and between the past and the present.

And in this case, the substance of the form expresses a hardness that manifests Rosamond's new relation to material objects—her greed, her irrepressible material desire that she enlists her father to help satisfy, marshaling him to accompany her to Chicago "to help her buy things for her country house," a shopping expedition that becomes an exhausting spree (151). When he returns home, he laments having been lured into the whole adventure. "Let's omit the verb 'to buy' in all forms for a time," he says to his wife (154). And he refuses to accompany Rosamond and Marsellus on their trip to Paris, where again they plan on "finding things for the house" (158–59). "We expect to pick up a good many things," they plead, hoping to use St. Peter's knowledge of history and of Paris as a crucial resource (159). St. Peter's effort to preserve his life as he knows it is experienced as an antipathy to irrepressible acquisition, possession, collection.

In the middle of this effort, in the middle section of the novel, Book Two, an altogether different site connects this story of objects to U.S. archeological history, as Cather re-writes the famous discovery of the Southwestern mesas. "Tom Outland's Story" is a story of "youthful defeat" about the college boy who became St. Peter's favorite student, who subsequently became an inventor and Rosamond's fiancé, and who finally died during World War I, killed fighting with the Foreign Legion (leaving her to marry Marsellus, but also leaving her as beneficiary of his inventions). His "defeat" designates not his untimely death but his failure to transform his discovery of the mesas into a properly national fascination. Working as a cattle driver with his friend Rodney Blake, Tom discovers, one dusk, "a number of straight mounds" (193). When he returns with a spade and discovers "some pieces of pottery, all of it broken, and arrow-heads, and a very neat, well-finished stone pick-ax" (194), he shares the news with Roddy, and the two of them begin excavating the site and living their lives there, camping in the cliffs. "To people off alone as we were," Tom explains to the professor, on the night when he finally tells the story he had withheld, "there is something stirring about finding evidences of human labour and care in the soil of an empty country. It comes to you as a sort of message, makes you feel differently about the ground you walk over every day" (194). This "message" from the past is the familiar message of occupation. As the boys continue to explore the area, they discover a "city of stone": "the city of some extinct civilization, hidden away for centuries," a mesa "full of little cliff-hung villages," where a "superior people" fashioned water and food bowls more accomplished "even than the pottery made at Acoma" (201, 202, 219, 220). Eager as they are to protect the site from "vulgar curiosity," Tom decides to go to the Smithsonian Institution, believing that the government will send a team of archeologists and will reward the young men for their work. But in Washington, with samples and photographs in hand, he is repeatedly rebuffed, and when he finally manages to meet with the director of the Smithsonian and his staff, he's told both that there is not a sufficient appropriation to conduct research in the New Mexican mesa, and that an "International Exposition of some sort in Europe the following summer" has commanded all their attention. "They were all pulling strings," he explains, "to get appointed on juries or sent to international congresses" (235). Within the novel, anthropology looks not like the epistemological ground for understanding the "object lessons" to be found in the relics of the Native American past, but like an institution unable, because unwilling, to recognize the power of those relics.

When Tom gives Mrs. St. Peter one of the "old pots" and explains that museums "don't care about our things," he speaks with the sensibility of someone whose own possessions have been denied any value (119). But the tragic aspect of this story of "youthful defeat" is in fact more personal, for Tom returns from Washington to discover that his buddy, Roddy, has sold their "curios" to a German, Fechtig, who has come to the Southwest to buy "up a lot of Indian things" (237), and who sneaks the artifacts out of the country through Mexico. Despite the intensity of their friendship, Roddy has failed to apprehend how much "those things [they] dug out together" meant to Tom (239). Recognizing that Tom's campaign was failing in Washington, and recognizing that "there's only one man in thousands that wants to buy relics and pay real money for them . . . [because] folks make a lot of fuss over such things, but they don't want to pay good money for them" (241–42), Roddy has made four thousand dollars on the sale. Although Roddy meant to share the money, thinking of Tom's portion as funds for the college education he still hoped to get, his friend's reaction is simple and it is adamant: "They belonged to boys like you and me, that have no other ancestors to inherit from. You've gone and sold them to a country that's got plenty of relics of its own. You've gone and sold your country's secrets, like Dreyfus" (242–43). In other words, the relics belong to no one as alienable property; they provoke a new mode of—a new meaning of—possession. In the final chapter of their romance of the New Mexican mesa, this story of "youthful defeat," Tom concludes by humiliating his friend unrelentingly. Roddy leaves the mesa and disappears from Tom's life.[121] Tom himself remains alone for the summer, clinging to the "Cliff City" that has become the center of his life and has centered his life. Although his story thus replicates (and diegetically anticipates) the story of the professor clinging to his study despite his house being emptied of its contents, it is only in the absence of the artifacts that Tom feels as though he is in true "possession" of the place and finds his "happiness unalloyed" (251). One might say of Tom Outland in the Blue Mesa what the narrator says of Paul in New York toward the end of Cather's "Paul's Case" (1905): "He felt now that his surroundings explained him."[122] In both cases, the point is that the explicatory scene (the triumph of the scene-agent ratio) depends on the character coming to find the appropriate setting, the way Jewett's narrator finds Dunnet Landing. It is not an original scene, but an eventual scene where the "dialectical pairing of people and things" makes sense.

"I wakened with the feeling that I had found everything," he reports, "instead of having lost everything" (251). His very capacity to confuse everything with nothing, or to imagine an everything without things, might be said to necessitate his physical absence from the novel's present. Tom's spiritual attachment to the Cliff City, which transcends his attachment to artifacts, is the culmination of his sense, as an orphan, of having finally found his ancestors.[123] And it is this ancestry, transforming him into a kind of Native American, that so utterly differentiates him from Marsellus, the Jew who both marries Tom's fiancé and lives off the money of his inventions. This is why, in Walter Benn Michaels's account of the "nativist modernism" of the 1920s, Cather's novel plays a paradigmatic role: identifying with the American Indian is a means of asserting an American identity that transcends legal citizenship, and thus of distinguishing assimilated immigrants from true Americans.[124] What Michaels calls "the production of Tom Outland as the descendant of Anasazi cliff dwellers" (45) works to spiritualize an affiliation that had been an affiliative displacement in *In the "Stranger People's" Country* and *The Country of the Pointed Firs* (and that spiritual affiliation, fantasized as a relation of blood, becomes a blood relation in Faulkner's fiction). But if, then, Cather writes the tragedy of the American subject, threatened by ethnic contamination, she does so while writing another tragedy—the tragedy of American objects: the failure on the part of the federal government to concern itself with the very artifacts that make aboriginal America palpable. For it is when the orphaned Tom finds in the cliffs the "pots and pans" of his "grandmothers," his "ancestors," that he most seriously imagines himself part of an aboriginal family. These are the refurbished relics that end up in German hands. In the postwar era, just as the U.S. government can no longer confer genuine American identity, so too it is unwilling to preserve aboriginal America, the remnants of that identity. Yet Cather's novel also makes it clear how the routines of museum work cannot fail to desacralize the nation's relics—to interrupt their power as a material medium through which to achieve some spiritual bond.

As the professor recalls Tom Outland's story, Cather retells what is no doubt the most exciting nineteenth-century episode of archeology in the American Southwest. Although previous explorers had found some ruins in the Mesa Verde and had discovered the existence of some cliff dwellings, and although the Hayden Survey of 1874–77 included a basic archeological account of the San Juan Drainage region (of northern New Mexico and Arizona, and southern Colorado), it was not until 1888 that Richard Wetherill and his friend Charles Mason discovered Cliff Palace. Stumbling upon some artifacts as they searched for stray cattle in the Marcos Canyon, they began to explore the region more thoroughly. Inspired by stories told by the Utes, they finally discovered the city built within an enormous cave among the highest cliffs. Camping for several seasons in the caves, they were joined by four other Wetherills and performed rudimentary excavation in Cliff Palace that unearthed an extraordinary number of prehistoric artifacts—pots and baskets and clothes and stonework—extraordinarily well preserved. Exhibiting their first collection of artifacts in Denver, they sold it for three thousand dollars, making it clear that there was money to be made in excavation. By 1891, cliff dwellings throughout the area became premier sites for both American and European archeologists. The Swedish archeologist Baron Gustav Nordenskïold employed the Wetherills, and displayed his resulting collection of Anasazi artifacts at the Columbian Exposition, a collection finally sold to the National Museum of Finland.[125] When silver mining slackened, provoked by the Federal Government's embrace of the gold standard in 1893, unemployed workers became "pothunters," trying, if not to replicate the success of the Wetherills, then to find and sell enough pots to feed their families. By the time Congress created Mesa Verde National Park in 1906, the great majority of treasures were gone from the site. *The Professor's House*, like the *Cliff Dwellers of America*, a popular documentary film released in 1926, marks a belated appreciation of just what the Wetherills had found.

No less than the politicians, anthropologists, and novelists of the era, American visual and plastic artists wrestled with "a crisis in American culture" that was "a crisis *of* culture" in the midst of postwar nativist nationalism,[126] experienced as the crisis of a modernism dominated by European paradigms. In this case as well, the Native American became the source of the solution. American Indian art, as Gail Levin argues, helped to satisfy the desire for a specifically American modernism, what Marsden Hartley called, in "Red Man Ceremonials: An American Plea for American Esthetics" (1920), a "national esthetic consciousness" for which "redman esthetics" could serve as the model, extricating American art from the European hegemony.[127] "The wide discrepancies between our earliest history and our present," Hartley argued, "make it an imperative issue for everyone loving the name America to cherish him while he remains among us as the only esthetic representative of our great country up to the present hour" (7). Like the anthropologist Edward Sapir, Hartley believed that only Indians possessed "genuine culture."[128] Although the story told about "primitivism" in the twentieth century remains most familiarly a story about the European post-impressionist, cubist, and surrealist engagement with artifacts from Africa and Oceania (displayed at the Paris exposition of 1889, later at the Musée d'Ethnographie du Trocadéro), Indian artifacts similarly helped to revitalize American modern art. Hartley, part of the Stieglitz circle, his work exhibited at "291," would have known about the new interest in primitivism from *Camera Work*, where Max Weber, in "The Fourth Dimension from a Plastic Point of View" (1910) had celebrated the grandeur of African statuary; as he reported to Steiglitz, he had found "the real thing" in the Trocadéro.[129] As Hartley put it, "Other nations of the world have long since accepted Congo originality. The world has yet to learn of the originality of the redman" (13). And yet for Hartley, it was not during a trip to the Southwest, but on a trip to Berlin (where he had gone to meet Kandinsky), that he discovered the source for his "Amerika" paintings. They were inspired by the objects he saw at the Museum für Völkerkunde in Berlin, where over thirty thousand specimens of Native American work were on exhibit. In *Indian Fantasy* (1914), Hopi and Plains Indian motifs from beadwork, sculpture, and pottery become part of the Americanized primitive phantasmagoria (fig. 15). Objects of knowledge have given way to objects of sensation, still mediated by the field of anthropology.

Murfree's and Cather's regional characters displace the Indians, who nonetheless linger, ghost-like, to confer the aura of culture. The displaced objects themselves inspire Hartley. And Tom Outland, himself displaced, exhibits full appreciation for Native American relics. Things in modernism may still appear to bond particular people to particular places—Outland to the Mesa, Hartley to America. But this is not because—as with Cather's professor, or Jewett's Mrs. Todd—the persons and the things have spent years occupying the same place; rather, it is because people and things have been displaced—because there is a circulation of people and a traffic in artifacts that fully reconfigures what we can mean by the scene-agent ratio. Indeed,

FIGURE 15

Marsden Hartley (1877–1943), *Indian Fantasy*, ca. 1914. Oil on canvas,
118.6 × 99.7 cm. North Carolina Museum of Art, Raleigh, Purchased
with funds from the State of North Carolina.

Ishmael's use of Queequeg's coffin as a float could be understood as prefiguring a modernist mode where people survive by "attaching themselves" to other people's things. And we might thus say that Joanna's tragedy, in *The Country of the Pointed Firs,* the tragedy of not being artifactually materialized in a proper place, points to the very possibility of being liberated from such propriety: of expropriations and dislocations that enable new affiliations, not restricted by things but inspired by them.

FOUR

The Decoration of Houses

Among the contemporary painters Henry James admired, he singled out John Singer Sargent, his fellow expatriate, for especially affectionate praise. Not only was Sargent "intelligent *en diable*"—"more intelligent about artistic things than all the painters" in London. He and James also became "excellent friends" from the moment they met in Paris, February 1884. The year before, Iza Boit had whispered pointedly to the novelist, during one salon, that the young painter was "de plus en plus fort." Though James had his doubts, he soon overcame them.[1]

Born in Florence and trained in France, Sargent traveled to the U.S. for the first time in 1887, which occasioned James's laudatory account of his work in *Harper's*. Though Sargent visited the U.S. so rarely that he ought to "count" as an American painter even less than James ought to "count" as an American novelist, the two expatriates share a subject matter that makes them seem, however continental, integral to America's Gilded Age. As Lewis Mumford put it, "America may be defined by its possessions, or by the things that it lacks," and the captains of industry in the Gilded Age tried to overcome the lack with a "predatory notion of culture," looking east to acquire the cultural objects of Europe just as they had looked west to acquire the land of the North American continent.[2] James wrote about this culture: Christopher Newman seeking to conquer Europe, Adam Verver amassing his incomparable European collection. Sargent painted it: the Curtis family in the Palazzo Barbaro (fig. 16), where the Bostonians first rented and then purchased the grand upstairs apartments, where Sargent (a family relation) spent much of his time in the early 1880s, and where James eventually set Milly Theale's residence in *The Wings of the Dove* (1902).[3] All but infatuated with his fellow cultural aristocrat—"I like him so much that . . . I don't attempt too much to judge him"—James pressed Sargent to leave Paris and to move to London, where he would find lucrative commissions and "magnificent subjects," including American subjects.[4] The painter settled into Chelsea the next year. "Is Mr. Sargent," James would go on to ask the readers of *Harper's*, "in very fact an American painter? The proper answer to such a question is doubtless that we shall be well advised to claim him."[5] During the subsequent vogue for Sargent, Americans (living in Paris or London, Boston or New York) claimed him as a kind of patriotic possession, the passion inspired not least by his august capacity to portray Americans at ease among their possessions, intimately, at times gloriously, at one with the sofa, the foot stool, the screen.[6]

James helped to stabilize the terms for appreciating Sargent. He wrote about the "immediacy" of the work: "It is as if painting were pure tact of vision."[7] He wrote about the technical facility and formal bravado. He wrote about Sargent's "idolatry" of Velasquez, going so far as to pronounce, comically and perspicaciously, that if anything unifies Sargent's output it is "the idea that it would be inspiring to know just how Velasquez would have treated the theme" (220). It is hardly surprising, then, that James singled out Sargent's most patent citation of Velasquez for extended commentary, a painting deeply indebted to *Las Meninas*, which Sargent had laboriously copied in Madrid in 1879. *The Daughters of Edward D. Boit* (1882), exhibited at the Salon of 1883, portrays the four children of the Bostonian expatriate painter and collector and his wife Iza (Charlotte Louisa Cushing), who organized a good portion of both the painter's and the novelist's Parisian social life (fig. 17). There were many personal reasons, then, along with art-historical reasons, why James was attracted to the painting. But these just begin to account for the attraction.

Always a bit unnerved by Sargent's accomplishment, his "*excess* of cleverness," James expressed his discomfort with the painting he called "The Hall with the Four Children" by describing the painter's precocity as a temporal disjunction.[8] To his eye the "astonishing" painting "offer[ed] the slightly 'uncanny' spectacle of a talent which on the very threshold of its career has nothing more to learn" (218). For James, then, the uncanniness *of* the image amounts to its manifestation of an indeterminate temporality, both the origin and end of an artistic career. And yet, when he comes to describing the figures *in* the image, he intimates the more familiar sense of the uncanny that I've invoked repeatedly in this book: an indeterminate ontology, the inability to distinguish between the animate and the inanimate. That intimation is nowhere evident in his opening assessment: "The artist has done nothing more felicitous and interesting than this view of a rich, dim, rather generalized French interior (the perspective of a hall with a shining

FIGURE 16

John Singer Sargent, R.A. (1856–1925), *An Interior in Venice*, 1899. Oil on canvas, 64.8 × 80.7 cm. © Royal Academy of Arts, London.

floor, where screens and tall Japanese vases shimmer and loom), which encloses the life and seems to form the happy play-world of a family of charming children" (222). But as he begins to remark on the square painting's "eminently unconventional" asymmetry, he begins to disclose something somehow wrong with this "happy play-world of a family." For although the "place is regarded as a whole," the pinafored daughters "detach themselves and live with a personal life." The eerie power of the painting resides, in marked contrast to *Las Meninas*, in the lack of relation (of interaction or interconnection) among the group—despite their depiction as a group—as though they were grouped as a set of inanimate objects. As for the girls standing in the shadows (who do not in fact hold hands, but rather touch without touching), they seem no more in company with one another than they are "in the delightful, the almost equal company of a pair of immensely tall emblazoned jars, which overtop them and seem also to partake of the life of the picture; the splendid porcelain and the aprons of the children shine to-

FIGURE 17
John Singer Sargent (1856–1925), *The Daughters of Edward Darley Boit*, 1882.
Oil on canvas, 87 3/8 × 87 5/8 in. Gift of Mary Louisa Boit, Julia Overing Boit,
Jane Hubbard Boit, and Florence D. Boit in memory of their father,
Edward Darley Boit (19.124). Courtesy, Museum of Fine Arts, Boston.
Reproduced with permission. © 2000 Museum of Fine Arts, Boston.
All Rights Reserved.

gether, while a mirror in the brown depth behind them catches the light"
(222). What we might call this ontological democratization of person and
thing—their equalization, to borrow James's formula—results both from
what a contemporaneous commentator called the "stiff, wooden forms" that
the children assume and from the vibrancy of the enormous Japanese urns.[9]
From the Jamesian point of view, if you don't imagine that Sargent here has

managed to paint a *portrait* of vases, then you ought to imagine that he has painted a *still-life* of girls.

Sargent's experiment with creating obscure empty spaces in his paintings has the effect, in this case, of evacuating the domestic space of any of the bric-a-brac that might make the children appear less diminutive. Indeed, the image is all but legible as a dresser top where the girls themselves assume the status of bric-a-brac, as though they were figurines (the sort of porcelain characters that come to life in *The Wizard of Oz*). In the context of Sargent's other paintings, and alone among them, *The Daughters of Edward D. Boit* depicts not the intimate possession of things, but an equation of humans and things that casts the human figures themselves as decorative objects among the Boit collection. What is arresting about the painting is the way it discloses how children, dolled-up, can be loved as material treasures, and how treasures can become objects of something like parental affection. Sargent suggests not just something of the sensibility with which Rosier, in *The Portrait of a Lady* (1881), thinks of Pansy "as he might have thought of a Dresden-china shepherdess," but also something of the sensibility with which Adam Verver, in *The Golden Bowl* (1904), cares for "precious vases only less than for precious daughters."[10]

All this is to say, then, that James may have found this painting "astonishing" less because of its "expressiveness of touch" (223) than because it is a "slightly 'uncanny' spectacle" that discloses a dialectic of person and thing, and a dynamic of materialist affectivity, central to James's own understanding of Americans abroad. And if Sargent and James are to be considered mirror images of one another,[11] they might be said to mirror in one another a proprietary understanding of character, what we've come to regard as the "degradation of *being* into *having*."[12]

It was such an understanding, William James believed, that grounded the "consciousness of self." Because "it is clear that between what a man calls *me* and what a man calls *mine* the line is very difficult to draw," a "*man's Self is the sum total of all he CAN call his,* not only his body and his psychic powers, but his clothes and his house, his wife and children, . . . his lands and horses, and yacht and bank-account."[13] No reader of Henry James, though, could be content to say that the novelist considers character reducible to possessions. It is, rather, some of the novelist's most notorious characters who voice that claim. It is Madame Merle, in *Portrait of a Lady*, who sounds like the precursor of James the psychologist: "What do you call one's self? Where does it begin? Where does it end? It overflows into everything that belongs to us—and then it flows back again. . . . I have a great respect for *things*" (397). Instead, the novelist's psychology posits the work of the mind as a great thing in excess of things, as it were, which can hardly be measured by any logic of possession or possessive individualism. Indeed, as he famously put it in his Preface to *The Portrait of a Lady,* he began with a character, to which such "usual elements" as "setting" had to be "superadded."[14] Still, readers of James have been perennially and proverbially fascinated by the topic of "things" in his fiction and the way that objects (a house, a statue, a cup) mediate the relations between characters, who *are* characters precisely in their relations.[15] Yet even as James thematizes "things" most obviously, he can effectively efface things from the descriptive register of a text. "Things" circulate as an idea in excess of any physical referent; the Jamesian sense of things can have nothing to do with the sensation of thingness. In the Jamesian lexicon, the word names a potent source of attraction, conflict, and anxiety; it does not (necessarily) name a group of physical objects. This is why James can be aligned so convincingly with the Heidegger and Derrida who posit a "thing" that is obscured by mere objects; this is why he can be aligned with the Lacan who posits a Thing that lies beyond the horizon of things, beyond representation.[16] Which is really to say that the novelist devotes himself to exploring the slippage or fluctuation between the physical and metaphysical referent.

In the effort to make sense of that exploration, I want to begin by demonstrating how one novel, *The Spoils of Poynton* (1896), participates in a new decorating impulse of the era; how James writes the novel as a Balzacian novel in excess of Balzac (whose "mighty passion for *things*" always fascinated James); and how he tests the limits of realism by evacuating the genre of, say, its material possessions. One of the effects of this evacuation is that characters and character, ideas and ideation, begin to assume a thing-like quality, as they do most elaborately in *The Golden Bowl,* where the collection of what we are asked to apprehend as materialized or externalized thoughts seems far more "massive" than any collection of objects. It is precisely within this text, though, where the eponymous object presents itself as something of a realist remainder, but one where the physical object, however meticulously specified, becomes no more than a placeholder for some thing that remains unspecifiable, some absent ground of Maggie Verver's new knowledge.

Throughout the chapter, I try to show how James was both obviously attracted to things yet somewhat embarrassed by them, eager to describe the physical object world yet eager to chart a kind of consciousness that transcends it. This kind of ambivalence emerges more casually when he writes about the visual arts, as in the opening essay of *Picture and Text* (1893), where he proclaims the writer's liberty from the tyranny of things, a freedom from things that is the freedom from having to render them in pencil or paint. When he describes the artistic attraction of the English countryside at Broadway, he explains that "the sky looks down on almost as many 'things' as the ceiling"; in other words, "the garden walls, the mossy roofs, the open doorways"—these all present themselves to the artist as objects that compel artistic attention.[17] But the *writer* can take pleasure in being "irresponsible," not having "to draw," allowing himself to "enjoy" the countryside with no ambition to "render" it (6–7). Still, even as he expresses this liberty from the countryside's "many 'things,'" he inexorably pursues them in print: "Everything is stone except the general greenness—a charming smooth local stone, which looks as if it had been meant for great constructions and appears even in dry weather to have been washed and varnished by the rain" (7–8). Whether James adds this description as a way of demonstrating the rival potency of the word, or, unconsciously, as a way of compensating for the liberty he's taken, it reads as a compulsive effort to represent things . . . written when Western painting, sculpture, and photography were about to liberate themselves from just that compulsion.

Décor

Reviewing *McTeague* in 1899, Willa Cather, one of the few critics who announced that "a great book has been written," lauded Frank Norris's descriptions as "a positive and active force," proof of the novelist's "power, imagination, and literary skill."[18] She also recognized that most writers resorted to description when they had nothing to say. In 1940, she described her own *The Professor's House* (1925) in relation to an exhibit of Dutch paintings she'd seen in Paris, portraying richly furnished rooms that nonetheless offered some means of visual egress, an open window looking out on the sea. "In my book I tried to make Professor St. Peter's house rather overcrowded and stuffy with new things; American proprieties, clothes, furs, petty ambitions, quivering jealousies—until one got rather stifled. Then I wanted to open the square window and let in the fresh air that blew off the Blue Mesa, and the fine disregard of trivialities which was in Tom Outland's face and in his behavior." Cather describes her formal experiment ("inserting the *Nouvelle* into the *Roman*") as an experiment in relation to things.[19] Three years before, she had published the signal American modernist manifesto about prose fiction—an attack, above all, on the way that the novel had "been overfurnished": "The property man has been so busy on its pages, the importance of material objects and their presentation have been so stressed" that the genre, by Cather's light, had been reduced to the act of observation, hopelessly confused for the art of writing.[20]

She characteristically quips that "we have had too much of the interior decorator," and she treasures the idea of a bold alternative: "How wonderful it would be if we could throw all the furniture out of the window" (47, 51). This assault on superfluous décor aligns with the modernism expressed by such classic arguments as those Le Corbusier published in *L'Esprit nouveau*, collected as *Vers une architecture* in 1923. He maintained that the new taste for "fresh air and clear daylight" found ornate décor anathema: "boudoirs embellished with 'poufs' in gold and black velvet, are now no more than the intolerable witnesses to a dead spirit."[21] And the architect's plea for a functionalist understanding of dwelling has a corresponding turn in Cather's plea for functional detail. One might thus argue that Cather could put the trope of the house of fiction to new use precisely because, by the 1920s, the house as such was being re-thought.

But it would be an oversight, of course, to suppose that this response to "boudoirs embellished with 'poufs'" emerged only as a full-fledged modernist harangue of the 1920s. Not only had Frank Lloyd Wright, in his first speaking engagement (1894), argued against "meaningless carpenter work and vulgar decoration," against "bric-a-brac" and "superfluous furniture," proclaiming that "too many houses are like notion stores, bazaars, and junk shops."[22] Also, in what remains one of the best-known American decorating texts, *The Decoration of Houses* (1897), Edith Wharton and Ogden Codman had begun their argument by denouncing the "superficial application of ornament totally independent of structure," the "vulgarity of current decoration" that amounts to "mere embellishments."[23] Although the book serves most impressively as a survey of European and English styles, Wharton and Codman repeatedly extol the "supreme excellence [of] simplicity" (192), which means eschewing "the accumulation of superfluous knick-knacks" (88). As though their point were not already clear, they reserve an especially caustic penultimate chapter for "Bric-à-Brac," denouncing the "indiscriminate amassing of 'ornaments'" and belittling the "amateur's tendency" to "buy too many things, or things out of proportion with the rooms for which they are intended" (182–83, 185).[24]

However archly recondite their will-to-distinction, Wharton and Codman thus seem to anticipate the modernist attack on so-called Victorian taste, what became the attack on kitsch. But they were hardly alone in being ahead of the times. As Lewis Mumford demonstrates in *The Brown Decades*, a modernist vilification of Victorian excess preceded modernism, as did the modernist celebration of function.[25] This protomodernism, moreover, was hardly confined to architects and artists. Edward Bok had used the *Ladies' Home Journal* to advocate domestic simplicity over and against ornateness.[26] And in a collection of essays on *Household Art*, for instance, published for the 1893 Columbian Exposition by the Board of Women Managers of the State of New York, arguments on behalf of bric-a-brac compete with considerably more arguments against it; it is a text where we witness the "leisure class" taking hold of a new aesthetic.[27] On the one hand, Candace Wheeler (a leader in the Arts and Crafts movement in the U.S.) maintains that "the final charm of any room lies in the addition of bits of things which give character as well as beauty—little treasures . . . a cup of Venetian glass" or "a smooth plaster copy of a Barye bronze" or "the latest and daintiest books."[28] On the other, Florence Morse bemoans the fashion for "meaningless bric-à-brac" and "indiscriminate riff-raff": "Bronzes, porcelains, glass, lamps, candles, sconces, flower-pots, vases, clocks, photograph frames, silver, statuary, curios, plaques, are huddled together on mantel, cabinet, bookcase, bracket, table, and shelf, regardless of shape, size, utility, color, or quality."[29] As with the typical modernist manifesto, her argument becomes fully proscriptive: "The mantel is not to be draped, nor is the patient piano to be loaded with bric-à-brac. Scarfs are not to hang over chairs, nor bows and ribbons perched where they do not belong" (185). In "The Limits of Decoration," Lucia Gilbert Runkle similarly maintains that "the elaborate and costly table naperies so generally adopted by fashionable hostesses during the last few years are worthy only of that decree of banishment which is certain to overtake them."[30] For both Runkle and Morse, the lesson had been learned from the Centennial Exhibition of 1876, precisely the kind of exposition meant to inculcate the passion for acquisition and display—a "place[] of pilgrimage to the commodity fetish," in Walter Benjamin's formulation; an event that gave rise to a wave of decorating literature and came to seem the opening event in "the real movement in favor of bric-à-brac."[31] Both women found themselves moved, though, by the Japanese Exhibit, where the serenity of the "quiet, airy, open rooms" depended on the scarcity of things (176). Like those modernists inspired by a Japanese aesthetic (Whistler, Wright, and Pound, among others) this group of fashionable New York women developed their own international style, a modernist domesticity *avant la lettre*. And just as it functioned for modernists, this appreciation for the "harmony" achieved by shunning any "profusion of costly and incongruous things" (176) helped to constitute them as a group, united foremost by their intense recognition of bad taste.

It is the profusion of costly and incongruous things at Waterbath that provokes Fleda Vetch's dismay within "the little tale" that Henry James called "The House Beautiful" while he worked on the manuscript that became *The Old Things* when it appeared serially in the *Atlantic* in 1896, and *The Spoils of Poynton* when it appeared as a book the following year. Though the final title underscores the martial metaphors that pervade the book, the original title helps to situate the text within the decorating discourse of the era, from Clarence Cook's *The House Beautiful: Essays on Beds and Tables, Stools and Candlesticks* (1878) to the magazine, *House Beautiful*, which began to appear in 1896, meant not simply to solidify notions of good taste, but to generate a public devoted to analyzing and expressing the aesthetics of the home.[32] By privately disclosing her dismay—"Isn't it too dreadful?"—the young Fleda initiates her friendship with Adela Gereth, a fellow guest who finds "the intimate ugliness of Waterbath" the source of comparable pain.[33] The older woman's "passion for the exquisite," responsible for the famous collection at Poynton, renders her acutely susceptible to aesthetic despair; she suffers from a "proneness to be rendered unhappy by the presence of the dreadful" (6). The Brigstocks have "smothered" Waterbath "with trumpery ornament and scrapbook art, with strange excrescences and bunchy draperies" (7). The house is "perversely full of souvenirs of places even more ugly than itself and of things it would have been a pious duty to forget" (7). In the midst of such perversity, her only solace takes the form of the new friendship, an aesthetic bond, a solidarity built on the mutual recognition of despicable décor. "Their drawing-room, Mrs. Gereth lowered her voice to mention, caused her face to burn, and each of the new friends confided to the other that in her own apartment she had given way to tears" (7).

Though there is something magnificently comic in all this, the emotional intensity of the shared aesthetic experience establishes the way that "things" mediate social relations in the novel—the way people circulate around them—and it establishes a politics of taste wherein "cultural capital," as we've come to call it, is utterly irreducible to class.[34] For the young woman who takes third-class train compartments, whose family doesn't "have at all good things," and "whose only treasure [is] her subtle mind" (162, 13) finds herself nonetheless embraced by the novel's embodiment of aristocratic sensibility. Mrs. Gereth "had only one question about persons: were they clever or stupid? To be clever meant to know the 'marks.' Fleda knew them by direct inspiration" (138). This impossible account of the role of nature, not nurture, in the education of cultural semiotics has the effect of naturalizing—that is, of universalizing—what reads like the novel's own discrimination, its own judgment, in the Kantian sense. As with so many of James's young women (Isabel Archer, Charlotte Stant), Fleda Vetch demonstrates a felicitousness that does not depend on fortune. She thus functions to demonstrate felicitousness as such, which is nonetheless tainted by the grandeur of Mrs. Gereth's materialism: "'Things' were of course the sum of the world; only, for Mrs. Gereth, the sum of the world was rare French furniture and oriental china. She could at a stretch imagine people's not 'having,' but she could n't imagine their not wanting and missing" (24–25). Fleda proves the exception because the issue of "wanting" does not concern her; her satisfaction derives from elaborate acts of appreciation. She proves the point argued by Vernon Lee, in *Art and Life* (1896), that the "aesthetic sentiment" replaces "the legal illusory act of owning by the real spiritual act of appreciation."[35]

The relationship between the two women develops in the context of Mrs. Gereth's expropriation, her sudden metamorphosis from "having" to "missing." Because she has lost her husband, she must lose her home, English law dictating that the intact estate will be inherited by her one son, Owen. Although granted another house (Ricks) in which to live, Mrs. Gereth must abandon the things she has devoted her life to acquiring, "things your father and I collected," as she says to her son, "things that we worked for and waited for and suffered for" (30). She substantiates the way that, as Susan Stewart puts it, "the collection presents a metaphor of 'production,'" not of consumption and not of luck.[36] And she theatricalizes what Jean Baudrillard terms "the miracle of collecting," the fact that "what you really collect is always yourself":[37] "They were our religion," Mrs. Gereth proclaims, "they were our life, they were *us*" (30–31). Nonetheless, aggrieved as she is by the nastiness of the law, it is more the thought of Poynton violated that provokes her outburst. Mona Brigstock, to whom her son is engaged, would "bring in her own little belongings and horrors! The world is full of cheap gimcracks in this awful age, and they're thrust in at one and every turn. They'd be thrust in here on top of my treasures, my own. Who'd save *them* for me?" (31). Mrs. Gereth understands the things at Poynton not as an accumulation of isolated objects she and her husband acquired, and she "care[s] nothing for mere possession" (214); she understands "the things" as a single work of art she has *produced*. This is why, in her case, it makes no sense to describe a "degradation of *being* into *having*": the "things" at Poynton are not so much objects as they are congealed actions, passionate acts of seeking, selecting, and situating. And this is why thinking "solely and incorruptibly of what [is] best for the objects themselves," she cannot help but think of herself, even as she invests taste with a fully ethical and all but ecological dimension (214). Exiled to Ricks, she has all the things secretly and swiftly transported from Poynton, only to comply with the law and return all the things when she believes that Fleda has supplanted Mona as the object of her son's affections.

But though Fleda and Owen have expressed their love to one another, Fleda will not interfere with his prior commitment, will not allow him, for her sake, to sever his ties to Mona: retaining both her own dignity and his, she forfeits both Owen and the spoils. Mrs. Gereth must forfeit Fleda as a potential member of the family, but not as the friend with whom, because she so thoroughly intuits the grandeur and grace of the woman's decorating touch, Mrs. Gereth has come to enjoy an inexpressible intimacy, an intimacy based on their joint superiority: "there are always things you and I can comfortably hate together" (245).

Although things thus compose the axle around which the plot turns, and through which this intimacy is achieved, the things at Poynton hardly appear in the novel's visual register. One reader records this fact by complaining that James "is distinctly weak about the specifications of one of the most beautiful houses in England."[38] After the first chapter's account of the décor at Waterbath, any reader of *Spoils* would expect the second chapter, given that it introduces Fleda to the home of her new friend, to provide a detailed account of Poynton, and to do so with something of the luxuriating attention that James had devoted to homes like Gardencourt, in *Portrait of a Lady*, or, more analogously, to Gilbert Osmond's Palazzo Roccanera. But we learn only that "the exquisite old house" is "early Jacobean, supreme in every part," and that "there were places much grander and richer, but no such complete work of art" (12–13). The details of this supremacy remain conspicuously absent. Despite the novel's eventual reference to two specific objects—a "great Italian cabinet" in the red saloon and the Maltese cross, described as "a small but marvelous crucifix of ivory, a masterpiece of delicacy" (71, 73–74)—Poynton, above all, is all awash in overarching characterization: "the shimmer of wrought substances spent itself in the brightness; the old golds and brasses, old ivories and bronzes, the fresh old tapestries and deep old damasks threw out a radiance" (58). Highly particularized objects appear elsewhere in the novel's domestic landscape—in Fleda's sister's and her father's house, and, above all, at Waterbath: a "stuffed cockatoo [was] fastened to a tropical bough and a waterless fountain composed of shells stuck with some hardened paste" (34). But as though such individuating description were to be preserved for the elements of bad taste alone, or as though it were in bad taste to visualize exquisite taste, James renders the mise-en-scène at Poynton as a matter of aura, not artifacts.[39]

By having the general effect of Poynton obscure particular objects—prohibiting access, as it were, to the apperception of things—James accomplishes several objectives. The novel appears to certify Mrs. Gereth's own conclusion that there is no way to choose a few things from among all the things. Though Owen grants her such a choice, "the general effect made preferences almost as impossible as if they had been shocks" (22). The lack of specifying, individuating attention also underscores how Mrs. Gereth's accomplishment lies not in the act of acquisition but in the art of composition. "It's your extraordinary genius," Fleda says to her, that "you make things 'compose' in spite of yourself" (249). It is when Mrs. Gereth has sent the things back to Poynton, when she has had to make do with the unexceptional stuff at Ricks, that her powers of arrangement become most clear, and when she demonstrates that her success does not depend on her medium, the material at hand. Fleda recognizes that it is in an "impression in which half the beauty resides," what she considers a kind of "poetry," the nature of which she can hardly begin to name: "It's a kind of fourth dimension. It's a presence, a perfume, a touch" (249). Finally, by emphasizing design over detail, the novel itself, as a manifestation of taste, participates in the aspirations outlined by the decorating discourse of the day, which ultimately advocated transforming the physical into something, say, metaphysical. Candace Wheeler writes of "a mysterious charm, a nameless something, an attractive ghost of harmony and tranquility" that transcends the objects in a room (3). Mrs. M. G. Van Rensselaer, insisting that Americans have devoted far too much attention "to secondary things," explains that "a mass of beautiful minor things" will not in themselves produce the "one large beautiful thing" toward which one should aspire.[40] In the midst of the unprecedented proliferation of things that tyrannized the American 1890s, the arbiters of taste sought some thing else. In Wharton and Codman's formulation this "beautiful thing," a Thing that names a kind of beauty in excess of things, becomes fully spiritualized: "that something, indefinable . . . which gives repose and distinction to a room" is, "in its effects as intangible as that all-pervading essence which the ancients called the soul" (33). To the degree that Mrs. Gereth's success lies in the "arrangement and effect of everything" she has performed the decorating feat of the day (249).

But of course it is not Mrs. Gereth's performance, but James's own, that makes *The Spoils of Poynton* such a pivotal text for apprehending the fate of things within fiction. Although readers of the novel may agree that Mrs. Gereth is morally vacuous—in the Preface, James himself describes her as "floundering . . . in the dusk of disproportionate passion"—she nonetheless represents much of the aesthetic achievement that James himself sought when he described life, on the one hand, as "all inclusion and confusion," and art, on the other, as "all discrimination and selection" (xvi, v). In other words, in the act of representing Mrs. Gereth's decorating acuity, he manifests what would become Cather's dictum that scenes must be presented by "suggestion rather than by enumeration" (48): "It is the inexplicable presence of the thing not named," she argues, "the emotional aura of the fact or the thing . . . that gives high quality to the novel" (50). In Fleda's words, "It's a presence, a perfume, a touch."

James's own capacity to generate aura and to eschew enumeration derives in large measure from his enlistment of the nonvisual senses. It remains customary to ascribe to the genre of the novel a specifically visual epistemic authority and to associate realism with other visualizing institutions: "If the realist novel flourished in the same age as the development of the great museums, it is because both seem to say, 'Look!'"[41] But *The Spoils of Poynton* never says "look," and an adequate apprehension of Mrs. Gereth's "effort toward completeness and perfection" could never reside in a visual register, not least because Poynton, all told, is a "matchless canvas for a picture" (50, 13). When James writes that the "beauty" of Poynton "throb[s] out like music" (26), he manages to collapse the distance that visual recognition entails. And when he describes human attention to exquisite objects, he does so through the medium of touch. "They're living things to me," Mrs. Gereth explains to her son, "they know me, they return the touch of my hand" (31). When Fleda recognizes that Mrs. Gereth has audaciously transported the things from Poynton to Ricks, her most intense recognition is tactile: "By this time the very fingers of her glove, resting on the seat of the sofa, had thrilled at the touch of an old velvet brocade, a wondrous texture she could recognize, would have recognized among a thousand, without dropping her eyes on it" (71). Their intimacy with the physical object world, an intimacy on which their intimacy is built, could not be rendered by the distantiating sense of sight, only by the tremble of the touch.

"Were they saving the things?" Fleda wants to know in quiet desperation when she learns that "Poynton's on fire" in the closing pages of the novel (213). But the contents of the estate, around which the plot of *The Spoils of Poynton* has turned, disappear without a trace. The conflagration retrospectively renders the war over the spoils more futile, even as it transforms the novel into a materialist tragedy. More important, though, this dramatic denouement theatricalizes the consumption of things with which the novel began. That is, it literalizes the absence of the spoils within the novel's descriptive register. Still, it may make more sense to say that this original absence itself provokes or necessitates the fire, as though the novel's chief narratological device—withholding things—finally motivated this melodramatic turn in the diegesis (which nonetheless resists melodrama by refusing to include any detail of specific objects lost to the flames). To recognize that James was writing a novel about things, but without things, is to appreciate the fire as an act (or rather a mark) of purification. Precisely because the novel is "weak about the specifications of one of the most beautiful houses in England," then, it has the strength to recommend itself as the James novel that most patently challenges realism—or challenges what Cather called the "popular superstition that 'realism' asserts itself in the cataloguing of a great number of material objects" (45).[42] Insofar as the fire marks this strength, it should be understood as the conflagration in which realism as such is consumed.

The Novel Démeublé

In her effort to rid the novel of its furniture, Cather singled out *The Scarlet Letter* as the exemplary instance of how to overcome narrative's reliance on the accretion of detail. One finds no information about Puritan "manners and dress and interiors" within the novel. The "material investiture of the story," she goes on to argue, "is presented as if unconsciously; by the reserved, fastidious hand of an artist, not by the gaudy fingers of a showman or the mechanical industry of a department-store window-dresser" (49). When it comes to focusing her disapprobation, she singles out Balzac, the showman who "tried out the value of literalness in the novel . . . with the inflamed zest of an unexampled curiosity" (46). Indeed, no one could argue that the *Comédie humaine* is anything but replete with physical objects, from the "poinards, quaint pistols, weapons with secret springs, . . . porcelain soup-tureens, Dresden china plates, translucent porcelain cups from China, antique salt-cellars, [and] comfit-dishes from feudal times" in the curiosity shop of *Le Peau de chagrin,* to the "stained glass, enamels, miniatures, and gold and silver snuff-boxes" in the bedroom of Sylvain Pons, described as an "expert judge of all those masterpieces, wrought by hand and brain, which in recent times have been popularly known as bric-à-brac."[43] In her objection to novelistic furniture, Cather no doubt had in mind the hypertrophy and hyperspecificity with which Balzac sets both his country and city scenes, like the dozens of paragraphs describing the house of Monsieur Grandet:[44]

> In each corner of the room stood a corner-cupboard, or rather a kind of sideboard topped by a tier of dirty shelves. An old inlaid card-table with a chessboard top was placed between the two windows. On the wall above this table hung an oval barometer set in a black frame decorated with a carved knot of ribbons, once gilt, on which the flies had frolicked so wantonly that the existence of gilding could now only be guessed at. Two portraits in pastel hung on the wall opposite the fireplace.

Though Cather fully recognizes the "stupendous ambition" of Balzac's effort to "reproduce" Paris ("the houses, the upholstery, the food, the wines"), she nonetheless condemns his very "succe[ss] in pouring out on his pages that mass of brick and mortar and furniture" as "unworthy of an artist" (46–47).

Although other critics have pursued Cather's basic question—Georg Lukács asks "how and why" description became the novel's "principal mode"—they have not all presented Balzac as the primary exhibit in the case against things.[45] In Lukács's light, Balzac's ability to render life in a new society depends on the attention to physical detail, and his particular kind of attention tends to infuse description with action. Instead, Lukács singles out Flaubert and Zola for their detached and unanimated observation, observation rendered independent of the destiny of characters, and thus symptomatic of the novelists' own surrender to fetishism. But for James, as for Cather, Balzac epitomizes the novelist devoted to environment—to things— and James considered Balzac's own "passion for bric-à-brac" as the source of the "enumerations of inanimate objects" in which he "often sins by extravagance."[46] Without a doubt, and despite Lukács, Balzac has become known as the enumerating author.

And just as "things" mediate the relation among so many of James's characters, so "things" mediate James's own relation to Balzac, both early and late in his career.[47] With the kind of ambivalence that Lukács and Cather both argue without, James considers Balzac "one of the finest of artists and one of the coarsest," whose "great general defect," as he puts it in *French Poets and Novelists* (1878), amounts to "the absence of fresh air."[48] However claustrophobic he found this atmosphere, though, James was clearly drawn to it like a drug, never ceasing "to wonder at the promptness with which he can 'get up' a furnished house," "often prefer[ing] his places to his people," and recognizing that, for Balzac, the "mise en scène" is no less significant than an "event" (50, 49). Though James thus appears to accord Balzac's material world the kind of animation accorded by Lukács, he does so with no historical reference to France; his argument about things in Balzac's fiction is not social or sociological but biographical, existential, and ontological. Concluding that "to live greatly in all one's senses, to have plenty of *things*—this was Balzac's infinite" (48), he begins by specifying this "living greatly" as a matter of human-being as such: "There is nothing in all imaginative literature that in the least resembles his mighty passion for *things*—for material objects, for furniture, upholstery, bricks and mortar. The world that contained these things filled his consciousness, and *being*, at its intensest, meant simply being thoroughly at home among them" (48). Although readers of Balzac should object that the novelist's exhaustive enumerations are more uncanny and more symptomatic than James believes,[49] his insight here is to sense that, for Balzac, the canny comfort of being-at-home with one's things—a comfort which *could* be dismissed as complacent bourgeois repose—might amount to an ongoing state of fervor. This is not, by James's light, an ontological economy where the desire for things is provoked by an unrelievable lack of being, but a drama of passionate plenitude. This is not Being disclosed by the thingness of things, but Being achieved among them.

This incomparable appreciation for Balzac's passion (James playing Fleda, let us say, to Balzac's Mrs. Gereth) helps to explain how, for James, things have a semiotic and social, but not a sociological, function: an index of character not class. In *Washington Square* (1880), to take a relatively simple example, James rivals Balzac in the efficiency of his mise-en-scène, and he makes things both the center of the plot and the measure of character. Although the plain and shy Catherine seeks "to be eloquent in her garments," James presents her in an inappropriate "red satin gown trimmed with gold fringe" that reveals her to be as awkward with things as she is with words.[50] Morris Townsend, who devotes himself to her in the hope of securing her father's things for himself, has all the taste that she lacks, expressed through acquisitive eyes that motivate the descriptions of the Doctor's house, extending and intensifying his every glance, such as his "glance at the long narrow mirror which adorned the space between the two windows, and which had at its base a little gilded bracket covered by a thin slab of white marble, supporting in its turn a backgammon board folded together in the shape of two volumes, two shining folios inscribed in letters of greenish gilt, *History of England*" (53). Such glances make it clear that he could gain a "devilish comfortable house" by marrying Catherine (89). But the price of the comfort is more than Morris Townsend is willing to pay. Wise to the man's designs on his daughter, the Doctor sweeps her away to Europe, where "all those celebrated things" will supposedly drive the young man from her thoughts (119). But because she returns from the trip still infatuated with the man and utterly unaffected by those things, Morris faces the fact that she is too "dull a woman" to marry—her relation to things is simply too unimaginative.

The more imaginative relation to things in *Washington Square* is what grants possessions their metonymic power to express character (70), and what makes them the sine qua non of being-at-home. When the Doctor and his daughter are in Europe, Morris gains access to the house and violates the Doctor's intimate abode: "He had his chair—a very easy one—at the fireside in the back-parlour (when the great mahogany sliding-doors, with silver knobs and hinges, which divided this apartment from its more formal neighbor, were closed), and he used to smoke cigars in the Doctor's study, where he often spent an hour turning over the curious collections of its absent proprietor" (121). Smoking here reads as a mode of male marking. If, as William James put it, collections "become, with different degrees of intimacy, parts of our empirical selves" (281), then Morris's disturbance of "all those things in the glass cases" reads like a violation of the Doctor himself (129). In turn, and as in any detective novel, that violation remains recorded. But in the case of the Doctor, no mere detective, he experiences the impressions left on his things as impressions left on his very psyche: "We doctors, you know, end by acquiring perception, and it is impressed upon my sensorium that he has sat in these chairs, in a very easy attitude, and warmed himself at that fire" (138).[51] This perceptiveness seems to result less from the Doctor's profession than from the quotidian intensity of his possession.

Only with such a sense of James's attraction to, and redeployment of, Balzac's materialism in the 1880s can a reader appreciate *The Spoils of Poynton* as a radical experiment in Balzacian realism. By the time James wrote his Preface to the New York Edition of the novel, this is how he himself had come to understand it. Having heard about a woman expropriated by the death of her husband, James describes himself as having recognized the story at once as a "perfect little workable thing," although only one "thing was 'in it,' in the sordid situation, on the first blush, and one thing only": "the sharp light it might project on that most modern of our current passions, the fierce appetite for the upholsterer's and joiner's and brazier's work, the chairs and tables, the cabinets and presses, the material odds and ends, of the more labouring ages" (vii, ix). The conception of the novel did not begin with a character. The project as he originally imagined it would have been a document in the history of taste, legible in the context of the new vogue for antiques, the Arts and Crafts movement, modern materialist nostalgia. But far from casting the story within a sociological light, he went on to imagine the book as having less do with people's passion for things than with the things themselves, which would animate the text even more than Sargent's grand Japanese jars animate *The Daughters of Edward D. Boit*. "On the face of it," James writes, "the 'things' themselves would form the very centre of such a crisis: these grouped objects, all conscious of their eminence and their price, would enjoy, in any picture of conflict, the heroic importance" (ix). Such centrality would require a Balzacian effort to render the things descriptively visible within the pages of the text. "They would have to be presented, they would have to be painted—arduous and desperate thought; something would have to be done for them not too ignobly unlike the great array in which Balzac, say, would have marshaled them" (ix). If it was Balzac who could make things come to life in a novel, then one should turn to Balzac to write a novel where they attain consciousness.

Given James's long history of success at "painting" things, this account of his desperation sounds decidedly forced, and he by no means proclaims the arduousness of the task as his rationale for abandoning it. Rather, once "the thing had 'come'" in conception, he faced an "editorial ruefulness" about the possible length of the installments to be published in *The Atlantic* (x). While the "real centre . . . *would have been* the felt beauty and value of the prize of the battle, the Things, always the splendid Things, placed in the middle light, figured and constituted, with each identity made vivid," in fact no "vigilant editor" would "allow[ ] room for" such a "rendered tribute" (xii, my emphasis). In other words, James blames the conditions of publishing for his own abandonment of Balzac. Whereas Lukács understood the commercialization of fiction—the complete transformation of the book into a commodity and the writer "into a salesman of his merchandise" (119)—as the reason for the triumph of description in the novel, James posits commercialization as the reason for its absence. Indeed, we might say that *The Spoils of Poynton* profoundly registers the effects of reification that accompany the ubiquity of the commodity form: that it "conceals above all the immediate— qualitative and material—character of things as things."[52] More precisely, in what James calls "the sublime economy of art" (vi), the physicality of the possessions have been supplanted by their (aesthetic) value; the objects have been supplanted by "things" just as things have been replaced by "Things." The things at Poynton attain their value (for Fleda and Mrs. Gereth, though not for Mona) outside the circulation of commodities, and their overwhelming value is aesthetically (that is, sensuously yet suprasensuously) determined. The extent to which, both in his novel and in his Preface, James never confuses "things"—"the Things, always the splendid Things"—with their merely physical particularization is the extent to which he suspends "things" as a concrete abstraction, physically experienced yet unspecifiable.

For James, the answer to the supposed editorial dilemma lay in finally replacing things with character, or, rather, displacing the physicality of objects with their effects, "lodg[ing] somewhere at the heart of one's complexity an irrepressible *appreciation*," which he fashioned in Fleda (xiv). Thus, though the spoils had "wondrous things to say," they could not be rendered "directly articulate" because it was too "costly to keep them up," whereas Fleda could be "maintained at less expense" (xii). In this textual economy, dialogue is the great bargain. According to the Preface, then, character as such comes into being as a system for registering the effectiveness of physical objects, which, as an effect, are not objects but "things." Whereas *Washington Square* is a novel about the impressions that people leave on objects, *The Spoils of Poynton* is about the impressions that things leave on people—which is really to say the impressions that constitute character.

However dubious this narrative of the novel's composition, it helps to explain why Fleda mediates the triumphant life of the spoils, why her fetishism animates the things that James already understands as animate and agential. When the things are returned to Poynton, she declares to herself that "[t]hey were nobody's at all—too proud, unlike base animals and humans, to be reducible to anything so narrow. It was Poynton that was theirs; they had simply recovered their own" (235). Fleda's claim, which relishes the moral superiority of these things, shows how seriously they remain at the center of the novel, however absent they seem to be. Though the novel itself maintains an utterly spare décor, James does not really interrupt Balzac's investment in things; rather, he intensifies that investment, granting things not a physical but a metaphysical potency. He concludes of the finished novel that the "'things' are radiant, shedding afar, with a merciless monotony, all their light, exerting their ravage, without remorse" (xiv–xv). The intensity of these things—which assume a status that really outstrips anything in Balzac, Flaubert, or Zola—transforms the novel into something inexplicable from a Lukácsian perspective. For when Lukács argues against unmotivated physical description, he imagines his readers asking "But what about the intensive existence of objects? The poetry of things?"—and these are questions to which he responds very bluntly: "only insofar as they furnish the indispensable vehicle for translating human relationships do they acquire poetic value" (135–36). But the idiosyncrasy of *Spoils*, of course, is the way in which human relationships become the medium for expressing things, for apprehending the intensity of their *being*, for recognizing that the being of things lies no more in the details of their mere physicality than does the being of humans.

Reification as Utopia

Having begrudgingly returned the things to Poynton, and anticipating Fleda's upcoming visit, Mrs. Gereth writes to her friend that, "with nothing else but my four walls, you'll at any rate be a bit of furniture. For that, a little, you know, I've always taken you—quite one of my best finds" (245). These words bluntly manifest the older woman's proprietary objectification of the younger. But far from being alarmed by the claim (as James's readers generally are), Fleda seems to appreciate the objectification, part of her overarching appreciation of all that Mrs. Gereth does with objects: "The position of a scrap of furniture was one that Fleda could conscientiously accept, and she by no means insisted on so high a place in the list. This communication made her easier, if only by its acknowledgment of the principle of property" (245–46). If her retention of the principle of property signals the woman's psychological stability, then her representation of Fleda as a bit of furniture, one of her "finds," might be said to signal her emotional health. For insofar as Mrs. Gereth exemplifies the "real collector" for whom, as Walter Benjamin put it, "ownership is the most intimate relationship that one can have to things," her proprietary objectification of Fleda amounts to her most genuine expression of warmth.[53] Apprehending the adequacy of her words (their adequacy from Fleda's point of view) requires thinking outside a familiar paradigm, where pieces of furniture attain their anthropomorphic value because they incarnate the "emotional bonds" of the family.[54] Instead, Mrs. Gereth's relation to furniture, her emotional bond with the physical object world, is the ground for feeling as such. Declaring Fleda a piece of furniture does not diminish her to the status of a commodity object; it elevates her to a status beyond (socially determined) value, and it envelops her in the kind of affection Mrs. Gereth generally reserves for objects (and does not expend, for instance, on her son). Indeed, given the woman's own status as an object among objects—"Wherever she was she was herself the great piece in the gallery"—the novel allows us to consider the relation between the two women as an intimacy between one thing and another (73).

This is hardly to suggest that, for James, the objectification of people as possessions can simply be considered beneficent or benign. Indeed, the persistence and power of the topic throughout James's career, and throughout the fiction I examine in this book, can be accounted for not least as the effort to rethink this possessiveness in the era just after human property, in the Southern U.S., existed literally and legally.[55] Nonetheless, when James treats this topic most extensively, in his last complete novel, *The Golden Bowl* (1904), proprietary objectification looks rather like an inescapable human condition: not a relation that *can* occur and might be avoided, but a relation that is the ground of any significant occurrence. However remote James was from American culture, this novel has thus served to illustrate the saturation of that culture with the commodity form, and to document the emergence of what Jean-Christophe Agnew describes as a "commodity aesthetic."[56] Attending to "literature of the interior" (decorating manuals, periodicals, and books), paintings, and works of fiction, Agnew defines the commodity aesthetic as "a way of seeing the world in general, and the self and society in particular, as so much raw space to be furnished with mobile, detachable, and transactionable goods" (135). For his concluding illustration, Agnew quotes the scene at the close of the novel where the magnificent objects at Fawns stand ready to be packed up. Adam Verver and his young wife, Charlotte Stant, prepare to sail for America to install his collection in a "museum of museums" in American City, leaving his daughter Maggie behind with her husband, the Prince, and thus severing the illicit intimacy between him and Charlotte (147). The father and daughter review the collection together:

> She had passed her arm into his, and the other objects in the room, the other pictures, the sofas, the chairs, the tables, the cabinets, the 'important' pieces, supreme in their way, stood out, round them, consciously, for recognition and applause. Their eyes moved together from piece to piece, taking in the whole nobleness—quite as if for him to measure the wisdom of old ideas. The two noble persons seated in conversation and at tea fell thus into the splendid effect and the general harmony: Mrs. Verver and the Prince fairly 'placed' themselves, however unwittingly, as high expressions of the human furniture required aesthetically by such a scene. The fusion of their presence with the decorative elements, their contribution to the triumph of selection, was complete and admirable; though, to a lingering view, a view more penetrating than the occasion really demanded, they also might have figured as concrete attestations of a rare power of purchase. (2:360)

However clearly this scene appears to illustrate a "commodity aesthetic," it does so only while staging—or momentarily resolving—the dynamics of objectification, possession, and commodification that the novel tracks from its outset. The couple's "fusion" with decorative objects (which, by standing out "consciously," seem slightly more cognizant than the couple who place themselves "unwittingly") fixes Charlotte and the Prince in the descriptive scene the way they have *not* been fixed previously by the proprietary imagination, even though both have been explicitly (indeed theatrically) objectified and commodified from the very outset of the novel. Their very status as "mobile, detachable goods"—that is, as commodities—has fostered their circulation; it has prevented them from attaining the status (or submitting to the status) of the genuinely and inalienably possessed. Indeed and instead, as Maggie laments, she and her father face "*their* complete possession . . . of our life" (2:74, my emphasis).

A world where all humans are objects, a novel that relentlessly metaphorizes people as things—these help illuminate both the difference between a commodity and a possession, and the spatial dynamics of collection. Benjamin, for one, understood the collector's labor as "the Sisyphean task of divesting things of their commodity character by taking possession of them," an unending task because the taint of purchase itself can never be wholly erased.[57] The act of collecting is one of conferring on the particular-ized object a value that derives from its place in the collection, not from its exchange within the world of fungible goods, nor as the manifestation of la-bor. The collector reobjectifies the object and relocates it from the commod-ity scene (the shop, the auction, the market) into an other space, a utopic or heterotopic space where value, far from being a mystery, is, to the collector, utterly transparent. When great capitalists like Adam Verver become great collectors, they are struggling, however paradoxically and futilely, to arrest the effects of capitalism, the full saturation of society with the commodity form. They struggle to buy a place beyond the market, by placing goods, re-arranging objects, somewhere else.[58] At the close of the first chapter, which relentlessly details the way the Prince is to "constitute a possession" (1:23), he himself, in the month prior to his wedding, figures himself as that which is meant to be extracted from circulation: "It was as if he had been some old embossed coin, of a purity of gold no longer used, stamped with glorious arms, mediaeval, wonderful, of which the 'worth' in mere modern change, sovereigns and half-crowns, would be great enough, but as to which, since there were finer ways of using it, such taking to pieces was superfluous" (1:23). This is gold coin that serves neither as money nor as a commodity but, doubly decirculated, as a piece of art.[59] From Adam and Maggie Verver's point of view, then, their aesthetic appreciation of the Prince is the antithesis of a commodity aesthetic: he is meant to be part of the collection of objects that have been rescued from circulation and stabilized within that collec-tion's autonomous world.

For Maggie, of course, the accomplishment of this goal entails loss as well as gain. Before the climactic scene at Fawns, she experiences "the perpetual throb of this sense of possession," and this sense underwrites her capacity to reorganize the relationships between the cast of four (2:207). But even if she might be said to attain possession of the Prince, she does so at the price of losing possession of her father—"possession" naming, as it does at the close of *Spoils*, a relation of profound intimacy. "Not yet since his marriage had Maggie so sharply and so formidably known her old possession of him as a thing divided and contested" (2:244). But even this "old possession" is new, for it is only in the course of recent events—the two marriages—that she has sufficiently objectified and estranged her father to the point where he ap-pears as an object of possession: "He was on her mind, he was even in a man-ner on her hands—as a distinct thing," no longer "too deep down, as it were, to be disengaged, contrasted or opposed, in short objectively presented" (1:154). Her father has been externalized from her, from within her, through a process of psychological disengagement that precedes their literal separation.

This novel opens by explicitly and theatrically emphasizing the Prince's new role as an object. Having strayed into Bond Street, he stops before the shop windows without interest in the "objects massive and lumpish, in silver and gold, . . . tumbled together as if, in the insolence of the Empire, they had been the loot of far-off victories" (1:3). He cannot concentrate on such objects because he's distracted by his new status as an object, an imperial purchase by Adam Verver meant to serve as his daughter's husband, rich in looks, charm, and "prenatal" history, if nothing else. Maggie has been playfully frank with her fiancé about the part he is meant to play: "You're at any rate a part of his collection . . . one of the things that can only be got over here. You're a rarity, an object of beauty, an object of price. . . . You're what they call a *morceau de musée*" (1:12). When she goes on to explain how her father stores his "bigger and more cumbrous" acquisitions throughout Europe, while saving some "smaller pieces" to travel with "to make the hotels we stay at and the houses we hire a little less ugly," the Prince cheerfully participates in the analogy: "I shall be one of the little pieces that you unpack at the hotel" (1:13, 14). The very fact that he will be on display, though, means that he will remain in circulation.

The first volume of the novel repeats variations on this theme about the Prince. "Representative precious objects, great ancient pictures and other works of art, fine eminent 'pieces' in gold, in silver, in enamel, majolica, ivory, bronze, had . . . so engaged" Adam Verver "that the instinct, the particular sharpened appetite of the collector, had fairly served as a basis for his acceptance of the Prince's suit" (1:140). If the first volume elaborates this dynamic, the second shows the work involved, beyond mere purchase, of transforming the Prince into a possession. Meanwhile, the dynamic has become so familiar that the novel can reproduce the same point about Charlotte with deft efficiency. Because Adam Verver applies "the same measure of value to such different pieces of property as old Persian carpets, say, and new human acquisitions" (1:196), he can appreciate Charlotte as the "real thing" (1:195). But acquisition is hardly a necessary condition for this logic of substitution. Adam Verver thinks about his daughter by analogizing her to a statue (1:187), and he thinks about her son, his only grandchild, as one of the "small pieces": "he had handled nothing so precious as the Principino, his daughter's first born . . . [whom he could] already almost toss and catch again, as he couldn't a correspondingly rare morsel of an earlier *pâte tendre*" (1:147).

While the novel thus offers an extensive portrait of the collector's imagination, where no person escapes his powers of objectification, such powers are hardly reserved for the collector himself. Maggie strikes the Prince, for instance, "in respect to the beautiful world, as one of the beautiful, the most beautiful things" (1:11). And during his first reencounter with Charlotte, she appears fully reified, affecting him "as a cluster of possessions . . . items in a full list, items recognized, each of them, as if, for the long interval, they had been 'stored'—wrapped up, numbered, put away in a cabinet. While she faced Mrs. Assingham the door of the cabinet had opened of itself; he took the relics out, one by one" (1:46). Among these relics, these reobjectified body parts, it is her waist that receives his greatest attention: "He knew above all the extraordinary fineness of her flexible waist, the stem of an expanded flower, which gave her a likeness also to some long loose silk purse, well filled with gold-pieces, but having been passed empty through a finger-ring that held it together. It was as if, before she turned to him, he had weighed the whole thing in his open palm and even heard a little the chink of the metal" (1:47). Though the image is far more tactile and far less exhibitionary than Adam Verver's images of the Prince, my point is simply that the process of imagining others as objects is ubiquitous in the novel: it is simply the way one imagines others. Yet it makes complete sense to say that the problem Maggie suffers is the problem of *not* being sufficiently objectified by the Prince's own proprietary imagination.

One way of explaining this ubiquity of metaphorization would be to say that reification has established the mode of human relation, and thus that the only way that affection can be expressed—or, indeed, felt—is through possessive predication. But another way of explaining it would be to say, simply, that this ubiquity of metaphorization explains itself. The point would be to underscore the novel's work as an extraordinary rhetorical machine, producing one analogy after another; from a formalist's point of view, the human relations within the diegesis would appear as the motivation for the rhetorical device. The Prince's face is described at length as a building, with his "dark blue eyes . . . resembl[ing] nothing so much as the high windows of a Roman palace, of an historic front by one of the great old designers, thrown open on feast-day to the golden air" (1:42). Described at length, Adam Verver's "neat colourless face" "resemble[s] a small decent room, clean-swept and unencumbered with furniture" (1:170). The "chamber of his brain" is described at length as "a strange workshop," as an elaborately detailed forge (1:127). What reads like an irrepressible impulse to describe people as things—an impulse that is not always focalized through a character—has the curious effect of producing a novel that is replete with objects that "exist" only within the Jamesian conceit. Unlike *The Spoils of Poynton*, the novel devotes considerable attention to cataloguing physical objects and detailing the mise-en-scène, but those catalogues and details assume nothing of the "breadth" and "mass" of the figural objects. It is as though, having unfurnished the novel in *Spoils*, James completely refurnishes it, but he refurnishes it with tropes. Moreover, though objects traditionally have a *metonymic* relation to characters in the realist novel—they are legible as indications of character—here they have an overwhelmingly *metaphorical* relation: they don't express characters, they substitute for them, they translate them into something visible, valuable, potentially possessible.

If the *Golden Bowl* finally feels as fully furnished as any novel by Balzac—not with superfluous objects but with the material weight of metaphor—this is because it is far more than physical features that get elaborated as inanimate objects; the novel hardly stops by describing bodies and faces as purses, coins, rooms, precious objects. Even Fanny Assingham, for instance, finds the Prince's "eloquence precious; there was n't a drop of it that she did n't in a manner catch, as it came, for immediate bottling, for future preservation. The crystal flas[k] of her innermost attention really received it on the spot, and she had already the vision of how, in the snug laboratory of her afterthought, she should be able chemically to analyze it" (1:271). As in the case of the forge that illustrates Adam Verver's mind, the novel transforms mental acts—attention, afterthought—into physical operations, externalizing the thought process by internalizing the physical world. This is why thought assumes such physical force in the novel—why, even casually, with a character like Fanny Assingham, we read that she can be found "wrapped in her thoughts still more closely than in the lemon-coloured mantle that protected her bare shoulders" (1:364). Thought assumes a physicality of its own. As Adam Verver thinks about his transformation from a businessman into a collector, his self-consciousness assumes an utterly physical dimension:

> *His* real friend, in all the business, was to have been his own mind, with which nobody had put him in relation. He had knocked at the door of that essentially private house, and his call, in truth, had not been immediately answered; so that when, after waiting and coming back, he had at last got in, it was, twirling his hat, as an embarrassed stranger, or, trying his keys, as a thief at night. He had gained confidence only with time, but when he had taken real possession of the place it had been never again to come away. (1:149)

James has extracted the private house from the realist novel and reinserted it as the locus of thought, literalizing the possessive individualism that demands that the self possess itself as a detachable entity. To become a self-possessed connoisseur, Adam Verver must take possession of his own mind, which is to say, in this case, to reify his mind in order to take possession of it—in order to step into his mind as though advancing, and advancing into, his own interiority. The image hardly squares with the sort of psychological insights William James had about collecting, his point that the "instinctive impulse [that] drives you to collect property" produces collections that become "parts of our empirical selves" (281). For the process of thinking has been empiricized, let us say, to the point where it makes no sense to describe a self or a subject who thinks; rather, a subject appears within the process of thinking and finds the opportunity there to enter a mind. Although readers of James may emphasize the way people are thought about as things, the novel's most striking and famous passages describe thinking itself as a kind of thing, or as a kind of thinging, that constitutes both the subject and the object of thought.

Things to Think With

Before turning to those passages, though, I want to return to the topic of collecting. Thus far in this chapter I've tried to show how the "things" in *The Spoils of Poynton* name a structuring absence—structuring in the sense that "their" lack of descriptive manifestation within the text legitimizes Mrs. Gereth's and James's own taste, organizes the novel's relation to Balzac, and transforms the physical presence of objects into a metaphysical potency, the power of "things." When it comes to *The Golden Bowl*, I've tried to show how the ubiquitous reification of people might be understood not just as a social condition, but also as a rhetorical maneuver, and as a phenomenology where one case of self-reification, however self-alienating, describes the self's relation to itself as a kind of intimacy: the canniness of finally settling into one's mind as though one were settling into one's study. Thoughts are no less physical than objects; thinking is no less physical than acting. James prompts us to imagine that, after the death of Adam Verver's first wife, the man all but literally collected himself, and became sufficiently self-possessed, to begin his extraordinary career as a collector.

As a collector, he participates in a familiar Jamesian pursuit, and in an increasingly ordinary and popular pursuit, as *The Spoils of Poynton* itself suggests. For when Fleda visits her father's house in West Kensington, for instance, she sits "in the company of the objects he was fond of saying he had collected—objects, shabby and battered, of a sort that appeared little to his daughter" (145). And there she must suffer his naïve efforts to prod her into "collecting something": "It did n't matter what. She would find it gave an interest to life—there was no end to the little curiosities one could easily pick up" (145). Collecting thus appears as the most immediately obvious mode of keeping boredom at bay, of transforming abstract longing—the desire for *something*—into a desire for some (particular) things. Even Mrs. Gereth recognizes that "one of the deepest mysteries of life" is the "way that—given certain natures—hideous objects could be loved" (55), the emphasis falling (in my reading of the novel) not so much on the hideousness as on the love: on the recognition that we use physical objects to arouse and organize our affection.

Of course, Adam Verver—incomparably rich, a "consummate collector" with "infallible high authority" (2:273)—belongs to that company of famous American collectors who threatened to drain England and Europe of their treasures.[60] But such figures were considered simply the elite victims of a "mania" that was widespread in both England and America. In his *Confessions of a Collector* (1897), for instance, William Hazlitt (the literary critic's grandson), tries to determine the source of "that strange, inexplicable cacoethes, which leads people to gather objects of art and curiosities," and he simply settles on an "inborn and indestructible trait."[61] In the inaugural issue of *The Curio* (1887), an American journal devoted to collecting, the editors make the familiar point that "there is nothing that is not collected," but they also make the observation inevitable by casting the collecting impulse as rudimentary, the collecting trope as primary, positing that the "acquirement of wealth" is simply one manifestation of the "collecting mania," and describing the Astors as collectors of real estate, Jay Gould as a collector of stock.[62] Collecting had become one of the topics of the day, but the psychology of collecting generally boiled down to a universalizing anthropology. Even the era's taste-makers, then, were willing to share the conclusions of child psychology, which, in the midst of children's veritably Balzacian enumeration of collected objects, came to insist, simply, that the collecting instinct is "practically universal"; the apparently spontaneous development of the collecting impulse testified to the fact that it is "no merely acquired trait."[63]

One way to read *The Golden Bowl*, then, would be to argue that James's portrait of the Ververs amounts to his contribution to the psychology of collecting. But you could also say that James intensifies and extends any understanding of the accumulating instinct by internalizing the operation—that is, by rendering thinking itself as a mode of accumulation, and thus making

Adam Verver's work of amassing European rarities seem like the merely physical version of a mental process, which is in large measure the process of making thoughts physical. In the first chapter of the second volume, awaiting her husband's return from his adventure with Charlotte at Matcham, Maggie finally assumes agency in the drama, she behaves with design and "an infinite sense of intention," and she effects the "great moment . . . for conscious repossession" by awaiting Amerigo's return not at her father's house, Eaton Square, but at her own house, Portland Place (2:9, 11). "[W]atching by his fireside for her husband's return," Maggie keeps asking herself questions about Charlotte that she cannot answer, questions that simply add to the "accumulations of the unanswered" (2:9, 14):

> They were *there*, these accumulations; they were like a roomful of confused objects, never as yet 'sorted,' which for some time now she had been passing and re-passing, along the corridor of her life. She passed it when she could without opening the door; then, on occasion, she turned the key to throw in a fresh contribution. So it was that she had been getting things out of the way. . . . What she should never know about Charlotte's thought—she tossed *that* in. It would find itself in company, and she might at last have been standing there long enough to see it fall into its corner. The sight moreover would doubtless have made her stare, had her attention been more free—the sight of the mass of vain things, congruous, incongruous, that awaited every addition. It made her in fact, with vague gasp, turn away, and what had further determined this was the final sharp extinction of the inward scene by the outward. The quite different door had opened and her husband was there. (2:14–15)

The deictic certainty with which these accumulated thoughts are externalized ("they were *there*"), which is the clarity with which Maggie's mental operations are spatialized, casts the passage as an elaborate account of containment, the first move of which is to materialize not just abstractions but negative abstractions: "what she does not know about Charlotte's thought." This is the will to figure (or to "remake") abstract anxiety concretely, however amorphous it remains. The task of "getting things out of the way" in this novel is, first off, a matter of turning things into things—more precisely, imaging abstract things as concrete objects. The image spatializes time ("the corridor of her life") and memory ("passing and re-passing") so that, however "confused" the objects are, there is some floor plan for managing them. James thus requires his readers to think not about the thingness of objects, as he had in *The Spoils of Poynton,* but about the objecthood of things, the transformation of the metaphysical into the physical. Peculiar as the image is, there is little doubt that it describes an increasingly powerful mode with which Maggie has come to organize her thoughts, and, indeed, to organize the thoughts of others. For when Maggie eventually recognizes how Charlotte suffers, trapped by having intuited Maggie's new intuitions, she detects in Charlotte "a new complication [that] had begotten a new anxiety—things these that she carried about with her done up in the napkin of her lover's accepted rebuke while she vainly hunted for some corner where she might put them down" (2:284). It is as though the intensity of the Ververs' collecting passion—"looking at things" was "almost as much a feature of their life as if they were bazaar-opening royalties" (2:144)—precipitates a capacity to objectify thoughts and emotions, and to imagine managing them physically.

In the most ambitious account we have of the power of thinking in James, Sharon Cameron describes the way that, in *The Golden Bowl*, "the presumed functions of speech and thought appear inverted" with thought becoming, in the second volume of the novel, "more audible and potent than speech."[64] But the potency of thinking might be weighed as well by the physicality and the physical force it seems to assume. In conversation with his daughter, Adam Verver, we're told, "might have been seeing things to say" (2:264). Thought and speech, speech and objects, objects and thought—the ontological distinction between these things, these "things," has been effectively erased. The very power of Maggie's thought is suggested by the fact that, even though the opening door interrupts her thinking about the roomful of confused objects, it is as though her thinking about the door of that room has conjured the opening of the other.[65] The materialization of thought—understood either as thought's externalization or as the internalization of the physical object world—serves not just to contain anxiety but to work on and in that world.

Which isn't to assert, unequivocally, that James means us to read the imagery as a product of Maggie's own image-making. Given the basic liberties of *style indirect libre* (the liberty, for instance, of describing a character's thoughts in a style he does not possess), it isn't easy to determine whether the image should be read, on the one hand, as a figure for Maggie's thinking or, on the other, as that thinking's own figure. The deictic certainty of the italicized demonstrative adverb—"They were *there*"—hardly makes it certain whether the thereness refers to a figure of the character's or a figure of the author's. The "accumulations," that is, might be *there* in Maggie's consciousness, specified as an "inward scene" or (as it were) *here* in James's conceit; it is precisely the spatial clarity insisted upon by the deictic, yet frustrated by both the "location" of the image and the spatial confusions within the image, that lends the novel's second volume so much of its uncanny energy.[66] Yet this thereness never exactly abandons the mimetic physicality of realism; it simply deploys this physicality otherwise, on behalf of consciousness.

All this is to suggest that the narrative of collecting (people and things) can be understood as a Jamesian feint, or as the diegetic motivation for the spatializing poetics of cognition, if not simply for the elaborate conceits as such. James's final novel thus redevelops the thematics of collection that preoccupied his French predecessors. Balzac's final novel, *Cousin Pons* (1848), details the complex machinations by which the friends, relatives, and employees of Sylvain Pons scheme to expropriate the dying man of his beloved collection, the way that the will of the collector is utterly frustrated before and after his death.[67] In his final (unfinished and, one might say, unfinishable) novel, *Bouvard et Pécuchet* (1881), Flaubert dooms two office clerks to a new adventure of accumulating knowledge and objects that never add up to the museum of their dreams. As Eugenio Donato put it, they are destined to "an indefinite wandering in a labyrinthine space," gathering up "a heap of meaningless and valueless fragments" that they can never organize into a system of "representation which is somehow adequate to a nonlinguistic universe."[68] The heterotopic achievement of collecting derives from the human capacity to generate an order of things; it is, as Susan Stewart has shown, a "mode of control and containment" (160). And museums, as Tony Bennett has shown at length, are "object lessons in power—the power to command and arrange things."[69] If Balzac and Flaubert might thus be said to conclude their respective careers by challenging this mode of control as a fantasy, James concludes his novel-writing career by exploring that mode in a different register. *The Golden Bowl* never questions Adam Verver's incomparable (and inexplicable) taste; it never challenges his well-meaning aspiration to create a "museum of museums" where he means to demonstrate "positively civilization condensed, concrete, consummate" (1:145). But the potency of the museal operation is as nothing in *The Golden Bowl* in contrast to the potency of reifying and organizing thoughts, and of a self-alienation that enables one to assemble and exhibit one's life. When, in the second volume of the novel, Maggie has the experience of "living over again" recent events, she finds that she can "choose them" and "fix them"; it is as though "a great picture hung on the wall of her daily life, for her to make what she would of" (2:10–11). She finds that scenes of her life are "*watchable* still"; she can "count" them, "parts of the experience," like "the firm pearls of a string" (2:11). The novel may exemplify James's dramatistic method at its most acute and astute, but, more momentously, the scenes of the drama become images and objects that the participant spectator can rearrange.

The elaborate conceit with which volume two opens makes it clear how

Maggie does not define herself through her possessions, but rather attains "conscious repossession" of herself as a mode of self-definition (2:11). The conceit begins as an image of the "situation so long present to her as practically unattackable":

> This situation had been occupying for months and months the very centre of the garden of her life, but it had reared itself there like some strange tall tower of ivory, or perhaps rather some wonderful beautiful but outlandish pagoda, a structure plated with hard bright porcelain, coloured and figured and adorned at the overhanging eaves with silver bells that tinkled ever so charmingly when stirred by chance airs. She had walked round and round it—that's what she felt; she had carried on her existence in the space left her for circulation, a space that sometimes seemed ample and sometimes narrow: looking up all the while at the fair structure that spread itself so amply and rose so high, but never quite making out as yet where she might have entered had she wished. She had n't wished till now—such was the odd case; and what was doubtless equally odd besides was that though her raised eyes seemed to distinguish places that must serve from within, and especially far aloft, as apertures and outlooks, no door appeared to give access from her convenient garden level. The great decorated surface had remained consistently impenetrable and inscrutable. At present however, to her considering mind, it was as if she had ceased merely to circle and to scan the elevation, ceased so vaguely, so quite helplessly to stare and wonder: she had caught herself distinctly in the act of pausing, then in that of lingering, and finally in that of stepping unprecedentedly near. . . . She had knocked in short—though she could scarce have said whether for admission or for what; she had applied her hand to a cool smooth spot and had waited to see what would happen. (2:3–4)

James tries to simplify the description (elaborated at much greater length) by saying that the "image" may "represent our young woman's consciousness of a recent change in her life" (2:4). "The pagoda in her blooming garden," he goes on to clarify, "figured the arrangement—how otherwise was it to be named?—by which, so strikingly, she had been able to marry without breaking, as she like to put it, with her past" (2:5), in other words the arrangement whereby the two marriages enable her to maintain her intimacy with her father, to live her life more with him than with the Prince. James's simplification and clarification of the conceit disclose his own sense of the difficulty of what he's trying to accomplish, or what his character accomplishes: not the objectification of people (a relatively easy matter, demonstrated throughout the text) but the objectification of the relations among them. A mode of sociality has become an "outlandish edifice." But the manifestation of those complex dynamics as a static physical form perpetuates the logic (indeed, in the second volume, it really initiates the logic) whereby familiar relationships become defamiliarized through the image-making process. Thus, the "arrangement" through which Maggie lives her daily life suddenly appears as strange to her as a "Mahometan mosque, with which no base heretic could take a liberty" (2:4). The orientalized building demonstrates less how foreign the arrangement is than how foreign Maggie feels. But that foreignness serves as the precondition for her capacity to *touch* the august exterior of the situation she's in.

Among the remarkable features of this image is its unequaled vivacity in the novel, a result of Maggie's motion round and round the pagoda, which, however "outlandish" and "inscrutable," is far more visualized than, say, the exterior of Fawns, which is why and how consciousness seems to dominate the novel, and to dominate it physically.[70] It is as though the pagoda were an exhibit from an international exposition, and one could trace its lineage back to the Exposition Universelle in Paris in 1889, which James reluctantly attended during his weeks in Paris that year, but which did, all told, make "a great impression."[71] But whereas any such exhibition hall would open its doors to the public, here, of course, no door seems to exist, although the "apertures and outlooks" make it seem as though Maggie herself has become the exhibit. If, as James put it in the Preface to the novel, Maggie's "exhibitional charm" "determines the view" in volume two (1:vii), the volume begins by describing her view of what amounts to a viewing apparatus for the "exhibitory vision of her" (1:vii). James has transposed the "exhibitionary complex" of the era into a private dramaturgy. If the point of the museums and exhibitions of the second half of the nineteenth century was to enable people to see "themselves from the side of power, both the subjects and objects of knowledge, knowing power and what power knows, and knowing themselves as (ideally) known by power,"[72] then James might be said to insist, in contrast, on recognizing how such seeing operates *within* consciousness. Whether or not the Paris exposition inspired the image of the pagoda, that image itself seems to have inspired James's trope of "the house of fiction," elaborated in the Preface to *Portrait of a Lady* (1908). The house has many "apertures, of dissimilar shape and size" that "hang . . . over the human scene," providing individual visions that remain distinct; the apertures are "but windows at the best, mere holes in a dead wall . . . not hinged doors opening straight upon life."[73] Read retrospectively, the *Golden Bowl's* pagoda might encourage us to imagine that we witness a character circling the house of fiction itself, or a character facing not so much her own exteriority to a social "arrangement" as her exteriority to a novelistic "arrangement," where houses have become not scenes of decoration but images with which to figure the "posted presence of the watcher" (1075), all the points of view from which one is constructed, the apertures from which one is known.

Golden Bowls

"What was your idea in suspending the four principle characters in 'The Golden Bowl' in the void?" Edith Wharton asked Henry James, to which he responded: "My dear—I didn't know I had."[74] Though his comment might attest to how James's own life of the mind had come to transcend or to ignore the physical world, it could testify no less to the fact that the novel *is* replete with objects, albeit objects—like the chimes outside the pagoda—that serve only as mental images, if not as the novel's own images of mentation. But to put the matter this way, which is to agree with Wharton's assessment, effectively evacuates the novel of its elaborately described physical objects, which we're clearly meant to see if not to feel. Above all, of course, the eponymous object, the golden bowl—a "capacious bowl, of old-looking, rather striking yellow gold, mounted by a short stem on an ample foot" (2:159)—occupies extensive textual space, described again and again, doted upon by several characters: "Simple but singularly elegant, it stood on a circular foot, a short pedestal with a slightly spreading base, and, though not of signal depth, justified its title by the charm of its shape as well as by the tone of its surface. It might have been a large goblet diminished, to the enhancement of its happy curve, by half its original height. As formed of solid gold it was impressive; it seemed indeed to warn off the prudent admirer" (1:112). Any reader might point to the gilded crystal bowl as evidence that this is still a universe of fiction where the circulation of objects and the circulation of characters around objects lie at the heart of the novelistic enterprise. It is, after all, the object around which the plot is organized. Whether or not you agree with Fanny Assingham—"Then it all depends on the bowl? I mean your future does? For that's what it comes to, I judge" (2:167)—there is no question that Maggie deploys the bowl as a prop in making her future, even as the bowl becomes the object through which she learns of her husband's past.

I have argued that the reification of Maggie's thinking—the physical shape given to thought, feeling, and memory—works to contain and control the crisis she faces. But she still seeks in the golden bowl some concrete incarnation of the mysterious "things" that confront her: "things that hadn't been told me," as she says to the Prince in their scene of confrontation, "and that gave their meaning, little by little, to other things that were before me"

(2:200); "the horror of the thing hideously *behind,* behind so much trusted, so much pretended, nobleness, cleverness, tenderness" (2:237). Maggie comes to imagine that all these undisclosed "things" have congealed in an object described as a "document," and which she herself describes as a "witness," a witness, that is, to the crime of intimacy between Charlotte and Amerigo.

Maggie discovers the bowl in her search through Bloomsbury (described with Balzacian detail) on her way home from having a visit with a Mr. Crichton, "custodian of one of the richest departments of the great national collection of precious things," who "could feel for the sincere private collector and urge him on his way even when condemned to be present at his capture of trophies sacrificed by the country to parliamentary thrift" (2:146). The value of a gift for her father, though, is irreducible to historical, aesthetic, or economic value. Indeed, his "sweet theory" maintains that the gift is always a "foredoomed aberration, and that the more it *was* so the more it showed, and the more one cherished·it for showing, how friendly it had been," making the "ugliest objects in fact as a general thing . . . the bravest, the tenderest mementoes" (2:156). The glass cases at Fawns thus display not only the sort of trophies identified by Mr. Crichton but also the mementos from Maggie: she "had come to be much represented in those receptacles" (2:156–57). From the father's and daughter's perspective, the objects amply represent her attention, affection, and devotion; and this is what she means the golden bowl to represent. It is a representation arrested before it ever begins when the shopkeeper, the antiquario, calls on Maggie to tell her he overcharged her, to confess to her that the bowl has a crack, and then, when he recognizes Amerigo and Charlotte from their photographs in the hall, to tell her about the couple who had considered purchasing the bowl long ago. Though the bowl can no longer represent Maggie's filial affection, it begins to represent everything else.

Throughout the novel, the bowl serves as a predictable vehicle for many metaphors. When Adam Verver claims to the Prince that "you're a pure and perfect crystal" (1:138), the Prince responds by saying, "Oh if I'm a crystal I'm delighted that I'm a perfect one, for I believe that they sometimes have cracks and flaws—in which case they're to be had very cheap!" (1:139) When they are about to launch on their illicit adventure to Gloucester, the Prince says to Charlotte that he feels "the day like a great gold cup that we must somehow drain together" (1:359). When Maggie explains to Fanny Assingham that the bowl has a crack, the older woman responds by saying "Then your whole idea has a crack" (2:178). In or out of view, the object appears so often within the expressions of the characters that it gradually assumes—or accretes—significance. As a gilded object that is cracked, or as the object desired first by Charlotte (as a wedding gift for her friend Maggie) then by Maggie (as a birthday gift for her father, after he has married Charlotte), it offers both readers of the novel and characters in the novel opportunities to read symbolically, metaphorically, or metonymically. But the pursuit of these opportunities hardly clarifies *what* the object means, though it powerfully demonstrates the extent to which readers of the novel, like Maggie herself, long for there to be some physical object with which, or through which, we can organize and stabilize knowledge and power, human emotion and human history. Indeed, the most salient way of reading *The Golden Bowl* as a collecting novel is to imagine that it documents not the way people collect objects, but the way that objects collect meaning, the way an object can seem to crystallize events, relations, situations.

Arguably, this longing to fill the bowl with significance is akin to the longing that precipitates the modernist conviction that there are "no ideas but in things," and the more recent, poststructuralist investment in material culture: the social life of things, the sex of things, the idea of "grasping things." But poets like William Carlos Williams and Marianne Moore aggressively tried to avoid making physical objects symbolic; James's bowl more obviously anticipates the objects in another modernist trajectory, from Heidegger's jug that gives man access to a cosmological poetics, to Lacan's vase, an object that represents the Thing as a signifier. Never does Lacan achieve such clarity about the Thing as when thinking about this vase. The Thing, he explains, "is that which in the real, the primordial real, I will say, suffers from the signifier—and you should understand that it is a real that we do not yet have to limit, the real in its totality, both the real of the subject and the real he has to deal with as exterior to him."[75] The Thing thus names the unknowable, unimaginable no-thing within both psychical and physical exteriority; the vase is "an object made to represent the existence of the emptiness at the center of the real that is called the Thing" (121), the emphasis resting on the fact that the potter cups (as it were) the nothing around which he creates the vase *ex nihilo*. James's bowl likewise incarnates a constitutive void, an absence of knowledge around which all the characters circulate, and by which they are defined; the bowl likewise obscures or sublimates that absence while compelling the characters to circle around it; and the bowl serves foremost as a "signifier of nothing other than of signifying as such or, in other words, of no particular signified" (120). With the same liberty that Lacan appropriates Heidegger's jar and turns it into a vase, we might appropriate Lacan's vase and turn it into a bowl, in a (decidedly non-Lacanian) effort to determine the overwhelming function of such physical objects in human lives. For it is as though James insists, in this final novel, that in the formal features of objects lies the form of human knowledge—not just the absences around which we manufacture some hard surface, and not just the multiple surfaces, but also the all but wholly hidden crack within that surface, a crack that calls into question the boundary between surface and interior, as between absence and presence, a crack through which the Thing might slowly seep. What is finally remarkable about the golden bowl in *The Golden Bowl* is that it seems to signify so much while it in fact signifies so little, precisely because it seems to signify so much.

When Charlotte had unexpectedly arrived from America for Maggie's wedding, and when she convinced the Prince to accompany her on her search for a suitable yet inexpensive wedding gift, she was fascinated by the bowl that the Prince himself dismissed by leaving the shop, explaining later that he had detected a crack in the crystal. "I saw the object itself. It told its story. No wonder it's cheap" (1:119). His way of making the point—seeing the 'object itself' amounts to eliciting a confession—initiates the effort to determine what other stories the object will tell. When Maggie says of the "incriminating piece" that she "want[s] it to meet him" and "him to meet it" (2:166, 164), she imagines the bowl prepared to tell the Prince a different story. When Maggie introduces Fanny Assingham to the object, now displayed on her mantel, the older woman expects some story not *of* it, but *from* it: "She looked at the precious thing—if precious it was—found herself in fact eyeing it as if, by her dim solicitation, to draw its secret from it" (2:167). Within the shop, the Prince had wondered whether he might purchase Charlotte something as a "small ricordo," to which she responded by insisting that a "ricordo from you—from you to me—is a ricordo of nothing. It has no reference" (1:108). But the bowl assumes reference; as a ricordo left behind, it comes to refer to their having been together in the shop; and its very physical features—the gilding, the hidden crack—generate a signifying structure that makes the bowl seem as though it both possesses and disguises a host of secrets. For Maggie, "the little word representing" the object—the demonstrative pronoun, *this*—"seemed to express and include for her the whole of her situation" (2:166). Whereas "situations" have been figured with elaborate images of town squares and pagodas, here a concrete object is meant to condense that work. But far from expressing her whole situation, the bowl seems to manifest the fact that Maggie's situation is anything but whole. Though she understands the bowl to mark "the outbreak of the definite" (2:169), there is little that is definite about the knowledge she learns; "there are many things," as Mrs. Assingham puts it, "that we shall never know" (2:175).

The value of the bowl may thus be said to lie in the history that it phantasmatically congeals, a value that Maggie herself effects by displaying the object and by projecting significance on it. From Fanny's perspective, "it was inscrutable in its rather stupid elegance, and yet, from the moment one had thus appraised it, vivid and definite in its domination of the scene" (2:165). When, in the novel's most dramatic moment, Fanny takes the bowl and "dashe[s] it boldly to the ground, where she ha[s] the thrill of seeing it lie shattered with the violence of the crash," she fantasizes that destroying the object will destroy knowledge: "Whatever you meant by it—and I don't want to know *now*—has ceased to exist" (2:179). But destroying the object hardly destroys all those things that have congealed there. Having gathered the pieces in her hands and having rearranged them on the mantel, Maggie says to the Prince, "you can handle them—don't be afraid—if you want to make sure the thing *is* the thing you and Charlotte saw together. Its having come apart makes an unfortunate difference for its beauty, its artistic value, but none for anything else. Its other value is just the same—I mean that of its having given me so much of the truth about you" (2:188–89). The apparent triumph of truth over beauty, though, is another phantasm, given that Maggie really learns so little about her husband's past. Nonetheless, the object, whole or broken, serves her as an emblem of *new* knowledge, and it serves to sublimate the gap in her knowledge, the gap in knowledge, the not known, around which James constructs so much of his novel both locally (within particular conversations) and overall. (What exactly, at the story's end, does Adam Verver know?) The issue is not what the bowl means, but the way in which Maggie uses the possession to reassure herself and others that she possesses concrete knowledge. Whereas, in *The Spoils of Poynton,* physical objects are abstracted into "things," in *The Golden Bowl* a physical object gets described and redescribed, intensely framed, doted upon, and thus becomes a thing, elevated to a significance that it hardly possesses on its own, yet a significance that it seems to have autonomously assumed.

On James's seventieth birthday in 1913, his friends in England honored him by organizing what he called "an extraordinary, prodigious, portentous, quite public Birthday," by commissioning Sargent to paint a portrait, and by presenting James with a golden bowl. The portrait has become one of Sargent's best-known works, and one of the best known images of James (fig. 18). By including James's topaz ring and his watch chain, by calling some attention to the stiff collar and to the sheer bulk of his body, Sargent hardly effaces the novelist's physicality; but it is the prominence of the shimmering forehead that lends the painting its authority as an expression of James's intellectual, creative power, over and against his accoutrements, as

FIGURE 18
John Singer Sargent (1856–1925), *Henry James*, 1913. Oil on canvas.
By courtesy of the National Portrait Gallery, London.

though he lived both comfortably within but also considerably beyond, his material context.[76] But James's own account of his other gift, a "really beautiful golden bowl," as one of the guests put it, suggests how important that context remained.[77] In a letter to his sister-in-law (William's wife Alice), the novelist described this "glittering tribute" at considerable length, proving (as he does over and over again in his letters) how adept he is at efficient and effective description. It is, he said,

> A really splendid 'golden bowl,' of the highest interest and most perfect taste, which would, in the extremity of its elegance, be too proudly false a note amid my small belongings here if it didn't happen to fit, or to sit, rather, with perfect grace and comfort, on the middle of my chimney-piece, where the rather good glass and some other happy accidents of tone most fortunately consort with it. It is a very brave and artistic (exact) reproduction of a piece of old Charles II plate; the bowl or cup having handles and a particularly charming lid or cover, and standing on an ample round tray or salver; the whole being wrought in solid silver-gilt and covered over with quaint incised little figures of a (in the taste of the time) Chinese intention.[78]

What is remarkable about James's letter is the length he goes to describing this bowl, lingering over it as though to suggest how much thought and affection it congealed, and never pausing to comment on the complexity or irony of the gift (an irony unintended, of course, by the gift-givers), or to suggest how, from another point of view, the bowl might appear as a bit of superfluous bric-a-brac cluttering the mantel, a souvenir of the occasion, a ricordo, compensating somewhat for his anguish at never having achieved financial success as a writer, a material pleasure, not unlike Sylvain Pons's, that could keep some sense of failure at bay.[79] Profoundly as James had wrested realism out of the Balzacian paradigm, he himself hardly lived beyond Balzac's "passion for things." When he returned to America shortly after competing *The Golden Bowl,* and after twenty years abroad, he engaged an altogether different power of the physical object world: in *The American Scene* (1907) people are no longer reified, but things are personified. In America, he discovers a land where things lead lives of their own.

FIGURE 19
Paul Strand, *Photograph* ("Wall Street"). Printed in *Camera Work*, December 1916.

CODA

The Death and Life of Things
Modernity and Modernism

> Warmth is ebbing from things. . . . We must compensate for their cold-
> ness with our warmth if they are not to freeze us to death.
> —Walter Benjamin, *One-Way Street*

> Seeing Manhattan from the 110th floor of the World Trade Center . . .
> the spectator can read in it a universe that is constantly exploding.
> —Michel de Certeau, "Walking in the City"

The most unnerving aspect of *The American Scene* (1907) is the volubility of
its buildings. Houses along the Jersey shore declare, "Oh yes; we are awfully
dear, for what we are and for what we do."[1] At Harvard, the older buildings
in the Yard propose a sophisticated summary of themselves (63). And in
New York, Trinity Church, putting "its tragic case" with "irresistible lucid-
ity," laments, "Yes, the wretched figure I am making is as little as you see my
fault—it is the fault of the buildings whose very first care is to deprive
churches of their visibility" (78). In the same city, City Hall "speak[s] volumes" (90). This proclivity for declamation extends beyond buildings: the
air in New Hampshire speaks its peace, as does the town of Concord. And
the book as a whole draws toward its close with a final question voiced by the
"monotonous rumble" of a Pullman train: "See what I'm making of all
this—see what I'm making, what I'm making!" (463). Which is hardly to say
that the train—or any of the rest of the animated inanimate object world—
has the last word, for that is a word, those are words, that Henry James reserves for himself: "I see what you are *not* making" (463).

His beef with the self-important Pullman, emblem of the economic and
social systems that have transformed the continent so readily, concerns neither the dispossession suffered by native inhabitants nor the disfigurement
suffered by the land. "I accept your ravage," James writes (463). Rather, he
excoriates the pretensions of a civilization that is no civilization, of a nation
where the "pretended message of civilization" cannot camouflage the "triumph of the superficial and the apotheosis of the raw" (463–65). And he
finds this ugly triumph registered foremost in the face and the fate of built
space, in the architectural record where he repeatedly reads neither the de-

structiveness of history nor the history of destruction, but the destruction of history itself.

Once respected by few readers (but readers who included W. H. Auden), *The American Scene* has now achieved a kind of literary-critical apotheosis, regarded both as an august exhibit of the "late James" and as a compelling commentary on America at the century's turn.[2] This encounter with America as a "revisiting spirit" (a spirit returning after twenty years) has come to seem vital to understanding James, modernity, and modernism; in each case, it is James's relation to the physical object world which mediates that understanding. Still, this reassessment of *The American Scene* has not begun to think through the observation that Auden made in 1946: "Outside of fairy tales, I know of no book in which things so often and so naturally become persons."[3]

I myself have argued that James, working with and against Balzac, evacuated the novel of things in *The Spoils of Poynton*, and that, in *The Golden Bowl*, he transformed thoughts into things: the reification of persons that gives volume one such thematic coherence becomes, in volume two, a reification of consciousness, the transformation of thought into substance. *The American Scene*, in turn, transforms substance into thought by giving voice to objects, by granting them consciousness. The intensity of its prosopopeia might be regarded, at first glance, as the return of the suppressed, a final return of objects, and monumental objects, to the Jamesian text. At the very least, you should be able to read its personification of things as the metathesis of *The Golden Bowl*'s reification of persons. The two texts, paired, seem to dramatize, in the late Jamesian register, Marx's understanding of the fundamental effects of capitalism.

And yet the speaking objects in James's text do not speak to one another, as they do at the close of Marx's dramatization of commodity fetishism. Instead, they speak to *him*. And they speak not of their exchange value, but of a value that is irreducible to exchange or use. To the degree that buildings serve as immobile property—not readily circulating through one or another scene of circulation but rather constituting that scene itself—they ought indeed to have other things to talk about. Just as, in his isolation, Thoreau discovered the sociality of nature, so James, erasing human companions from the story he tells, renders built space interactive.[4] But this interactivity has the strange effect, in *The American Scene*, of abandoning the visible on behalf of the audible, and fashioning a scene that, despite or because of its assumed agency, is anything but scenic, anything but scopic. It is as though there were no point of view from which to see the buildings because James insists on seeing the world from the buildings' point of view. All told, then, it is difficult to tell whether the prosopopeia grants priority to objects, saving them from what Jean Baudrillard has called the long history of the object's passivity and abjection, its status as no more than the "alienated, accursed part of the subject."[5] Or whether the ventriloquist's performance dramatizes (or simply enacts) the subject's splendor—at the object's expense. Or whether, perhaps, in this case, the Jamesian dramaturgy insists on apprehending the world without the subject/object dichotomy and the dialectic it generates.

The difficulty of resolving these questions makes it difficult indeed to accept Hugh Kenner's argument about the place of *The American Scene* in the history of American modernism. Though the "modernism" of the modernist novel most readily brings to mind the concentrated disclosure of the subject (in, for instance, Conrad, Proust, Joyce, Woolf, and Faulkner), the "modernism" of lyric and plastic media brings to mind the restless reclamation of objects (in, for instance, Dadaism, Constructivism, Precisionism, and Objectivism). And though James's fiction and (crucially) his prefaces to the New York edition (1909) had long been central to discussions of modernist fiction, Kenner saw in *The American Scene* the origin of a new aesthetic attitude toward the physical world. He began *The Pound Era* (1975) by describing an encounter, in Chelsea, summer 1914, between James (age 71), showing his niece around London, and Ezra Pound, running errands with his wife Dorothy, who recounted the meeting years later. Although biographers might smile (or cringe) at the image of James's fastidious civility confronting Pound's brashness, Kenner used the serendipitous encounter to dramatize an unruffled transition, one famous American expatriate passing the baton of literary ingenuity to the next. Not only does he argue that Pound assimilated both James's syntactic idiosyncrasies and his sensibility— "the *Homage to Sextus Propertius* (1917) was achieved by a mind filled with James's prose"; he also concludes that "James's great sensibility brought in a generation," responsible as it was for Pound's *Mauberly*, Eliot's *Prufrock*, and even William Carlos Williams's *Spring and All*.[6]

Kenner reads in *The American Scene* a mind holding "converse with particulars, mute mental particulars, the act of perception and the act of articulation inextricably one," and he thus sees there the anticipation of Williams's dictum, "Say it, no ideas but in things" (18), first published in 1926, and repeated at the outset of the first volume of *Paterson* (1946). When Kenner turns his full attention to Williams, he argues that this dictum held sway for the poet in the intervening decades, and rightly claims that this motto defines not just an aesthetic but "an epistemology (what you can know is in front of you)" and "a statement of American limitation (things are multiple in their opaque thinghood, no Duccio having transfigured the local stone)" (510). At this stage of his discussion, Kenner reinvokes James: "In more than 400 pages without dialogue, *The American Scene* has no ideas but in things" (512). The poet from New Jersey and the novelist from abroad suddenly seem to speak with a single voice.

Of course, there *is* dialogue in *The American Scene*, although there is no dialogue between people. But despite the exchange between James and the physical world, it is hard to read the text without longing for more "particulars" and more "opaque thinghood"—without wondering how the loquacious buildings, for instance, remain so disembodied, so undescribed. Indeed, James inhabits an epistemology where knowledge can derive from no particulars whatever. In Baltimore, he is faced with the "predicament" of finding no particulars that comprise his impression of the city. Recognizing that "character" derives from "so many particular parts which conduce to an expression," he walks "about the city looking for the particular parts—all with the singular effect of rather failing to find them and with [his] impression of felicity at the same time persistently growing" (308). You could hardly imagine a less vivid portrait of Baltimore (or any city) if by vividness you meant pictorial amplitude. James everywhere violates those imagist doctrines that would come to have such an impact on Williams—F. S. Flint's "direct treatment of the 'thing,'" Pound's "go in fear of abstractions"—just as he stands opposed to what would become *Spring and All*'s cult of destruction and celebration of the "NEW."[7] In fact, James would seem like an obvious target in Williams's "annihilation of strained association" and in his effort, on behalf of the "actual," to discard "complicated ritualistic forms."[8] Not even the calculated slippage in Kenner's formulation from "particulars" to "mute mental particulars" can legitimate the affinity he claims between James and the early Williams, who so willfully and skillfully provides particulars that add up to no impression: "The red paper box / hinged with cloth / is lined / inside and out / with imitation / leather."[9]

In contrast to Williams, the overall *impressions* that James has of America (to underscore that term on which he methodically insists) are formed as much by absence (what has not been made) as by any particular presence. His most aggressive lexical strategy for imparting this impression (of what isn't) deploys the word "thing" to denote not an object at hand but a lack. In the record of rural New Hampshire, for instance, he describes the impression of "a particular thing that, more than any other, had been pulled out of the view" (23). He circles round this "thing," clarifying the objection. "This particular thing was exactly the fact of the *importance*, the significance, imputable, in a degree, to appearances" (23). What doesn't appear in this countryside is the generalized care for appearances; that is, the rude arrangement of the buildings, like the shabbiness of the farms, precludes the view from exuding that "ineffable glow" of an English countryside. James works to generalize the point: "Perpetually, inevitably, moreover, as the restless analyst wandered, the eliminated thing *par excellence* was the thing most absent to sight" (24). More simply put, the "ugliness" amounts to the "complete abolition of *forms*" (25). But James's idiosyncratic formulation—the thing most absent is an expunged thing—emphasizes the extent to which the problem isn't really the not made ("I see what you are not making"), but the unmade: the pulled out, the abolished, the eliminated. It is as though the aura of objects were immanent, inherent, and had been villainously denied or crudely exorcised; this is why "not making" seems to carry the charge of violently destroying; this is why the book seems so curiously nostalgic—curious because James often mourns the loss of what never was.

Moreover, when James writes of New York, he faces a more exacerbating problem of particularity: he faces a "too-defiant scale of numerosity and quantity" that prohibits pictorial representation (121). Momentarily engaged by imagining what Zola might have done with New York, he comes to recognize that the "monstrous phenomena" of the city have "gotten ahead" of "any possibility of poetic, of dramatic capture" (83). The "confusion" has been "carried to chaos for any intelligence, any perception" (83). Disoriented by the absence of once familiar, memorable, and stabilizing sites, the novelist becomes a theorist of what Kevin Lynch has termed the "imageability of city form," suffering from the formlessness he finds all around him and unable himself, despite the perceptual acuity of his earlier travel writing, to render it realistically.[10] (Though James writes of the "the intensity of the material picture in the dense Yiddish Quarter" [130], for instance, or, more generally, of the "New York phantasmagoria" [133], novels by Howells or Cahan, Dreiser or Wharton, provide much more intense *pictures* of the city.)

It is hardly surprising, then, that the kind of distress and disorientation that James feels resurfaces in the no less canonical depiction of the postmodern cityscape, Fredric Jameson's account of the "mutation of built space" for which the human subject is perceptually unequipped.[11] But rather than arguing that James in New York uncannily anticipates Jameson's state of disorientation in Los Angeles, you might point out how Jameson's claim—that "there has been a mutation in the object unaccompanied as yet by any equivalent mutation in the subject"—is in fact an updated version of Georg Simmel's claim, published in 1900, about the "preponderance of objective over subjective culture," about how the pace of "material culture," the "culture of things," has left "individual culture" lagging far behind, the individual as such suffering a state of shock.[12] But making such a point would really require placing both James and Simmel in a trajectory (running, say, from Baudelaire to Jameson) where the subject is repeatedly overwhelmed in its encounter with the turbulence of urban transformation. My point is merely to direct attention to both an epistemological and an experiential rationale for why James, however much he may converse with objects, does not really "converse with particulars."[13]

Sharon Cameron, though, offers a very different rationale, insisting that, in *The American Scene*, consciousness subordinates "the objects being contemplated to consciousness itself, until consciousness attends only to its own workings" (18). In her reading, the problems of modernity, like the problems of America, are really beside the point, serving merely as occasions for James to diversify the propagation and investigation of consciousness. "The journey across the country," she writes, "is less the occasion for exploring aspects of places than it is for examining aspects of consciousness" (2). By consciousness, she means consciousness dissociated from psychology, consciousness understood outside the confines of a psychological self, detached from the body, from character, and from the environment. This is the consciousness that Edmund Husserl theorized as a new object of inquiry that eradicates any distinction between "inner" experience and the "outer" world, reduces the world to consciousness, and argues that things must be understood only as things-in-thought (26). In a stroke, Cameron goes far toward explaining the absence of pictorial vividness in the book by arguing that "James, as if recoiling from what he sees, almost, it seems, stops seeing at all" (3–4).

The power of her claim challenges any faith that James concerns himself with the physical object world. Yet this power itself depends on having dispensed with scenes where James stages the very dichotomous thinking, the very psychology, that phenomenology seeks to overcome. For just as he fully thematizes the absence of particulars, so too he dramatizes a consciousness ruptured by psychology; that is, he explicitly deploys a psychology structured by the inner/outer dichotomy. Exactly because he finds in Washington Square, as distinct from the rest of Manhattan, "the pretense that nearly nothing was changed," he feels one particular change as a bodily assault. "The effect for me," he writes, "was of having been amputated of half my history": "The grey and more or less 'hallowed' University building— wasn't it somehow, with a desperate bravery, both castellated and gabled?— has vanished from the earth, and vanished with it the two or three adjacent houses, of which the birthplace was one. This was the snub, for the complacency of retrospect, that, whereas the inner sense had positively erected there for its private contemplation a commemorative mural tablet, the very wall that should have borne this inscription had been smashed as for demonstration that tablets, in New York, are unthinkable" (91). "Private contemplation" fully expects to find itself productively engaged by public "demonstration"; powerful as the "inner sense" may be, it longs to be confirmed externally. In accord with the book's extensive metaphorics of writing, the loss here is expressed and generalized as the absence of writing matter, the absence of surfaces on which the inner sense might externalize itself. This particular episode—which seems indescribable outside the structures of psychological realism—might be said to underwrite, affectively, the bulk of the book.[14] It not only testifies to the insufficiency of the merely internal object; it also predicts why the object world as such proves insufficient. For what suddenly seems futile is the whole dynamic by which one trusts the durability of built space. "Where, in fact, is the point of inserting a mural tablet, at any legible height, in a building certain to be destroyed to make room for a sky-scraper" (92)? Objects cannot be depended on as a source of continuity in the midst of human flux because objects, too, are mutable. They too have lives (and deaths) of their own.

Yet from Cameron's point of view, James's assertions about his own powerlessness and his protests against the power and vulgarity of American materialism exist as a kind of feint, an excuse to put consciousness in play. All but needless to add, such a reading evacuates *The American Scene* of all pathos: James turns out to be "intoxicated by his new found alienation," and consciousness "embraces its embattlement so as to free itself of the given, effectively to banish it, and to substitute for what is there what is *wanted* to be there" (3). The lack that seems to constitute so much of the book—the thing missed, the missing thing—gets replaced by amplitude. But this is really because, from the phenomenological point of view, consciousness of what is absent nevertheless marks the full presence of consciousness; it is still consciousness of something.[15] Which is why, for Cameron, *The American Scene* appears as the embodiment of power, not only manifest in "the ability of consciousness to dominate objects," but also demonstrated by "consciousness's skill in *dispensing* with objects, so that what is being contemplated by consciousness is something like itself" (6–7).

Nonetheless, the moment you glimpse this power outside phenomenology's frame, it begins to read as a symptom of its obverse. Thus, if, in a fantasy of omnipotence, consciousness at times dominates or dispenses with objects in *The American Scene*, it does so in a mode of revenge against the revenge of the object, against the way in which the object seems to subject the subject to a longing it cannot fulfill. And if it makes some sense to say, as Cameron does, that James's ventriloquism transforms the physical object world into a "dummy for the voicings of consciousness" (23), it makes no less sense to say that this ventriloquism demonstrates how consciousness needs objects to mediate its own relation to itself. And more than any other text by James, *The American Scene* insists on the impossibility of preventing historical, social, and economic considerations from saturating that mediation. This is why any retreat into consciousness reads, more specifically, as a symptom of what Simmel called "hyperaesthesia," a sensitivity to the "shocks and confusions" provoked by modern life, which typically induce one or another anaesthetizing prophylaxis (474).[16] Insofar as James, "recoiling from what he sees, almost, it seems, stops seeing at all," *The American Scene* could be read as a textbook case of how art copes with this pathological state: "reality is touched not with direct confidence," Simmel argues, "but with fingertips that are immediately withdrawn" (474). The "most extreme refinement of our literary style avoids the direct characterization of objects; it touches only a remote corner of them with the word" (474). After the full-fledged emergence of phenomenology, Theodor Adorno perceived its "exaltation" of the mind's "domination" as no more than a desperate effort to compensate for the individual's degradation within systematized society.[17] All told, then, the absence of particulars in James's text can't quite be read as the mind's domination of objects, for it may in fact signify how objective culture (both the culture of things and the thingness of culture) has overwhelmed the mind.

Of course phrasing the critical quandary in such blunt terms keeps cornering James as a subject (or cornering consciousness, freed from the subject) into a wholly adversarial posture toward the physical object world, and this is a posture that *The American Scene* does not in fact sustain. Indeed, James's ventriloquism seems to confer not simply voice but something like rights onto the built environment. Or, rather, he seems to confer rights in the mode of conferring voice in order to grant objects some belated yet originary right to narrate their own stories, and thus to express the longing to have their rights realized. Determined as their fate seems to be, they nonetheless retain, in this animating vocalization, some agency, however ghostly. James not only asks a simple question—What do objects want? They also muster a straight-forward answer.

That answer comes during his account of New York, which, witnessed from the bay, looms as a "monstrous organism," its skyscrapers, "giants of the mere market," hovering as a "thousand glassy eyes" (75–77). New York is the scene of the crime of modernity, and the crime of modernity is its relentless, pecuniary pursuit of novelty. It is the foreclosure of any possibility that experience, memory, and history can be lodged in static physical structures. It is the incessant volatility, the will to "move, move, move, as an end in itself," in which the sole constant is the "perpetual passionate pecuniary purpose which plays with all forms, which derides and devours them," resting only to create the "illusion of finality" amid the facts of formlessness (84, 111). Among the buildings that speak in *The American Scene,* Trinity Church, a "poor ineffectual thing" that "aches and throbs," speaks most poignantly, obscured as it is by the buildings that have come to surround it, subject as it is to "that inexorable law of the growing invisibility of churches" (78–79, 83). Though James *hears* the church (78–79), he *sees* the "sky-scraper that overhangs" it, the "vast money-making structure quite horribly, quite romantically justif[ying] itself, looking through the weather with an insolent cliff-like sublimity" (83). The very fact that the churches of lower Manhattan have survived at all, their "mere exemption from the 'squashed' condition," is made the more poignant by the "vision of the doom that does descend, that had descended all round" (94). James reads this scene of modernity as a disaster site where little survives among the wreckage.

That reading is James's version of Marx's claim that "all that is solid melts into air," a claim ultimately voiced by irrepressible "powers above" the city that speak to the city itself: "I build you up but to tear you down" (112).[18] For the "revisiting spirit" in New York, this means that "you learn, on the occasion of a kindly glance up and down a quiet cross-street . . . that such and such a house, or a row, is 'coming down'; and you gasp, in the presence of the elements involved, at the strangeness of the moral so pointed," the moral that New York will do its best to prevent "sincerity and sentiment" from "tak[ing] root," will prevent objects from transcending their merely physical instantiation—will prevent them, in the terms I've deployed in this book, from becoming things (111–12). The history of modernity, propelled both by capital and by instrumental reason, is the history of proscribing objects from attaining the status of things, proscribing any value but that of use or exchange, secularizing the object's animation by restricting it to *commodity fetishism* alone.

The counter-animation enacted and explored by *The American Scene* insists on defining nonpecuniary value, and it exhibits an exchange between the physical object world and its human subjects that stands outside the structure of ownership. Whereas Mark Twain, for instance, considered his house "sentient matter" because of the life his family lived there, and whereas the stove in *Vandover and the Brute* assumes a personality because of Vandover's intimacy with this prized possession, it is James's nonproprietary "relation to New York" that is "almost inexpressibly intimate" (117), and he quickens built space on other grounds. City Hall, the one edifice that "lives on securely" in New York, speaks on behalf of "the exquisite truth of the *conferred* value of interesting objects, the value derived from the social, the civilizing function for which they have happened to find their opportunity" (96). In James's political economy, value may not amount to the quantity of human labor congealed within an object, but it does amount to the sociality, the history and habits congealed there. In the midst of the "vision of eternal waste" that New York has become—where the "conscious, sentient-looking houses and rows" are forbidden "the true taste of history"—a "particular place only asks, as a human home, to lead the life it has begun, only asks to enfold generations and gather in traditions, to show itself capable of growing up to character and authority" (113). What buildings want is the aura of history, "the shimmer of association" (154), the time and the peace to become historical. They long for their longevity. They want to belong and even to belong to. Just as people collect objects to manifest themselves physically in space, so objects incorporate people to define themselves metaphysically in and over time. This is how they attain a ritual value beyond the exigencies of exchange and use. But the "perpetual repudiation of the past" and the "democratic broom" that James witnesses throughout the "great commercial democracy" have cleansed objects of any such "poetry of association" (55, 92, 31).[19]

Still, in his patently nostalgic response to this democratic destructiveness, James effects a more radical democracy of his own. His vivification of the inanimate world—his dominant trope and his thoroughgoing indulgence in the pathetic fallacy—might be read, in Benjaminian terms, as the effort to combat the coldness of the material world by infusing it with human warmth.[20] But by suffusing so many components of the American scene with a voice—with affect and with consciousness—the personification of things in *The American Scene* would seem itself to entail a reification of persons. It is as though James must assume the status of an object to speak his own mind. Adorno wrote that "everything must metamorphose into a thing in order to break the catastrophic spell of things."[21] Yet it seems no less true, from James's point of view, that everything must metamorphose into a human in order to interrupt the catastrophe that humans are in the process of wreaking. In James's case, this ontological homogenization, which is the radical gesture within his reactionary cause, is a matter neither of collapsing the inner and the outer, nor of preserving the otherness and particularity of objects; it is a matter of taking a nonproprietary possession of objects that simultaneously requires being possessed by them. That is, if *The American Scene* patently differentiates itself from the nineteenth-century novel by not addressing possessions, it everywhere entails possession nonetheless;

James's haunting habit of giving voice to buildings and their no less ghostly habit of possessing him—these re-enchant modernity's disenchanted world of objects. Within the illogic of projection and introjection, the animate and the inanimate, like the subject and object, become indistinct.[22] And this lack of distinction can be cast as an elaborate obstruction of that modernity which insists on an ontological distinction, arbitrary and artificial, between inanimate objects and human subjects.[23]

Neither the paradigm of Williams's aesthetic modernism (where ideas are embodied only in things) nor the paradigm of Husserl's philosophical modernism (where things are embodied only as ideas) explains how *The American Scene* anticipates a modernism that knows we have never been modern, that we have not and cannot sustain that ontological divide. This is the modernism that appears in such efforts as the Constructivist attempt to revolutionize the quotidian interactions with the physical object world, to overcome the "rupture between Things and people," which meant both encouraging the "psyche" to become "more thing like" and "dynamiz[ing]" things to become "equals, comrades."[24] More ubiquitously, this is a modernism where the medium of the Jamesian consciousness is supplanted by other media that energize the physical world's animation. In his essay "On Décor" (1918), Louis Aragon describes how cinema invigorates "common objects," how "each inanimate object" can become "a living thing."[25] Siegfried Kracauer insists that the experience of the cinematic object not only increases our knowledge of it, "but in a manner of speaking incorporate[s] it into us so that we grasp its being and its dynamics from within."[26] And indeed, though Williams, in the 1920s, wrote against the kind of value James sought to preserve, James's prosopopeia might be said to prefigure Williams's own epic equation of Paterson the city and Paterson the man: "Paterson lies in the valley under the Passaic Falls / its spent waters forming the outline of his back."[27]

The American Scene reads as a transitional text between one American generation's fascination with objects of possession and the next generation's engagement with objects as such. But its power lies in James's capacity to re-energize an obsolete trope—a trope that realism eschews, a trope we associate with the sentimental and gothic traditions—on behalf of exposing the ontological grounds on which modernity proceeds in the name of progress, and on behalf of literalizing the common sense that tells us that "an attack on architecture . . . is an attack on man."[28] At the same time, James's plea on behalf of architecture (which he hears as architecture's self-defense) cannot be reduced to a claim on behalf of the authority of merely static physical structure, for the structures are anything but static and they are rendered as something less and more than physical.[29] His animation of the world might even be said to hark back to those premodern times and places where objects were anything but inert, where "things themselves had a personality and an inherent power"—even as it anticipates modernism's capacity to vivify the physical object world by other means, means that themselves literalize the work of prosopopeia.[30]

From our historical vantage point, *The American Scene* can be seen striving for an effect that only subsequent technologies could fully realize. For James had really begun to describe a more recent future, a future where verbal performance has been disjoined from human embodiment, and where knowledge has expanded far beyond the confines of the autonomous subject.[31] Everyday life now presents us not with phenomenology's reduction of the world to consciousness, but with consciousness reconceived as something dispersed throughout the material world. This is a future that we will continue to need help describing as we wonder whether our sense of things can ever begin to apprehend their sense of us.

September 2001

NOTES

INTRODUCTION

1. Mark Baldwin, "The Origin of a 'Thing' and its Nature," *The Psychological Review* 2 (1895): 551–52.

2. Louis Zukofsky, *"A"* (Berkeley: University of California Press, 1978), 61.

3. Theodor W. Adorno, *Negative Dialectics,* trans. E. B. Ashton (New York: Continuum, 1997), 140, 185. Further references provided parenthetically.

4. G. W. F. Hegel, "Perception: Or Things and Their Deceptiveness," *Phenomenology of Mind,* trans. J. B. Baillie (New York: Harper & Row, 1967), 161–78. My somewhat flip remark relies on a caricature version of what is, of course, a complex dialectic whereby consciousness struggles to resolve the contradiction between the singularity and multiplicity that constitutes the Thing which exhibits itself for apprehension.

5. William Carlos Williams, *A Novelette,* in *Imaginations* (New York: New Directions, 1970), 295–96. Further references will be provided in the text.

6. William Carlos Williams, *Spring and All,* in *Imaginations,* 110. Further references will be provided in the text.

7. William Carlos Williams, *A Novelette,* 295–96. In other words, Williams moves from the project of refining perception to the project of attaining a new kind of production. See Donald W. Markos, *Ideas in Things: The Poems of William Carlos Williams* (Rutherford, N.J.: Farleigh Dickinson University Press, 1994), 121–31.

8. For recent approaches to this history, see, for instance, the essays collected by Cristina Giorcelli in *The Idea and the Thing in Modernist American Poetry* (Palermo: ILA Palma, 2001).

9. Ralph Waldo Emerson, *Nature* (1836), *Essays and Lectures* (New York: Library of America, 1983), 34.

10. Nonetheless, because this opposition and this distinction are not *staged* by Williams, we can say that he works outside the Romantic tradition that includes Emerson. See J. Hillis Miller, *Poets of Reality: Six Twentieth-Century Writers* (Cambridge, Mass.: Harvard University Press, 1966), 285–359.

11. Georges Bataille, *The Accursed Share: An Essay on General Economy,* trans. Robert Hurley (New York: Zone Books, 1988), vol. 1, pp. 136, 129.

12. Attention to this "material support" assumed an urgent pitch in the advice to writers that proliferated at the turn of the century—in journals like *The Writer*—as writing came to be understood more ubiquitously as a profession. In his advice to "the ambitious amateur," Frank Norris obviates the typical admonitions about legibility by suggesting that you "have your manuscripts typewritten. . . . The time [is] too short to expect the reader to decipher script" ("The 'Volunteer Manuscript': Plain Talk to the Ambitious Amateur" [1901], *The Literary Criticism of Frank Norris*, ed. Donald Pizer [Austin: University of Texas Press, 1964], 141). By now, much advice from the era sounds rather comic: "There is no better way to keep a steel pen in good condition than by sticking it in a common potato" ("Helpful Hints and Suggestions," *The Writer* 8 [May 1895]: 72). Friedrich Kittler's overture on Nietzsche and the typewriter (which blinds the writer to the writing act) provides an exemplary instance of a new technological history of writing (*Discourse Networks 1800/1900*, trans. Michael Metteer and Chris Cullens [Stanford: Stanford University Press, 1990], 177–205). In a book about things I have noticeably ignored the thingness of books. To begin considering that topic, see Adrian Johns, *The Nature of the Book: Print and Knowledge in the Making* (Chicago: University of Chicago Press, 1998). On the physical process of producing modernist texts, see George Bornstein, *Material Modernism: The Politics of the Page* (New York: Cambridge University Press, 2001).

13. Catherine Gallagher and Stephen Greenblatt, *Practicing New Historicism* (Chicago: University of Chicago Press, 2000), 54. Michel Serres, *Statues* (Paris: François Bourin, 1987), 111.

14. In 1978, René Girard lamented that "it has now become more or less axiomatic that 'words' and 'things' must go their separate ways," provoked to do so by the Saussurian theory of the sign (*"To Double Business Bound": Essays on Literature, Mimesis, and Anthropology* [Baltimore: Johns Hopkins University Press, 1978], viii). Though Saussure is certainly less of a presence and pressure in current critical practice, words and things continue to go their own separate ways; or, rather, the attention to the discursive, iterative materialization of the world reduces things to the effect of words. For the most influential version of such attention, see Judith Butler, *Bodies That Matter: On the Discursive Limits of Sex* (New York: Routledge, 1993), 1–23. For a recent and powerful introduction to the deconstructive engagement with "materialism," see the essays collected by Tom Cohen et al., *Material Events: Paul de Man and the Afterlife of Theory* (Minneapolis: University of Minnesota Press, 2001).

15. See, for instance, David Frisby and Mike Featherstone, eds. *Simmel on Culture: Selected Writings* (London: Sage, 1997); Gaston Bachelard, *The Poetics of Space*, trans. Maria Jolas (Boston: Beacon Press, 1969); Walter Benjamin, *One-Way Street*, trans. Edmund Jephcott, *Selected Writings*, vol. 1, *1913–1926*, ed. Marcus Bullock and Michael W. Jennings (Cambridge, Mass.: Harvard University Press, 1996), 444–88, and Benjamin, "Paris, Capital of the Nineteenth Century," *The Arcades Project*, trans. Howard Eiland and Kevin McLaughlin (Cambridge, Mass.: Harvard University Press, 1999), 14–26; and Siegfried Kracauer, *The Mass Ornament: Weimar Essays*, trans. Thomas Y. Levin (Cambridge, Mass.: Harvard University Press, 1995).

16. Arjun Appadurai, ed., *The Social Life of Things: Commodities in Cultural*

Perspective (New York: Cambridge University Press, 1986); Steven Lubar and W. David Kingery, eds., *History from Things: Essays on Material Culture* (Washington: Smithsonian Institution Press, 1993); Victoria de Grazia, ed. *The Sex of Things: Gender and Consumption in Historical Perspective* (Berkeley: University of California Press, 1996); Daniel Miller, ed., *Material Cultures: Why Some Things Matter* (Chicago: University of Chicago Press, 1998). See also Mihaly Csikszentmihalyi and Eugene Rochberg-Halton, *The Meaning of Things: Domestic Symbols and the Self* (New York: Cambridge University Press, 1981); and Susan M. Pearce, ed., *Experiencing Material Culture in the Western World* (London: Leicester University Press, 1997). More recent efforts to produce material objects (and the materiality of objects) as a new object of knowledge include Michael Taussig, *Mimesis and Alterity: A Particular History of the Senses* (New York: Routledge, 1993); Daniel Tiffany, *Toy Medium: Materialism and Modern Lyric* (Berkeley: University of California Press, 2000); Miguel Tamen, *Friends of Interpretable Objects* (Cambridge, Mass.: Harvard University Press, 2001); Bill Brown, ed., *Things*, a special issue of *Critical Inquiry* (Fall 2001). An especially profound influence on much of this work, and an important leavening of literary criticism's more typical concerns in the 1970s and 1980s, is to be found in Susan Stewart, *On Longing: Narratives of the Miniature, the Gigantic, the Souvenir, the Collection* (Baltimore: Johns Hopkins, 1984). In the fields of American history and art history, attention to objects has been newly energized. See, for instance, Laurel Thatcher Ulrich, *The Age of Homespun: Objects and Stories in the Creation of an American Myth* (New York: Knopf, 2001), and Alexander Nemerov, *The Body of Raphaelle Peale: Still Life and Selfhood, 1812–1824* (Berkeley: University of California Press, 2001).

17. Albert S. Bolles, *The Financial History of the United States, from 1861 to 1885* (New York: D. Appleton and Company, 1886), 446.

18. Henry James, *Washington Square* (1881), in *Henry James: Novels 1881–1886* (New York: Library of America, 1985), 26.

19. Alfred D. Chandler Jr., *The Visible Hand: The Managerial Revolution in American Business* (Cambridge, Mass.: Belknap Press, 1977), 235. See all of Part III, pp. 207–84. Further references will be provided in the text.

20. On the production of mass markets, see Richard Ohmann, *Selling Culture: Magazines, Markets, and Class at the Turn of the Century* (New York: Verso, 1996).

21. Anon., "The Contributor's Club: The Tyranny of Things," *Atlantic Monthly* 97 (May 1906): 716.

22. William James, *A Pluralistic Universe* (Cambridge, Mass.: Harvard University Press, 1977), 97.

23. Herman Melville, *Moby-Dick or, The Whale* (New York: Penguin, 1992), 470.

24. Charles Baudelaire, "A Philosophy of Toys," *The Painter of Modern Life and Other Essays*, trans. Jonathan Mayne (London: Phaidon Press, 1964), 202–3.

25. Walter Benjamin, "Russian Toys," trans. Gary Smith, *Moscow Diary* (Cambridge, Mass.: Harvard University Press, 1986), 123.

26. Toni Morrison, *The Bluest Eye* (New York: Holt, Rinehart and Winston, 1972), 20–21.

27. André Breton, *Nadja*, trans. Richard Howard (New York: Grove Press, 1960), 89.

28. Walt Whitman, "Song of the Open Road," in *Complete Poetry and Collected Prose*, ed. Justin Kaplan (New York: Library of America, 1982), 301.

29. Vladimir Nabokov, *Transparent Things* (1972; New York: Vintage, 1989), 1. Further references will be provided in the text.

30. Martin Heidegger, "The Thing" (1950), in *Poetry, Language, Thought*, trans. Albert Hofstadter (New York: Harper Colophon Books, 1975), 165–82. See, in contrast, Georg Simmel's attention to the handle: "The Handle" (1911), trans. Rudolph H. Weingartner, in *Georg Simmel, 1858–1918: A Collection of Essays, with Translations and a Bibliography*, ed. Kurt H. Wolff (Columbus: Ohio State University Press, 1959), 267–75.

31. Jacques Lacan, *The Ethics of Psychoanalysis 1959–1960, The Seminar of Jacques Lacan, Book VII*, trans. Dennis Porter (New York: W. W. Norton, 1992), 115–27.

32. Gaston Bachelard, *The Poetics of Space*, 74–89.

33. Fernand Léger, *"Ballet Mécanique"* (1924), trans. Alexandra Anderson, in *Functions of Painting*, ed. Edward F. Fry (New York: Viking Press, 1973), 50. The more full-fledged, modernist version of this projection appears in the Constructivist project. Aleksandr Rodchenko, for instance, argued, in 1925, that "Our things in our hands must be equals, comrades" (quoted by Christina Kiaer, "Rodchenko in Paris," *October* 75 [Winter 1996]: 3).

34. Karl Marx, *Capital*, trans. Ben Fowkes (New York: Penguin, 1976), vol. 1, 163.

35. David Hounshell, *From the American System to Mass Production, 1800–1932* (Baltimore: Johns Hopkins University Press, 1984), 303–30. On the cultural impact of Fordism, see Terry Smith, *Making the Modern: Industry, Art, and Design in America* (Chicago: University of Chicago Press, 1993). The literature on the international appeal of Fordism is vast. As Peter Wollen has put it, in "the 1920s Fordism became a worldview," as important to the Soviet Union as to Germany, part of an Americanism that seemed to overcome the burden of tradition (Wollen, "Cinema/ Americanism/the Robot," in James Naremore and Patrick Brantlinger, eds., *Modernity and Mass Culture* [Bloomington: Indiana University Press, 1991], 43).

36. William Carlos Williams, *Paterson* (New York: New Directions, 1958), 6. He began to write *Paterson*, he says, because "a man is indeed a city, and for the poet there are no ideas but in things" (ii). And the poem, just as it begins, interrupts itself:

> —Say it, no ideas but in things—nothing but the blank faces of the houses
> and cylindrical trees
> bent, forked by preconception and accident—
> split, furrowed, creased, mottled, stained—
> secret—into the body of the light! (6)

There is no secret about the fact that the ideas in things, as rendered in or by this image, are irreducible to the ideas we might express in words. Indeed, a prominent strain in Williams criticism would argue that the nominalist point here is that there are only material objects themselves and no thing that realizes any idea. But the point lurks in the visualized distinction between, on the one hand, the featurelessness of the designed landscape (blank houses, cylindrical trees) and its abrupt disformation, the (furrowed, mottled) pattern wrought by chance. The idea in these things—or, more precisely and more generally throughout Williams's work, the idea expressed by the relation between them—amounts to the conviction that the life of things will never correspond to our preconceived ideas, and that this life of things is the life on which our happiness depends. For it is only when (by accident) something materializes that did not already exist (as an idea) that we can rest assured that the world is not destined to remain only as it is. In the absence of accident, this landscape of blank houses and cylindrical trees has no more vitality than suburban design.

However one reads Williams—as a realist (he would say "actualist") or an Objectivist, as a nominalist or a materialist—one must concede that he was willing to portray a world where ideas attain physical manifestation: "Inside the bus one sees / his thoughts sitting and standing" (9). And yet the ideas in this case don't achieve physical realization because they are, more simply and strikingly, physical. Not ideas *in* things, but ideas *as* things, the things we call human bodies. If you take a man to be a city, then you can understand the things circulating through the city as his thoughts. Still, this effort to translate Williams's non sequitur ("a man is indeed a city, and for the poet there are no ideas but in things") is a rationalization he himself would resist.

37. Paul Strand, "Photography," *Camera Work* no. 49/50 (1917): 4.

38. These details are taken from Maria Morris Hambourg, *Paul Strand, Circa 1916* (New York: Metropolitan Museum of Art, 1998), 12–26. See also Naomi Rosenblum, "Paul Strand: The Early Years, 1910–32" (Ph.D. diss., City University of New York, 1978).

39. Strand, quoted by Hambourg, 32. Strand explained his intentions in an interview with William Innes Homer in 1974, which Hambourg quotes, 34.

40. Fernand Léger, *"Ballet Mécanique, "* 50.

41. Water Benjamin, "Little History of Photography," trans. Edmund Jephcott and Kingsley Shorter, *Selected Writings*, vol. 2, *1927–1934*, ed. Michael W. Jennings, Howard Eiland, and Gary Smith (Cambridge, Mass.: Harvard University Press, 1999), 518.

42. Paul Strand, interview with William Innes Homer, quoted by Maria Morris Hambourg, *Paul Strand, Circa 1916*, 34.

43. Georges Poulet, "Criticism and the Experience of Interiority," *The Structuralist Controversy: The Languages of Criticism and the Sciences of Man*, ed. Richard Macksey and Eugenio Donato (Baltimore: The Johns Hopkins Press, 1970), 57.

44. Walter Benjamin, *Berliner Kindheit um neunzehnhundert*, in *Gesammelte Schriften*, ed. Rolf Tiedemann and Hermann Schweppenhäuser, vol. 7 (Frankfurt am Main: Suhrkamp Verlag, 1989), 416–17. Translation by Brice Cantrell.

45. Leo Stein, *The A-B-C of Aesthetics* (New York: Boni & Liveright, 1927), 44.

46. Max Weber, *Essays on Art* (New York: William Edwin Rudge, 1916), 32, 36.

47. F. S. Flint, "Imagisme," *Poetry*, March 1913, reprinted in *Imagist Poetry*, ed. Peter Jones (London: Penguin Books, 1972), 129.

48. See Theodor Adorno, *Aesthetic Theory*, trans. Robert Hullot-Kentor (Minneapolis: University of Minnesota Press, 1997), 226. On the two strains of American modernism in its relation to object culture, as an art that would "save the world from enslavement to things," and as an art that imagined a "harmonious alignment with the new world of glass, steel, and geometry," see Wanda M. Corn, *The Great American Thing: Modern Art and National Identity, 1915–1935* (Berkeley: University

of California Press, 1999), quotation pp. 17–18. For a wide-ranging cultural history, see Miles Orvell, *The Real Thing: Imitation and Authenticity in American Culture, 1880–1940* (Chapel Hill: University of North Carolina Press, 1989). On the productivist ambitions of modernism and the "struggle against the mass-produced commodity on behalf of the handcrafted thing," see Douglas Mao, *Solid Objects: Modernism and the Test of Production* (Princeton: Princeton University Press, 1998), quotation p. 11.

49. Fernand Léger, "The New Realism" (1935), trans. Harold Rosenberg, in Léger, *Functions of Painting*, 112.

50. See, for instance, Simon J. Bronner, ed., *Consuming Visions: Accumulation and Display of Goods in America, 1880–1920* (New York: Norton, 1989); Richard Wightman Fox and T. J. Jackson Lears, eds., *The Culture of Consumption: Critical Essays in American History, 1880–1980* (New York: Pantheon Books, 1983); Jackson Lears, *Fables of Abundance: A Cultural History of Advertising in America* (New York: Basic Books, 1994); Walter Benn Michaels, *The Gold Standard and the Logic of Naturalism: American Literature at the Turn of the Century* (Berkeley: University of California Press, 1987); Richard Ohmann, *Selling Culture: Magazines, Markets, and Class at the Turn of the Century* (New York: Verso, 1996).

51. George Santayana, "The Elements and Function of Poetry," *Interpretations of Poetry and Religion* (New York: Charles Scribner's Sons, 1900), 263. It is easy to detect, within this essay, just how far Santayana is from the modernist engagement with things: "The strain of attention, the concentration and focussing [*sic*] of thought on the unfamiliar immediacy of things, usually brings about nothing but confusion. We are dazed, we are filled with a sense of unutterable things, luminous yet indistinguishable, many yet one" (269). On the "objective correlative," see T. S. Eliot ("Hamlet," *Selected Essays* [London: Faber and Faber, 1932]), who explains it as "a set of objects, a situation, a chain of events which shall be the formula" of a "*particular* emotion," and which can thus evoke that emotion (145).

52. Gertrude Stein, "How Writing Is Written" (1935), *How Writing is Written: Volume II of the Previously Uncollected Writings of Gertrude Stein*, ed. Robert Bartlett Hass (Los Angeles: Black Sparrow Press, 1974), 152.

53. Ralph Waldo Emerson, "Experience," *Essays and Lectures* (New York: Library of America, 1996), 473.

54. Walt Whitman, "Song for Occupations," *Complete Poetry and Collected Prose*, 95–96, 94.

55. Henry David Thoreau, *Walden; or, Life in the Woods* (1854), in Thoreau, *A Week on the Concord and Merrimack Rivers; Walden, or, Life in the Woods; The Maine Woods; Cape Cod*, ed. Robert F. Sayre (New York: Library of America, 1985), 417.

56. Henry James, "Honoré de Balzac" (1875), *Literary Criticism, Volume Two* (New York: Library of America, 1984), 48–49.

57. Jean-François Lyotard complains of psychoanalytic interpretations that works of art "are there only in place of a missing object, as the accepted formula has it; and they are there only *because* the object is missing" ("Beyond Representation," trans. Jonathan Culler, in *The Lyotard Reader*, ed. Andrew Benjamin [Oxford: Basil Blackwell, 1989], 158).

58. François Dagognet, *Éloge de l'objet: Pour une philosophie de la marchandise* (Paris: Librairie Philosophique, 1989), 9.

59. Jean Baudrillard, *Fatal Strategies*, trans. Phillip Beitchman and W. G. J. Niesluchowski (New York: Semiotext[e], 1990), 111.

60. Theodor Adorno, *Negative Dialectics*, 193.

61. Willa Cather, *Not Under Forty* (New York: Knopf, 1936), 47, 43.

62. Hugh Kenner, *The Pound Era: The Age of Ezra Pound, T. S. Eliot, James Joyce and Wyndham Lewis* (Berkeley: University of California Press, 1971), 18-20.

63. Donald Judd, "Claes Oldenberg" (1966), in *Compete Writings 1959-1975* (New York: New York University Press, 1975), 192.

64. Slavoj Žižek, *The Plague of Fantasies* (London: Verso, 1997), 1. Žižek's point is that the familiar antagonism between abstraction and concreteness does not quite characterize our epoch: "In the good old days of traditional *Ideologiekritik*, the paradigmatic critical procedure was to regress from 'abstract' (religious, legal . . .) notions to the concrete social reality in which these notions were rooted; today, it seems more and more that the critical procedure is forced to follow the opposite path, from pseudo-concrete imagery to abstract (digital, market . . .) processes which effectively structure our living experience" (1).

CHAPTER ONE

1. See Justin Kaplan, *Mr. Clemens and Mark Twain* (New York: Simon and Schuster, 1966), 228.

2. The house was built in Hartford's literary colony, Nook Farm, where the Clemenses had such neighbors as Harriet Beecher Stowe and Charles Dudley Warner. Details of the house can be found in Kenneth R. Andrews, *Nook Farm: Mark Twain's Hartford Circle* (Seattle: University of Washington Press, 1969); Wilson H. Faude, "Mark Twain's Connecticut Home," *Historic Preservation* 26, no. 2 (1974): 16-20; Wilson H. Faude, *The Renaissance of Mark Twain's House* (Larchmont, N.Y.: Queens House, 1978); and Hugh F. McKean, *The "Lost" Treasures of Louis Comfort Tiffany* (Garden City: Doubleday & Company, 1980), 103.

3. Clarence Chatham Cook, *The House Beautiful: Essays on Beds and Tables, Stools and Candlesticks* (New York: Scribner, Armstrong and Co., 1878), 96.

4. The Cook source, and a comparison of the House Beautiful description in *Life on the Mississippi* with the description of the Grangerford parlor in *The Adventures of Huckleberry Finn*, were crucial components of the compositional chronology for *Huckleberry Finn* that Walter Blair established in *Mark Twain and Huck Finn* (Berkeley: University of California Press, 1960). For an account of the relation of these descriptions to one another, see Lucille M. Schultz, "Parlor Talk in Mark Twain: The Grangerford Parlor and the House Beautiful," *Mark Twain Journal* 19 (1979): 14-19.

5. Samuel L. Clemens, letters to Charles Warren Stoddard, 26 Oct. 1881, and to William Dean Howells, 28 Jan. 1882, *Mark Twain's Letters*, ed. Albert Bigelow Paine, 2 vols. (New York: Harper & Brothers, 1917), vol. 1, pp. 404-5, 416.

6. Anon., "The Contributor's Club: The Tyranny of Things," *Atlantic Monthly* 97 (May 1906): 716-17.

7. See Alexis de Tocqueville, "Author's Preface to the Twelfth Edition," *Democracy in America*, trans. George Lawrence, ed. J. P. Mayer, 2 vols. in 1 (New York: Doubleday, 1969), xiv; Ralph Waldo Emerson, *Nature, Essays and Lectures*, ed. Joel Porte (New York: Library of America, 1983), 25. Tocqueville hereafter cited parenthetically.

8. Charlotte Perkins Gilman, *Women and Economics: A Study of the Economic Relation Between Men and Women as a Factor in Social Evolution* (1898; New York: Dover, 1998), 60.

9. Henry David Thoreau, *Walden; or, Life in the Woods* (1854), in Thoreau, *A Week on the Concord and Merrimack Rivers; Walden, or, Life in the Woods; The Maine Woods; Cape Cod*, ed. Robert F. Sayre (New York: Library of America, 1985), 375, 350.

10. Clemens, *Mark Twain's Autobiography*, 2 vols. (New York: Harper and Brothers, 1924), 1:227, 226.

11. Quoted in Kaplan, *Mr. Clemens and Mark Twain*, 228.

12. See *Consuming Visions: Accumulation and Display of Goods in America, 1880−1920*, ed. Simon J. Bronner (New York: Norton, 1989); *The Culture of Consumption: Critical Essays in American History, 1880−1980*, ed. Richard Wightman Fox and T. J. Jackson Lears (New York: Pantheon Books, 1983); and Lears, *Fables of Abundance: A Cultural History of Advertising in America* (New York: Basic Books, 1994).

13. Karl Marx, *Capital*, trans. Ben Fowkes, 3 vols. (London: Penguin, 1990), 1:163; hereafter cited parenthetically.

14. William James, review of *The Sense of Beauty*, by George Santayana, *Essays, Comments and Reviews*, vol. 17 of *The Works of William James*, ed. Frederick H. Burkhardt et al. (Cambridge, Mass.: Harvard University Press, 1987), 536.

15. George Santayana, *The Sense of Beauty: Being the Outlines of Aesthetic Theory* (1896; New York: Charles Scribner's Sons, 1936), 30; hereafter cited parenthetically. The book is based on a course of lectures Santayana delivered at Harvard between 1892 and 1895.

16. In Kant's view, aesthetics as such concerns representation and not objects: the feeling of pleasure "denotes nothing in the object, but is a feeling which the Subject has of itself and of the manner in which it is affected by the representation." *The Critique of Judgement*, trans. James Creed Meredith (Oxford: Clarendon Press, 1928), 42 (I.1); hereafter cited parenthetically. On the suppression of the object in Kant's *Critique* and in aesthetics more generally, see Martin Jay, "Drifting into Dangerous Waters: The Separation of Aesthetic Experience from the Work of Art," in *Aesthetic Subjects*, ed. David McWhirter and Pamela Matthews (Minneapolis: University of Minnesota Press, 2002). For a different account of Kant, though, see Frances Ferguson, *Solitude and the Sublime: Romanticism and the Aesthetics of Individuation* (New York: Routledge, 1992), chap. 3. For an important overview of the topic of aesthetic value, see John Guillory, "The Discourse of Value: From Adam Smith to Barbara Hernstein Smith," *Cultural Capital: The Problem of Literary Canon Formation* (Chicago: University of Chicago Press, 1993), chap. 5.

17. Grant Allen, *Physiological Aesthetics* (New York: Appleton, 1877), 2. See, also, Henry Rutgers Marshall, *Pain, Pleasure, and Aesthetics: An Essay Concerning the Psychology of Pain and Pleasure, with Special Reference to Aesthetics* (London: Macmillan, 1894). Physiological aesthetics—understood as the physiological ground of either aesthetic appreciation or artistic production—had considerable currency in the late nineteenth century. James, for instance, taught a course on physiological aesthetics at Harvard. For a discussion and account of his syllabus, see Francesca Bordogna, "Historical Contexts of James's Pragmatist Epistemology," Ph.D. diss., University of Chicago, 1998, chap. 1. Santayana marks his difference from the

coarser brands of physiological aesthetics by emphasizing the difference between bodily and aesthetic pleasure, the latter providing an "exhilarating" "illusion of disembodiment" (29). In this way, he struggles to return aesthetics to the senses, but not to the body.

18. The Penguin editor includes a note by Marx: "One may recall that China and the tables began to dance when the rest of the world appeared to be standing still— *pour encourager les autres.*" Fowkes explains that this reference is "to the simultaneous emergence in the 1850s of the Taiping revolt in China and the craze for spiritualism which swept over upper-class German society. The rest of the world was 'standing still' in the period of reaction immediately after the defeat of the 1848 Revolutions" (1:164).

19. Marx is citing an authority for this definition of wealth, but the authority he cites is himself, *The Critique of Political Economy.*

20. The mystery of the commodity form requires an act of demystification to unveil its truth; the fetishism of commodities necessitates an act of defetishization to disclose their actual content. For an extensive account of this relation between essence and appearance, see Moishe Postone, *Time, Labor, and Social Domination* (New York: Cambridge University Press, 1993), esp. 58–61, 166–71.

21. Marx does in fact mention desire, but only in a footnote, where he defers to Nicholas Barbon: "Desire implies want; it is the appetite of the mind, and as natural as hunger to the body" (1:125). What accounts of consumer culture have insistently claimed and shown is that "desire" is anything but natural. It is important to add that Marx's argument against abstraction, against the mystification that occults the human history of the object, hardly amounts to a stand against consumer goods. See Peter Stallybrass, "Marx's Coat," in *Border Fetishisms,* ed. Patricia Spyer (London: Routledge, 1998), 183–207.

22. Georg Lukács, *History and Class Consciousness: Studies in Marxist Dialectics,* trans. Rodney Livingstone (Cambridge, Mass.: MIT Press, 1971), 83; hereafter cited parenthetically.

23. That is, Lukács fails to describe what we are to understand by the "character of things as things" in the same way that, as Heidegger objected (without ever specifying Lukács), he fails to describe for us what "we are to understand *positively* when we think of unreified *Being*" (Martin Heidegger, *Being and Time,* trans. John Macquarrie and Edward Robinson [New York: Harper and Row, 1962], 72). For a reading of *Being and Time* as a response to Lukács, see Lucien Goldmann, *Lukács and Heidegger: Towards a New Philosophy,* trans. William Q. Boelhower (London: Routledge and Kegan Paul, 1977).

24. Walter Benjamin, "Paris, Capital of the Nineteenth Century" (1935), *The Arcades Project,* trans. Howard Eiland and Kevin McLaughlin (Cambridge, Mass.: Harvard University Press, 1999), 7; my emphasis; hereafter cited parenthetically. Benjamin's understanding of the commodity is far more complex than I can suggest here. See, for instance, the points made by Susan Buck-Morss, *The Dialectics of Seeing: Walter Benjamin and the Arcades Project* (Cambridge, Mass.: MIT Press, 1986).

25. Simmel made something of the same point when he wrote about "The Berlin Trade Exhibition" in 1909. Explaining how the fair assembles "the products of the entire world in a confined space as if in a single picture," he describes how the competition between such a surplus of goods within that picture necessitates presenting

something other then their "usefulness and intrinsic properties": "the interest of the buyer has to be aroused by the external stimulus of the object, even the manner of presentation." But Simmel's account of commodity aesthetics remains untroubled by a Marxist perspective because Simmel, as he clarifies at length in the second chapter of *The Philosophy of Money*, had no faith whatsoever in the concept of use value (or the labor theory of value to which it is bound) (Georg Simmel, "The Berlin Trade Exhibition," trans. Sam Whimster, *Simmel on Culture: Selected Writings*, trans. David Frisby et al., ed. Frisby and Mike Featherstone [London: Sage Publications, 1997], 256–57.) See Simmel, *The Philosophy of Money*, trans. Tom Bottomore and David Frisby (London: Routledge, 1990), 79–100. I should note, in passing, that several chapters from the book appeared in the U.S. as essays, translated and published mostly by the University of Chicago sociologists, above all Albion Small. For an overview, see Donald N. Levine, Ellwood B. Carter, and Eleanor Miller Gorman, "Simmel's Influence on American Sociology," *American Journal of Sociology* 81 (1976): 813–45, 1112–32. And see Gary D. Jaworski, *George Simmel and the American Prospect* (Albany: State University of New York Press, 1997). If one were going to extend the present study into twentieth-century American sociology, Simmel's work would be the obvious place to begin.

26. For an extensive account of the schisms between psychological and economistic accounts of value, see Jack Amariglio and Antonio Callari, "Marxian Value Theory and the Problem of the Subject: the Role of Commodity Fetishism," *Fetishism as Cultural Discourse*, ed. Emily Apter and William Pietz (Ithaca: Cornell University Press, 1993), 186–216. Given the fact that "aesthetics is Marx's blind spot," as W. J. T. Mitchell puts it, there's nothing surprising about the fact that commodity aesthetics has no place in *Capital*. See Mitchell, *Iconology: Image, Text, Ideology* (Chicago: University of Chicago Press, 1986), chap. 6.

27. On the department store, see Ralph M. Hower, *History of Macy's of New York, 1858–1919: Chapters in the Evolution of the Department Store* (Cambridge, Mass.: Harvard University Press, 1943); Robert W. Twyman, *History of Marshall Field & Co., 1852–1906* (Philadelphia: University of Pennsylvania Press, 1954); Susan Porter Benson, *Counter Cultures: Saleswomen, Managers, and Customers in American Department Stores 1890–1940* (Chicago: University of Illinois Press, 1986); and William Leach, *Land of Desire: Merchants, Power, and the Rise of a New American Culture* (New York: Pantheon Books, 1993), chaps. 1–8.

28. James Livingston provides a good example of cultural historians who write as though things come to life—become "not unsentient matter"—only as commodities; he writes as though fetishism were only an economic, and not an anthropological, fact (*Pragmatism and the Political Economy of Cultural Revolution, 1850–1940* [Chapel Hill: University of North Carolina Press, 1994], 204; hereafter cited parenthetically). This is why he seriously misconstrues the famous lines that close Whitman's "Song for Occupations":

> When the psalm sings instead of the singer,
> When the script preaches instead of the preacher,
> When the pulpit descends and goes instead of the carver that
>   carved the supporting desk, . . .

When a university course convinces like a slumbering woman
and child convince,
When the minted gold in the vault smiles like the
nightwatchman's daughter,
When warrantee deeds loaf in chairs opposite and are my
friendly companions,
I intend to reach them my hand and make as much of them
as I do of men and women. (98—99)

Livingston isn't exactly wrong to say that Whitman is "willing to endow the teem-
ing world of objects with a weird life of its own." But how can this be understood
as Whitman's act of taking "commodity fetishism as his point of departure"
(204)? For, on the hand, "commodity fetishism" designates the production of
phantasmatically autonomous value. On the other, Whitman's scene follows his
conviction that men and women in the here and now are more sacred than the
hereafter ("Happiness not in another place, but this place . . . not for another hour,
but this hour"). As the poem closes, then, the poet denies that the component parts
of organized religion, education, economy, and government possess any of the
animation of men and women (who themselves are the only sources of animation). You could call it an argument against the fetishism of institutions. But
"commodity fetishism" has been fetishized to the point where any hint of an uncanny animation of material objects (even a hint denied) immediately conjures up
"commodity fetishism." *The end result, of course, is that "commodity fetishism"—
as a concept—might be said to veil the complex history of the human interaction with
the phenomenal object world in much the same way that commodity fetishism as such
veils the history of social relations between humans.* Whitman quotations from *Complete Poetry and Collected Prose*, ed. Justin Kaplan (New York: Library of America, 1982), 98—99.

29. Émile Zola, *The Ladies' Paradise* (Berkeley: University of California Press,
1992), 6; hereafter cited parenthetically. On the department store in France, see
Michael B. Miller, *The Bon Marché: Bourgeois Culture and the Department Store,
1869—1920* (Princeton: Princeton University Press, 1981); Rosalind Williams,
Dream Worlds: Mass Consumption in Late Nineteenth-Century France (Berkeley: University of California Press, 1982).

30. Kristin Ross, "Introduction: Shopping," Zola, *The Ladies' Paradise*, xxii.
See also Rachel Bowlby, *Just Looking: Consumer Culture in Dreiser, Gissing and Zola*
(London: Methuen, 1985), chap. 5.

31. Anon., "Zola," *The Literary World*, 14 July 1883, p. 228.

32. For an especially vicious attack, see anon., "Zola's New Novel," review of
The Ladies Paradise, by Zola, *The Critic*, 10 March 1883, p. 104. For a comprehensive
account of Zola's reception in America, see Albert J. Salvan, *Zola aux États-Unis*
(Providence: Brown University Press, 1943).

33. *Sister Carrie* (1900; New York: Penguin, 1981), 78, 22; hereafter cited parenthetically.

34. Not only is this animation unclarified by Marx's account of commodity
fetishism; moreover, though Marx understands money as the abstracting abstract

medium par excellence (as do, for instance, Simmel and Lukács), Dreiser renders Carrie's relation to money—"two soft, green, handsome ten-dollar bills" (62)—as a physical relation, among other things.

35. The crucial difference that divides the American case from the French is that Zola contains the complex and contradictory aspirations in his novel with a love plot, between Octave Mouret, triumphant proprietor of the new store in Paris, and Denise, who comes to work as a shop girl. The plot ultimately resolves itself in domestic union, and the erotic relation between humans and consumer objects is finally displaced by a relationship between humans. Despite his having invented "this mechanism for crushing the world," she "loved him for the grandeur of his work, she loved him still more every excess of his power" (345). In contrast, Carrie doesn't love people; she loves things: listening to Hurstwood, she hears "instead the voices of the things which he represented" (118). No resolvable love plot threatens the course of what Walter Benn Michaels terms "perpetual desire" (*The Gold Standard and the Logic of Naturalism* [Berkeley: University of California Press, 1987], 42).

36. Dreiser's novel thus marks the end of a relation to objects that had structured the first example of American Realism, Rebecca Harding Davis's *Life in the Iron Mills* (1861). Written in the genre of the "factory tour" and with the sort of muckraking objective that became customary as the century closed, *Life in the Iron Mills* depicts the pitiful lives of Welsh immigrants: "Incessant labor, sleeping in kennel-like rooms, eating rank pork and molasses" (Rebecca Harding Davis, *Life in the Iron Mills and Other Stories*, ed. Tillie Olson [New York: The Feminist Press of the City of New York, 1985], 15). In his hours of relief from laboring at the fiery furnaces, one of the mill hands, Hugh Wolfe, expresses what little spirit he has by working on statues of korl, "chipping and moulding figures,—hideous, fantastic enough, but sometimes strangely beautiful"—from the "great heaps of the refuse from the ore after the pig-metal is run" (24). Reduced by the mill to the status of a mindless beast, he nonetheless expresses his humanity—expresses himself—when he creates such figures as the "woman, white, of giant proportions, crouching on the ground, her arms flung out in some wild gesture of warning" (31). The story clearly narrates a distinction Hannah Arendt makes between labor and work, between *animal laborans* and *homo faber*, the former compelled to an "effort that leaves no trace" because it incessantly produces objects that are incessantly consumed, the latter free to assure the "worldly character of the produced thing" (*The Human Condition* [Chicago: The University of Chicago Press, 1958], 81, 94). But the point I wish to emphasize is how the novella assumes as its fundamental inquiry the question of how human-being expresses itself (or fails to) in the objects humans create—not, for instance, in the objects they purchase or display. Indeed, the novella inscribes Wolfe's self-destruction, his suicide, within the paradigm of making: "he lay down on the bed, taking the bit of tin, which he had rasped to a tolerable degree of sharpness, in his hand,—to play with, it may be. He bared his arms, looking intently at their corded veins and sinews" (59). That is, Davis renders this act of self-reification and self-destruction as a pathological act of art. For an account of Davis in the realist trajectory, see Sharon M. Harris, *Rebecca Harding Davis and American Realism* (Philadelphia: University of Pennsylvania Press), 1991.

37. Simon Nelson Patten, *The New Basis of Civilization*, ed. Daniel M. Fox (1907; Cambridge, Mass.: Belknap Press, 1968), 139.

38. Neil Harris, "Museums, Merchandising, and Popular Taste: The Struggle for Influence," in Ian M. G. Quimby, *Material Culture and the Study of American Life* (New York: Norton, 1978), 154.

39. Paul Bourget, *Outre-Mer: Impressions of America* (New York: C. Scribner's Sons, 1895), 231. Quoted by Neil Harris, "Museums, Merchandising, and Popular Taste," 149.

40. See, for instance, John Dewey, "The University School" (1896), *The Early Works, 1882–1898* (Carbondale: Southern Illinois University Press, 1972), vol. 5, p. 440; and "The Place of Manual Training in the Elementary Course of Study" (1901), *The Middle Works, 1899–1924* (Carbondale: Southern Illinois University Press, 1976), vol. 1, ed. Jo Ann Boydston, pp. 230–37. Dewey's insistence on attending to material things doesn't quite square with his early emphasis on exchange (see below), but the point of the thing is always its place in some process. For the importance of Froebel blocks to Wright, see *An Autobiography* (New York: Longmans, Green, and Co., 1932), 11–14.

41. Simon J. Bronner, "Object Lessons: The Work of Ethnological Museums and Collections," in *Consuming Visions*, 217–54. See also Steven Conn, *Museums and American Intellectual Life, 1876–1926* (Chicago: University of Chicago Press, 1998).

42. See "Half a Century of Inventions," *Popular Science Monthly* 37 (July 1890): 428.

43. Frederick G. Bourne, "American Sewing-Machines," in *One Hundred Years of American Commerce*, ed. Chauncey M. Depew (New York: D. O. Haynes, 1895), vol. 2, p. 530. Margo J. Anderson, *The American Census: A Social History* (New Haven: Yale University Press, 1988), 102.

44. David A. Hounshell, *From the American System to Mass Production, 1800–1932* (Baltimore: Johns Hopkins University Press, 1984), 201.

45. Steven Crane, "New York's Bicycle Speedway" (1896), *The University of Virginia Edition of the Works of Stephen Crane*, 10 vols., ed. Fredson Bowers (Charlottesville: University Press of Virginia, 1969–1974), vol. 8, p. 371.

46. As much as this material and visual productivity could crowd the most fashionable streets of the city, elsewhere it was the inexplicably mounting refuse from the circuit of production and consumption that seemed to threaten people's sense of control over their environment, giving birth to the new science of waste management. And in the tenements described by Jacob Riis, Abraham Cahan, and Upton Sinclair, among others, the lack of human freedom is rendered not least as the incapacity to free oneself from the sight and smell of the city's detritus. Though the problem of this excess could be considered the problem of not being able to keep the residue of consumption out of sight, excess had also become a problem to be resolved by economists. Macroeconomic theory addressed the problem of "overproduction" with the invention of marginalist economics, and the recognition that business could be regularized by attending to the issue of distribution and consumption. See Livingston, *Pragmatism*, 49–62.

47. Georg Simmel, *The Philosophy of Money*, 474.

48. Simon Bronner, "Object Lessons," 219.

49. Lears, *Fables of Abundance*, 6; Daniel J. Boorstin, *The Americans: The Democratic Experience* (New York: Random House, 1973), 89–90.

50. For reasons that will become clear, my quotations are from the photographic facsimile of a copy of the first American edition, Mark Twain, *The Prince and the Pauper* (1881; New York: Oxford, 1996), 44; hereafter cited parenthetically. The University of California Press published a scholarly edition in 1979.

51. Clemens, letter to Howells, 11 March 1880, *Mark Twain's Letters*, 1:377.

52. A more psychological account of this novel might read it in relation to William James's account of "The Consciousness of Self," where he tries to describe how, for instance, Peter, waking up in the same bed with Paul, believes he has dreamt his own dream and not Paul's. See William James, *The Principles of Psychology* (1890; Cambridge: Harvard University Press, 1983), 317.

53. Anon. "Mark Twain's 'The Prince and the Pauper,'" *The Century* 23 (March 1882): 784. Despite the book's critical success in America, it was not popular by Twain's standards.

54. For the most sustained engagement with Twain's own strategies of impersonation, see Kaplan, *Mr. Clemens and Mark Twain;* and Susan Gillman, *Dark Twins: Imposture and Identity in Mark Twain's America* (Chicago: University of Chicago Press, 1989).

55. Nonetheless, *The Prince and the Pauper* has a prominent place in Howard G. Baetzhold, *Mark Twain and John Bull: The British Connection* (Bloomington: Indiana University Press, 1970); and Sherwood Cummings, *Mark Twain and Science: Adventures of a Mind* (Baton Rouge: Louisiana State University Press, 1988).

56. On Twain's attitudes toward England in the 1870s, see Howard G. Baetzhold, "Mark Twain: England's Advocate," *American Literature* 28 (Nov. 1956): 328–46. On his Medievalism more generally, see Kim Moreland, *The Medievalist Impulse in American Literature: Twain, Adams, Fitzgerald, and Hemingway* (Charlottesville: University Press of Virginia, 1996), 28–76.

57. See Henry-Russell Hitchcock, *The Architecture of H. H. Richardson and His Times* (1936; Cambridge, Mass.: MIT Press, 1966); Douglass Shand Tucci, *Ralph Adams Cram: American Medievalist* (Boston: Boston Public Library, 1975); Robert Mane, *Henry Adams on the Road to Chartres* (Cambridge, Mass.: Harvard University Press, 1971). For a brief introduction, see Peter W. Williams, "The Varieties of American Medievalism," *Studies in Medievalism* 1 (Spring 1982): 7–20. For the most influential recent account, see T. J. Jackson Lears, *No Place of Grace: Antimodernism and the Transformation of American Culture* (New York: Pantheon Books, 1981).

58. In his note on the curiousness of the determinations of reflection, Marx writes: "For instance, one man is king only because other men stand in the relation of subjects to him. They, on the other hand, imagine that they are subjects because he is king" (*Capital* 1:149 n. 22). Slavoj Žižek usefully extrapolates: "'Being-a-King is an effect of the network of social relations between a 'king' and his 'subjects'; but—and here is the fetishistic misrecognition—to the participants of this social bond, the relationship appears necessarily in an inverse form: they think that they are subjects giving the king royal treatment because the king is already in himself, outside the relationship to his subjects, a king" (Slavoj Žižek, *The Sublime Object of Ideology* [London: Verso, 1989], 25). From Žižek's perspective, the fetishistic relation between humans gives way, with the advent of capital, to the defetishization of this relation and the fetishization of the relation between humans and objects. Twain, however,

collapses the difference by inserting a mediating object within the fetishistic relation between humans.

59. See Ernst Kantorowicz, *The King's Two Bodies: A Study in Medieval Political Theology* (Princeton: Princeton University Press, 1957). And see Claude Lefort, "The Image of the Body and Totalitarianism," in *The Political Forms of Modern Society: Bureaucracy, Democracy, Totalitarianism*, ed. John B. Thompson (Cambridge, Mass.: MIT Press, 1986), 302; and *Democracy and Political Theory*, trans. David Macey (Minneapolis: University of Minnesota Press, 1988), 244. Of the totem, Durkheim writes that "in general a collective sentiment can become conscious of itself only by being fixed upon some material object; but by virtue of this very fact, it participates in the nature of this object, and reciprocally, the object participates in its nature" (*Elementary Forms of Religious Life*, trans. Joseph Ward Swain [New York: Free Press, 1965], 269).

60. William Shakespeare, *Henry V*, in *The Complete Works of William Shakespeare*, ed. David Bevington, 6 vols. (New York: Bantam Books, 1988), vol. 3, 4.1.232. On *King Richard II*, see Kantorowicz, *The King's Two Bodies*, 24–41.

61. Žižek, *For They Know Not What They Do: Enjoyment as a Political Factor* (New York: Verso, 1991), 255, 257. See Jacques Lacan, "Desire and the Interpretation of Desire in *Hamlet*," trans. James Hulbert, ed. Jacques-Alain Miller, in *Literature and Psychoanalysis*, ed. Shoshana Felman (Baltimore: Johns Hopkins University Press, 1982).

62. See Lefort, *Democracy and Political Theory*, 244.

63. Clemens, letter to Benjamin Ticknor, 14 August 1881, *Mark Twain's Letter's to His Publishers, 1867–1894*, ed. Hamlin Hill (Berkeley: University of California Press, 1967), 140. For further information on the illustrations, see Beverly R. David and Ray Sapirstein, "Reading the Illustrations in *The Prince and the Pauper*," in the Oxford edition, 22–26.

64. Engels writes of the apparently "incorporeal alien powers" that seem to control men's lives, experienced when the "product rul[es] the producer" (Friedrich Engels, *The Origin of the Family, Private Property and the State*, trans. Alick West [New York: International Publishers, 1972], 233, 234). In my effort to simplify this reading of Twain, I have elided three Renaissance contexts: the first is the emergence of the concept of fetishism in the sixteenth century (see William Pietz, "The Problem of the Fetish, I," *Res* 9 [Spring 1985]: 5–17); the second is the place of commodity objects (see Douglas Bruster, *Drama and the Market in the Age of Shakespeare* [New York: Cambridge University Press, 1992], chaps. 6 and 7; and Ann Rosalind Jones and Peter Stallybrass, *Renaissance Clothing and the Materials of Memory* [New York: Cambridge University Press, 2000]); and the third is the transition from feudalism to capitalism (see Richard Halpern, *The Poetics of Primitive Accumulation: English Renaissance Culture and the Genealogy of Capital* [Ithaca: Cornell University Press, 1991]).

65. Anon., "Seals," *American Law Review* 1 (1867): 638–52.

66. Anon., "Looked Upon with Veneration," *Green Bag* 3 (1891): 395.

67. G. H. Parkinson, "The Great Seal," *The Leisure Hour* 31 (1882): 371.

68. Annette B. Weiner, *Inalienable Possessions: The Paradox of Keeping-While-Giving* (Berkeley: University of California Press, 1992), 6.

69. Indeed Twain was afraid of having the seal illustrated because he thought he might somehow be accused of forgery.

70. David Starkey, "Court and Government," in *Revolution Reassessed: Revisions in the History of Tudor Government and Administration,* ed. Christopher Coleman and David Starkey (Oxford: Clarendon Press, 1986), 46. Starkey's essay (pp. 29–58) is the best account of the struggles over the signet, the various seals, and the sign manual, and Cromwell's effort to establish and then circumvent standard sealing procedures. My thanks to Jonathan Goldberg for pointing me to this essay.

71. Hamlet's metaphor (5.2.53) implicitly invokes an analogy between the act of imprinting and the act of conception that is commonplace in Shakespeare and Renaissance writing more generally, and that harks back to Plato and to Aristotle. See Margreta de Grazia, "Imprints: Shakespeare, Gutenberg and Descartes," in *Alternative Shakespeares II,* ed. Terence Hawkes (New York: Routledge, 1996), 63–94. De Grazia concludes her essay by showing how the readily gendered act of sealing helped to anthropomorphize the most significant reproductive mechanism of the Renaissance, the printing press. Thinking of Twain in relation to the history that de Grazia charts, it is difficult not to imagine that his use of the "trivial thing" to structure the denouement of the novel doesn't bear some relation to his disastrous infatuation with printing technology. In 1880, Twain invested heavily in the Kaolatype printing process, and the year after he began to invest in the infamous Paige Typesetter. For one account of this infatuation, see Hamlin Hill, "Mark Twain: Texts and Technology," in *Cultural Artifacts and the Production of Meaning: The Page, The Image, The Body,* ed. Margaret J. M. Ezell and Katherine O'Brien O'Keefe (Ann Arbor: University of Michigan Press, 1994), 71–84.

72. Aristotle, *De Anima,* trans. R. D. Hicks (Amsterdam: Hakkert, 1965), 424.a.17, p. 105.

73. Descartes, *Rules for the Direction of the Natural Intelligence,* trans. and ed. George Heffernan (Atlanta: Rodopi, 1998), 141.

74. Neil Hertz, "Dr. Johnson's Forgetfulness, Descartes' Piece of Wax," *Eighteenth Century Life* 16 (November 1992): 176. My point is deeply indebted to this essay, as to Bernard Williams, *Descartes: The Project of Pure Inquiry* (London: Penguin, 1978).

75. Lefort, *Democracy and Political Theory,* 17.

76. Thomas Paine, *Rights of Man,* in *Collected Writings* (New York: Library of America, 1995), 472, 467.

77. John Dewey, "The Scholastic and the Speculator," *The Early Works, 1882– 1898,* vol. 3, p. 149. All but needless to add, one can regard Dewey's essay as an example of how the "Protestant ethic" had become obsolete in the decades before Weber theorized its centrality.

78. James Livingston, *Pragmatism,* 81. Livingston's point, all along, is that this new subjectivity conceptually underwrote a new *"social* self" (66). Further references will be provided parenthetically.

79. Although Livingston's argument squares with recent work that has emphasized the liberatory, self-fashioning potential of consumer culture, his book idiosyncratically and importantly tracks one genealogy of the very "postmodern personality" (his term) which capacitates that work (*Pragmatism,* 215). That is, his argument shows the way recent reconceptualizations of consumer culture were in

fact original conceptualizations that facilitated the emergence of that culture. The destabilized subject may seem like a (French) concept that helps us assess (American) consumer culture, but it was also the concept on which—or the "mode of acceptance" through which—that culture was built, the foundation of the cultural revolution that did not simply accompany, but helped to effect, the transition from proprietary to corporate capitalism and the consumerist regime. I should add that I am uninterested here in participating in the debate about when "consumer culture" in fact emerged in the West (the American 1890s, the English eighteenth century, the Dutch seventeenth century, the Venetian Renaissance, etc.) except to say that there has been considerable agreement that the nature of capitalism significantly changed in the closing two decades of the nineteenth century, and agreement that this change was theorized (by the marginalists) at the time. For a general discussion of the historical question, see Jean-Christophe Agnew, "Coming Up for Air," in *Consumption and the World of Goods,* ed. John Brewer and Roy Porter (New York: Routledge, 1993), 19–39.

80. See Raymond Williams, "Advertising: The Magic System," in *The Cultural Studies Reader,* ed. Simon During (London: Routledge, 1993), 335.

81. See Annette B. Weiner, *Inalienable Possessions.* Weiner writes in the effort to arrest the long history of anthropological attention to exchange as the only meaningful fate of objects. "Exchange does not produce a homogeneous totality, but rather is an arena where heterogeneity is determined. . . . In other words, things exchanged are about things kept" (10).

82. Daniel Greenleaf Thompson, *Politics in a Democracy: An Essay* (New York: Longmans, Green, and Co., 1893), 3.

83. Ibid., 2.

84. Lefort, *Democracy and Political Theory,* 15.

85. Tocqueville, *Democracy in America,* 430. See Slavoj Žižek, "Formal Democracy and Its Discontents," *Looking Awry: An Introduction to Jacques Lacan through Popular Culture* (Cambridge, Mass., MIT Press, 1991), 154–70. The abstract character of the democratic subject, the liberal subject, the Enlightenment subject, the public subject, the citizen—this can be told in many different registers, and grounded in Kant or Marx ("On the Jewish Question") no less than in Descartes. Because the Cartesian subject can be said to be both the subject of democracy and the subject of psychoanalysis, pointing to Descartes (through Tocqueville) seems the most appropriate gesture within this essay. See especially Joan Copjec, who incorporates the insights of Lefort and Jacques Alain Miller, *Read My Desire: Lacan against the Historicists* (Cambridge, Mass.: MIT Press, 1994), 141–61; and David Lloyd and Paul Thomas, *Culture and the State* (New York: Routledge, 1998). On American abstraction more particularly, see Philip Fisher, "Democratic Social Space: Whitman, Melville, and the Promise of American Transparency," *The New American Studies: Essays from Representations,* ed. Philip Fisher (Berkeley: University of California Press, 1991), 70–111. On Abstraction as the condition of U.S. citizenship—a condition which, however enabling, perpetually compromises the status and role of citizens embodied by gender, race, ethnicity, or sexuality, see Lauren Berlant, "National Brands/National Bodies: *Imitation of Life,*" *The Phantom Public Sphere,* ed. Bruce Robbins (Minneapolis: University of Minnesota Press, 1993), 173–208; and Michael Warner, "The Mass Public and the Mass Subject," *The Phantom Public Sphere,* 234–

56. We might say that whereas the racialized subject in America suffers from the distinction of embodiment, Tocqueville, Veblen, and Lefort address the specular problem (for the homogenized, white bourgeois subject—for Twain) of never feeling distinct enough.

86. Mark Twain, *Life on the Mississippi* (New York: Oxford University Press, 1996), 400−406.

87. Edgar Allan Poe, "Philosophy of Furniture," *Selected Writings of Edgar Allan Poe: Poems, Tales, Essays, and Reviews*, ed. David Galloway (Harmondsworth: Penguin, 1967), 414, 415.

88. William Leach, *Land of Desire: Merchants, Power, and the Rise of a New American Culture* (New York: Pantheon Books, 1993), 3, 6. Thus, John Bates Clark and other economists of the era began to insist that only a free market could insure democracy (and thus Americans today continue to confuse free markets with freedom). On Clark, see Dorothy Ross, *The Origins of American Social Sciences* (New York: Cambridge University Press, 1991), 121, 157.

89. Thorstein Veblen, *The Theory of the Leisure Class: An Economic Study of Institutions* (1889; New York: Penguin, 1979), 242.

90. Tocqueville, *Democracy in America*, 537.

91. Albert Bigelow Paine, introduction to Clemens, *Mark Twain's Autobiography*, vii.

92. The incomparable filmic account of this desperate yet vain effort to accumulate things is of course Orson Welles's *Citizen Kane*.

93. Marx, *Contribution to the Critique of Hegel's Philosophy of Right*, in *The Marx-Engels Reader*, ed. Robert C. Tucker (New York: Norton, 1978), 19.

94. This comment is quoted and discussed in the context of other such metaphors by Thomas M. Grant, "The Curious Houses that Mark Built: Twain's Architectural Imagination," *Mark Twain Journal* 20 (Summer 1981): 1−10.

95. Clemens, *Mark Twain's Autobiography*, 2:34.

96. Sigmund Freud, "Mourning and Melancholia," in *The Standard Edition of the Complete Psychological Works of Sigmund Freud*, trans. and ed. James Strachey, 24 vols. (London: Hogarth, 1953−74), 14:245. To begin understanding Twain's curious expression of grief in the context of American proscriptions against the uncontrollable attachment to the dead, one would begin with Mitchell Robert Breitwieser's extraordinary *American Puritanism and the Defense of Mourning: Religion, Grief, and Ethnology in Mary White Rowlandson's Captivity Narrative* (Madison: University of Wisconsin Press, 1991).

97. Tocqueville, *Democracy in America*, 2:538; my emphasis.

98. Emerson, "Experience," *Essays and Lectures*, 473.

CHAPTER TWO

1. Charles Monroe Sheldon's *In His Steps; "What Would Jesus Do?"* was not just *a* best-seller in 1897; it was one of the top best-sellers in the nineteenth century. For an overview of social gospel fiction, see Robert Glenn Wright, *The Social Christian Novel* (New York: Greenwood Press, 1989).

2. Frank Norris, *The Joyous Miracle* (New York: Doubleday, Page, 1906), 1−3. Mervius goes on to tell Jerome a story from his youth, about how the strange carpenter's son turned a clay bird to life. Jerome has no faith in the eyewitness account.

3. "How to Make Our Ideas Clear," *The Collected Papers of Charles Sanders Peirce*, ed. Charles Hartshorne and Paul Weiss (Cambridge, Mass.: Harvard University Press, 1934), 6 vols., 5, par. 398; hereafter, citations by volume and paragraph will be provided parenthetically.

4. See Jacques Derrida, *Of Grammatology*, trans. Gayatri Chakravorty Spivak (Baltimore: John Hopkins University Press, 1976); Judith Butler, *Bodies That Matter: On The Discursive Limits of "Sex"* (New York: Routledge, 1993), 1−23, 27−55; Michel de Certeau, *The Writing of History*, trans. Tom Conley (New York: Columbia University Press, 1988). On the "repeatable materiality that characterizes the enunciate function" (105), see Michel Foucault, *The Archaeology of Knowledge*, trans. A. M. Sheridan Smith (New York: Harper and Row, 1972), 88−105.

5. In this chapter, it may begin to seem as though I consider repetition the only tool in the novelist's bag for convincing readers of the reality of the referent. That is hardly the case, of course. In an essay I silently invoke throughout this book, Roland Barthes argues that gratuitous, unmotivated detail is meant to confirm the existence of the scene "outside" the text ("The reality effect," *French Literary Theory Today*, ed. Tzvetan Todorov, trans. R. Carter [Cambridge: Cambridge University Press, 1982], 11−17). Reading Thomas Hardy, Gillian Beer points out the way the "eye of the writing moves far and near" to create the shifts in space and scale the disclose the "plentitude of experience" (*Darwin's Plots: Evolutionary Narrative in Darwin, George Eliot and Nineteenth-Century Fiction* [London: Routledge and Kegan Paul, 1985], 247−48). Elaine Scarry also uses Hardy as an example when she discusses how writing achieves "the vivacity of perception" that convinces the reader of the solidity of the described object ("On Vivacity: The Difference Between Daydreaming and Imagining-Under-Authorial-Instruction," *Representations* 52 [Fall 1995]: 1−26.

6. W. D. Howells, "Editor's Easy Chair," *Harper's Monthly Magazine* 103 (Oct 1901): 824. My emphasis.

7. J. Hillis Miller, *Fiction and Repetition: Seven English Novelists* (Cambridge, Mass.: Harvard University Press, 1982), 2−3.

8. Anon., "A Story of San Francisco," *The New York Times—Saturday Review*, 11 March 1899, rpt. *The New York Times Book Review* (New York: Arno Press, 1968), 150.

9. A. S. van Westrum, "A Novelist with a Future," *The Book Buyer* 22 (May 1901): 326.

10. By this I certainly don't mean to say that critics haven't done a powerful job tracing the impact of Darwinian theory on the *plot* of narrative fiction. Gillian Beer, for instance, after showing how scientific *description* gave way to *narration*, examines how the tensions between natural law and human individuality (or taxonomy and morphology), and questions of origin and inheritance, structure the plots of George Eliot's and Thomas Hardy's novels (*Darwin's Plots*). Similarly, for June Howard (*Form and History in American Literary Naturalism* [Chapel Hill: University of North Carolina Press, 1985]), the question of form is foremost the question of plot.

11. For the standard characterological reading (in the context of Darwin and Spencer), see Donald Pizer, *The Novels of Frank Norris* (Bloomington: Indiana University Press, 1966), 23−85. In the eponymous chapter of *The Gold Standard and the Logic of Naturalism* (Berkeley: University of California Press, 1987), Walter Benn Michaels identifies a "naturalist ontology" shared by the miser Trina and the Gold-

bugs, both committed to gold over and against any representative paper. Despite his use of the term "naturalist ontology" (167), Michaels is eager to deny that naturalism expresses any one ontological position. Rather, he wants to say that the "discourse of naturalism" is constituted by conflicts that it does not resolve (172–73).

12. Josiah Royce, "Self-Consciousness, Social Consciousness and Nature," in *The Basic Writings of Josiah Royce*, ed. John J. McDermott (Chicago: University of Chicago Press, 1969), vol. 1, p. 452; hereafter cited parenthetically.

13. Marcel Proust, *À la recherche du temps perdu* (Paris: Gallimard, 1987), 3.

14. Proust, *À la recherche du temps perdu*, 4. *Remembrance of Things Past*, trans. Terence Kilmartin (New York: Random House, 1981), 3 vols., 1:4.

15. W. D. Howells, "American Letter," *Literature*, 8 April 1899, p. 371.

16. Frank Norris, *McTeague: A Story of San Francisco* (New York: Penguin, 1982), 9, 5; hereafter cited parenthetically.

17. Quoted as Theme number 23 in *A Novelist in the Making*, ed. James D. Hart (Cambridge, Mass.: Harvard University Press, 1970), 78.

18. Gérard Genette, *Narrative Discourse: An Essay in Method*, trans. Jane E. Lewin (Ithaca: Cornell University Press, 1980), 123, 160.

19. Of course, a good formalist would argue that such a confrontation serves only to motivate and foreground the orchestration of singulative and iterative modes. (On the singulative, see Genette, *Narrative Discourse*, 114.) Whether one wishes to emphasize how the technique serves to represent the action or to emphasize how the action serves as an alibi for the technical endeavor, there's little doubt that diegetic action and narrative technique are productively fused here, not a typical feat for Norris, who generally succeeds as a novelist despite technique. In his words: "It's the life that we want, the vigorous, real thing. . . . Damn the 'style'" ("An Opening for Novelists: Great Opportunities for Fiction Writers in San Francisco," *The Literary Criticism of Frank Norris*, ed. Donald Pizer [Austin: University of Texas Press, 1964], 30). All but needless to add, much of the point of this chapter is to expose the literary "style" by which he tried to manufacture the sense of extra-literary "life."

20. For useful commentaries, see George Gentry, "Habit and the Logical Interpretant," *Studies in the Philosophy of Charles Sanders Peirce*, ed. Philip R. Wiener and Fredric H. Young (Cambridge, Mass.: Harvard University Press, 1952), 75–92; A. J. Ayer, *The Origins of Pragmatism: Studies in the Philosophy of Charles Sanders Peirce and William James* (London: Macmillan, 1968), 40–49. For an important discussion of Peirce's understanding of habit in relation to the Derridean understanding of iteration, see Samuel Weber, "Closure and Exclusion," *Diacritics* 10 (Summer 1980): 34–52.

21. Charles Sanders Peirce, "Man's Glassy Essence," 6:262.

22. Lamarck's impact in America extended far beyond the late nineteenth-century neo-Lamarckians, with Herbert Spencer's version of the story more widely read than Lamarck's itself: "While the modified bodily structure produced by new habits of life is bequeathed to future generations, the modified nervous tendencies produced by such new habits of life are also bequeathed; and if the new habits of life become permanent, the tendencies become permanent. . . . It needs only to contrast national characters to see that mental peculiarities caused by habit become heredi-

tary." See George W. Stocking Jr. (who quotes Spencer), "Lamarckianism in American Social Science, 1890–1915," *Race, Culture, and Evolution: Essays in the History of Anthropology* (Chicago: University of Chicago Press, 1982), 234–69. On the literary-critical scene, see Donald Pizer, "Evolutionary Ideas in Late Nineteenth-Century English and American Literary Criticism," in *Realism and Naturalism in Nineteenth-Century American Literature* (Carbondale: Southern Illinois University Press, 1984), 86–95.

23. Charles Sanders Peirce, "Evolutionary Love," 6:300. On Le Conte and Norris's other evolutionist teachers at Berkeley, see Pizer, *The Novels of Frank Norris*, 3–22. For a brief contemporaneous review of the literature on "inherited habit," see C. Lloyd Morgan, *Animal Behaviour* (London: Edward Arnold, 1900), 106–16.

24. J. B. Lamarck, *Zoological Philosophy: An Exposition with Regard to the Natural History of Animals* (1809), trans. Hugh Elliot (Chicago: University of Chicago Press, 1984), 122.

25. Charles Sanders Peirce, *Reasoning and the Logic of Things* (Cambridge, Mass.: Harvard University Press, 1992), 240–41. At times, the most recent cosmology seems to accord with the Peircian formulation.

26. William James, *Principles of Psychology* (1890; Cambridge, Mass.: Harvard University Press, 1981), 109, 110; hereafter cited parenthetically.

27. Frank Norris, *Blix* (New York: Doubleday & McClure Co., 1899), 109; hereafter cited parenthetically.

28. Norris and James share the same emphasis on the priority of the physiological over the emotional: in his famous metaleptic account of emotion, James argues that we don't cry because we are sad; rather, our crying makes us sad; and in *McTeague*, it is "only *after* her marriage with the dentist," for instance, that Trina begins "to love him" (183). The same logic underlies Pascal's interest in habit: ritual can engender faith, which is to say that "habit provides the strongest truths and those that are most believed" (*Pensées*, trans. A. J. Krailsheimer [Harmondsworth: Penguin, 1966], pensée 821, p. 274.) It is not affect or conviction that generates action, but action that predicates conviction and affect.

29. Pascal, *Pensées*, pensée 821, p. 274. Pascal also writes: "Habit is a second nature that destroys the first. But what is nature? Why is habit not natural? I am very much afraid that nature itself is only a first habit, just as habit is a second nature" (pensée 126, p. 61).

30. In his semiconscious waking, Marcel encounters the walls of his room shifting about, rearranging themselves to become other rooms where he has slept, and in one such room the decor (violet curtains, a rectangular cheval-glass) are both uncannily animate and hostile, the memory of which prompts an exclamation: "Habit! that skillful but slow-moving arranger who begins by letting our minds suffer for weeks on end in temporary quarters, but whom our minds are none the less only too happy to discover at last, for without it, reduced to their own devices, they would be powerless to make any room seem habitable" (Proust, *Remembrance of Things Past*, 1:9). Because our habits habituate us to certain contexts, our minds experience novel space as an excruciating shock. But because habit as such can finally make the strange familiar, the initial shock can be overcome. The exclamation precedes the moment when semiconsciousness becomes full consciousness and in Marcel's bedroom "the

surrounding objects stand still" (1:9), as though the very consideration of habit had arrested the world into physical equilibrium. As a "slow-moving arranger," habit puts things in place and keeps them there.

31. For a discussion of the role of habit in the novel as a shield against personal loss, see Barbara Hochman, "Loss, Habit, Obsession: The Governing Dynamic of *McTeague*," *Studies in American Fiction* 14 (Autumn 1986): 179–90.

32. In the novel as I want to describe it, it is important to note in such sentences that McTeague does not *think*. He *feels*.

33. Lamarck, *Zoological Philosophy*, 350.

34. And it is precisely McTeague's lack of understanding about habit, one might conclude, that spells his ruin with Trina from the start. When she explains that picnicking is one of one her family's customs, he says, nodding, "Yes, yes, a custom. . . . a custom—that's the word" (67).

35. Lamarck, *Zoological Philosophy*, 350.

36. Frank Norris, *Vandover and the Brute* (Lincoln: University of Nebraska Press, 1978), 181; hereafter cited parenthetically.

37. This is the specular case of Vandover's father, who abandons his retirement and reenters the "sordid round of business" because it is "the only escape from the mortal *ennui* and weariness of the spirit" that he suffers in leisure (6).

38. For a contrasting figure, we can consider Cowperwood in Dreiser's *The Financier*, who loses all his possessions following the market crash but loses no sense of himself.

39. On gambling narratives, see Ann Fabian, *Card Sharps, Dream Books, and Bucket Shops: Gambling in Nineteenth-Century America* (Ithaca: Cornell University Press, 1990). On the paradigmatic results of addiction, see John C. Burnham, *Bad Habits: Drinking, Smoking, Taking Drugs, Sexual Misbehavior, and Swearing in American History* (New York: New York University Press, 1993).

40. The metaphor of the worn path and the channel of water—though not located physiologically as a path or channel in the nervous system—had become customary in the wake of John Locke and Bishop Richard Watley. For a discussion of these and other sources, including Hume, see Joseph M. Thomas, "Figures of Habit in William James," *New England Quarterly* 66 (March 1993): 7–11.

41. On the toy industry and marketing for children see William Leach, "A New Child World and 'Paradise in the Toy Department,'" *Land of Desire: Merchants, Power, and the Rise of a New American Culture* (New York: Pantheon Books, 1993), 85–90; and Bill Brown, "American Childhood and Stephen Crane's Toys," *The Material Unconscious: American Amusement, Stephen Crane, and the Economies of Play* (Cambridge, Mass., Harvard University Press, 1996), 167–98.

42. Walter Benn Michaels, *The Gold Standard and the Logic of Naturalism*, 158.

43. Anon., "A Story of San Francisco," 150.

44. Frank Norris, *A Man's Woman* (Doubleday & McClure Co., 1900), 132, 196; hereafter cited parenthetically.

45. I should emphasize that events still occur within Norris's "philosophy of habit": as Bennett and Lloyd's "new life" of writing together "settle[s] quietly and evenly into its grooves a routine beg[ins] to develop," and there is "little variation in their daily life" (251, 263). But during the routine, this man's woman resuscitates his

ambition; she recapacitates him to be "a man, and not a professor" (255) by conjuring up the adventurer within him, refamiliarizing him with his former habits of body and mind, reminding him of an instinct that is no longer instinctual.

46. For an extended discussion of the writing in the novel in the context of impressionism's "fixation on the scene of writing," see Michael Fried, "Almayer's Face: On 'Impressionism' in Conrad, Crane, and Norris," *Critical Inquiry* 17 (Autumn 1990): 193–236.

47. Drawing attention to the repetition in Stephen Crane's *The Red Badge of Courage*, I myself have argued that "the novel's self-quotation instantiates the reproducibility we have come to associate foremost with photography." Bill Brown, *The Material Unconscious*, 157.

48. Gertrude Stein, "Portraits and Repetition," *Lectures in America* (1935; New York: Virago, 1985), 176–77.

49. This is what Lacan suggests in his beautiful "fable" of Prévert's collecting impulse. Eager as he is to differentiate Freud's collecting habits from Freud's psychoanalytic work, and eager to differentiate what "is called an object in the domain of collecting . . . from the meaning of object in psychoanalysis," Lacan nonetheless slips quickly from the phenomenological to the psychoanalytic. Prévert's matchboxes "were all the same and were laid out in an extremely agreeable way that involved each one being so close to the one next to it that the little drawer was slightly displaced. As a result, they were all threaded together so as to form a continuous ribbon that ran along the mantelpiece, climbed the wall, extended to the molding . . . I don't say that it went to infinity but it was extremely satisfying from an ornamental point of view." The point is that the matchboxes transcend their status as objects, "that in the form of an *Erscheneinung,* as it appeared in its truly imposing multiplicity, it may be a Thing." What Lacan recognizes about the matchbox, the thing he recognizes, could never be detected by seeing one matchbox in isolation. But if "the absurd character of this collection pointed to the thingness as match box . . . the Thing that subsists in a match box," Lacan goes on to proclaim that this "thing is not, of course, the Thing," which is fundamentally veiled and names the unsymbolizable Real in its totality (as interiority and exteriority). The story of the Thing that is not the Thing is another version of the story of an object-based epistemology that comes to have no faith in the epistemological power of objects, which is still the story of how anxieties and aspirations, frustrations and desires, are sublimated through the mediation of material objects. *The Ethics of Psychoanalysis 1959–60, The Seminar of Jacques Lacan, Book VII*, trans. Dennis Porter (New York: Norton, 1992), 113–14.

50. Gertrude Stein, *The Making of Americans: Being a History of a Family's Progress* (Normal, Ill.: Dalkey Archive Press, 1995), 146; hereafter cited parenthetically.

51. Just as iterative narration ("they *would leave* him") is replaced by the singulative ("they left him"), so the subject ("they") gradually shifts: "every one mostly left him to his fighting, to his brushing people away from around him . . . " (146).

52. "The feeling is of words themselves," Williams argues, "a curious immediate quality quite apart from their meaning." This is hardly to say, however, that Stein's work isn't mimetic; it just operates according to a different logic of mimesis: "Stein's pages have become like the United States viewed from an airplane—the

same senseless repetitions, the endless multiplications of toneless words." William Carlos Williams, "The Work of Gertrude Stein," in *Imaginations* (New York: New Directions, 1970), 345, 350.

53. Gertrude Stein, "Portraits and Repetition," 166; Proust, *Remembrance of Things Past*, 3:261.

54. Gilles Deleuze, *Difference and Repetition*, trans. Paul Patton (New York: Columbia University Press, 1994) 1, 5.

55. John Dewey, *Human Nature and Conduct* (New York: Henry Holt, 1922), 42; *Democracy and Education* (New York: Macmillan, 1916), 35. Habit, as Dewey originally understood it, emerges from a serial association that "has been so often performed that one act not only serves as a sign to consciousness that the next must be performed, but when the sign has become fused with the act signified" (*Psychology* [1887], *The Early Works 1882–1898* [Carbondale: Southern Illinois University Press, 1967], vol. 2, p. 101). "Habit" remains a profoundly important aspect of Dewey's philosophy as it develops from his psychological work (which attempts to orchestrate the experimental research of others) to his work in education and ethics. For a succinct overview, see John Thomas Kilbridge, "The Concept of Habit in the Philosophy of John Dewey," Ph.D. diss., University of Chicago, 1949.

56. Gertrude Stein, *A Long Gay Book*, in *A Stein Reader*, ed. Ulla E. Dydo (Evanston: Northwestern University Press, 1993), 159, 160, 245; hereafter cited parenthetically.

57. Leo Stein, *The A-B-C of Aesthetics* (New York: Boni and Liveright, 1927), 45, 49; hereafter cited parenthetically. This is what we might call a plain-spoken version of Heidegger's argument about how the hammer, in the moment that it breaks, calls our attention to itself as an object. Stein also uses the hammer as an example (48).

58. On the modernist antipathy to habit, see, for instance, Phil Fisher, who defines the modernist "gothic of everyday life" as that which "reanimates the terrifying and yet illuminating otherness of things, of our double connection to things as they are and things as we have diminished them in our structures of use and habit" ("The Failure of Habit," *Uses of Literature*, Harvard English Studies 4, ed. Monroe Engel [Cambridge, Mass.: Harvard University Press, 1973], 10). Within Fisher's essay, William James gets demonized as a rigid advocate of habit, which he is—with some notable exceptions. On the antipathy to habit in Western philosophy, see Paul Connerton, *How Societies Remember* (Cambridge: Cambridge University Press, 1989).

59. As Dewey would later put it, only a "hitch" in habit "provokes thought" (*Human Nature and Conduct*, 178).

60. George Santayana, *Interpretations of Poetry and Religion* (New York: Charles Scribner's Sons, 1900), 260.

61. Karl Marx, *Capital*, trans. Ben Fowkes (London: Penguin, 1990), vol. 1, p. 128. Georg Lukács, *History and Class Consciousness: Studies in Marxist Dialectics*, trans. Rodney Livingstone (Cambridge, Mass.: MIT Press, 1971), 92.

62. Theodor Adorno, *Minima Moralia: Reflections from Damaged Life*, trans. E. F. N. Jephcott (New York: Verso, 1978), 40. I am extrapolating the concept of "misuse value"—a value that resides outside (or in violation) of the dictates of use and exchange—from Adorno's characterization of children at play (227–28) as from

Walter Benjamin's prior characterization in *One-Way Street*, trans. Edmund Jeph-cott, *Selected Writings*, vol. 1, *1913–1926*, ed. Marcus Bullock and Michael W. Jennings [Cambridge, Mass.: Harvard University Press, 1996], 449–50, 464–66). On the role of the ludic for Benjamin, see Miriam Bratu Hansen, "Benjamin and Cinema: Not a One-Way Street," *Critical Inquiry* 25 (Winter 1999): 324. For other efforts to track the values of "misuse," see Bill Brown, "How To Do Things with Things (A Toy Story)," *Critical Inquiry* 24 (Summer 1998): 935–64; and Brown, "The Secret Life of Things (Virginia Woolf and the Matter of Modernism)," *Modernism and Modernity* 6 (Summer 1999): 1–28.

63. William Carlos Williams, *The Collected Earlier Poems* (New York: New Directions, 1966), 381. In one of the best accounts of that aesthetic in America, *The Real Thing: Imitation and Authenticity in American Culture, 1880–1940* (Chapel Hill: University of North Carolina Press, 1989), Miles Orvell concludes by addressing the "reframing, or simply framing" (292) that enabled Williams and Evans, Joseph Cornell, and Claes Oldenburg, to produce art out of quotidian waste. For a useful overview of the conceptualization of waste, see Jonathan Culler, "Rubbish Theory," *Framing the Sign: Criticism and its Institutions* (Norman: University of Oklahoma Press, 1988), 168–82.

64. Mary Douglass, *Purity and Danger: An Analysis of the Concepts of Pollution and Taboo* (London: ARK, 1984), 40.

65. David Hume, *An Enquiry Concerning Human Understanding* (Oxford: Oxford University Press, 1999), 109.

66. Immanuel Kant, *Prolegomena to Any Future Metaphysics*, trans. Paul Carus (Indianapolis: Hackett, 1977), par. 30.

CHAPTER THREE

1. *Sarah Orne Jewett Letters*, ed. Richard Cary (Waterville, Maine: Colby College Press, 1967), 108.

2. Richard H. Brodhead, *Cultures of Letters: Scenes of Reading and Writing in Nineteenth-Century America* (Chicago: University of Chicago Press, 1993), 176.

3. Willa Cather, "148 Charles Street," *Not Under Forty* (New York: Alfred A. Knopf, 1936), 61; Henry James, "Mr. And Mrs. James T. Fields," *Literary Criticism*, 2 vols. (New York: Library of America, 1984), vol. 1, pp. 165–66. Richard Brodhead quotes both remarks (*Cultures of Letters*, 234, n. 23).

4. Richard Brodhead, *Cultures of Letters*, 173.

5. *Sarah Orne Jewett Letters*, 95.

6. Paul Shorey, "Present Conditions of Literary Production," *Atlantic Monthly*, August 1896, p. 156. Shorey goes on to say that local color stories and sketches are the "most prosperous forms of literature to-day and contain the most promise for the immediate future" (164).

7. Willa Cather, "148 Charles Street," 63.

8. Richard Brodhead, *Cultures of Letters*, 134. All but needless to add, Brodhead is fully self-conscious about the maneuver. As he refrains from reading any of the sketches, and thus enables us to appreciate the sociological import of regionalism, Jewett becomes legible in and as the "Jewett-Fields milieu" (156), which doesn't mean her work is reducible to this milieu, only that this milieu was a condition of its circulability. The "genre defined by these place-centered literary features," Brod-

head writes, "served as the principal place of literary access in America in the post-bellum decades"; and he describes Jewett as the writer who "shows that literary regionalism" became "the site for the reconstruction of women's authorship on these terms" (116, 174). The region produced by regionalism as such, then, is the region of high culture, where "a new attention to the craftedly verbal or *formal* features of the work of art" make "the 'work' of art more a self-contained wrought object" (173).

9. Kenneth Burke, *A Grammar of Motives* (New York: Prentice Hall, 1945), 9.

10. Marcia McClintock Folsom, "'Tact Is a Kind of Mind-Reading': Emphatic Style in Sarah Orne Jewett's *The Country of the Pointed Firs*," *Colby Library Quarterly* 18, no. 1 (1982): 66–78; Richard Brodhead, *Cultures of Letters*, 147. As Brodhead adds parenthetically, "Jewett follows Wordsworth and George Eliot in this cult of an object world humanized through continuous association" (147). One could add several authors to Brodhead's list, and this is the place to mark my recognition of how extensive the "object matter of literature" is as a topic.

11. The phrase is from Steven Conn, *Museums and American Intellectual Life, 1876–1926* (Chicago: University of Chicago Press, 1998).

12. G. Staniland Wake, ed., *Memoirs of the International Congress of Anthropology* (Chicago: Schulte, 1894), vii.

13. Quoted by Robert W. Rydell, *All the World's a Fair: Visions of Empire at American International Expositions, 1876–1916* (Chicago: University of Chicago Press, 1984), 64. Putnam had been hired to direct the Exposition's anthropological exhibits.

14. The best sense of this era is provided by the essays in George W. Stocking Jr., ed., *Objects and Others: Essays on Museums and Material Culture* (Madison: University of Wisconsin Press, 1985). See also Steven Conn, *Museums and American Intellectual Life*, 75–114.

15. *Sarah Orne Jewett Letters*, 95. A slightly (but significantly) different version—"Don't try to write *about* people and things, tell them just as they are"—appears in Jewett, "Looking Back on Girlhood," in *Novels and Stories*, ed. Michael Davitt Bell (New York: Library of America, 1994), 759.

16. Otis Mason, quoted by Curtis M. Hinsley, *The Smithsonian and the American Indian: Making a Moral Anthropology in Victorian America* (Washington, D.C.: Smithsonian Institution Press, 1981), 89.

17. Barbara Kirshenblatt-Gimblett, "Objects of Ethnography," in *Exhibiting Cultures: The Poetics and Politics of Museum Display*, ed. Ivan Karp and Steven D. Lavine (Washington: Smithsonian Institution Press, 1991), 388.

18. Otis T. Mason, "Report on the Department of Ethnology in the U.S. National Museum 1885," *Annual Report of the United States National Museum, 1885* (Washington, D.C.: Government Printing Office, 1886), 63.

19. Clifford Geertz, *The Interpretation of Cultures* (New York: Basic Books, 1973), 412, 5. For an account of the costs of this "rapport," see George E. Marcus, "The Uses of Complicity in the Changing Mise-en-Scène of Anthropological Fieldwork," *Representations* 59 (Summer 1997): 85–108.

20. Frank Hamilton Cushing, "The Germ of Shore-Land Pottery: An Experimental Study," in *Memoirs of the International Congress of Anthropology*, ed. G. Staniland Wake, 217–34. On Cushing's work for *Century*, see Brad Evans, "Cushing's Zuni Sketchbooks: Literature, Anthropology, and American Notions of Culture," *American Quarterly* 49 (December 1997): 717–45. Despite my claim here, Cushing

also worked to make cultural (not technological) sense of objects in, for instance, his work on *Zuni Fetishes* (1883; rpt. Las Vegas: KC Publications, 1994). Of course, depending on how loosely one wishes to define "ethnographic writing," one could say that versions of it appear in the captivity narratives, in travel writing such as John Bartram's, and in Herodotus's *Histories*. Though this chapter will not address genres of ethnographic writing, I should say that Franz Boas's "A Year Among the Eskimo" (1887) begins with the kind of generic apologia that could serve as a preface to any of Jewett's collections of sketches: he explains that he will not be providing "exciting adventures, such as shipwrecks and narrow escapes" but rather must be content to describe "the daily life of the inhabitants of these ice-bound coasts" (George W. Stocking Jr., ed., *A Franz Boas Reader: The Shaping of American Anthropology, 1883–1911* [Chicago: University of Chicago Press, 1974], 44).

21. It is difficult to overemphasize the popularity of local-color writing in America in the closing three decades of the century, and this includes writing that is irreducible to regionalist fiction. While the public taste for the local is clearly supplanted by the taste for romance in the late 1890s—the serialization of *The Tory Lover* (1900–1901), Jewett's own effort in the genre, conveniently marks the end of an era—the taste is in fact satisfied by other literary and nonliterary forms: the Western (which in the hands of writers like Zane Gray effectively combines local colorism and romance), books of photographic views, filmic travelogues, etc. Moreover, we may think of the temporal remoteness of the historical romance as a substitute for the spatial remoteness of regionalism, no doubt satisfying some of the same desires.

22. Eric Sundquist, "Realism and Regionalism," *Columbia Literary History of the United States*, ed. Emory Elliott (New York: Columbia University Press, 1988), 503; Amy Kaplan, "Nation, Region, Empire," *The Columbia History of the American Novel*, ed. Emory Elliott (New York: Columbia University Press, 1991), 252; Richard Brodhead, *Cultures of Letters*, 121. See also Sandra A. Zagarell, "Troubling Regionalism: Rural Life and the Cosmopolitan Eye in Jewett's *Deephaven*," *American Literary History* 10 (1998): 639–63. A notable exception to the casualness of the equation between ethnographic and regionalist writing is to be found in Brad Evans, "The Ethnographic Imagination in American Literature: A Genealogy of Cultures, 1865–1930," Ph.D. diss., University of Chicago, 1997.

23. Sarah Orne Jewett, *The Country of the Pointed Firs*, in *Novels and Stories*, 399.

24. Sarah Orne Jewett, *Deephaven*, in *Novels and Stories*, 111, 16–17.

25. See any historical portion of the *Annual Report*, for instance, G. Brown Goode, "Report Upon the Condition and Progress of the United States National Museum During the Year Ending June 30, 1893," *Annual Report of the U.S. National Museum, 1893* (Washington, D.C.: Government Printing Office, 1895), 3–10.

26. G. Brown Goode, "Museum-History and Museums in History" (1888), *Annual Report of the U. S. National Museum, 1897*. Part II. (Washington:, D.C.: Government Printing Office, 1901), 72; Goode, "The Museums of the Future," *Annual Report of the U.S. National Museum, 1889* (Washington, D.C.: Government Printing Office, 1891), 427.

27. Curtis Hinsley, "From Shell-Heaps to Stellae: Early Anthropology at the Peabody Museum," in George W. Stocking Jr., *Objects and Others*, 60.

28. G. Brown Goode, "The Museums of the Future," 427.

NOTES TO PAGES 88-91

29. The classic account of this estrangement appears in Georg Simmel, *The Philosophy of Money*, trans. Tom Bottomore, David Frisby, and Kaethe Mengelberg (New York: Routledge, 1990), 448-52.

30. Ralph Waldo Emerson, "The Uses of Natural History," *The Early Lectures of Ralph Waldo Emerson*, ed. Stephen Whicher, Robert E. Spiller, and Wallace E. Williams (Cambridge, Mass.: Harvard University Press, 1959), vol. 1, p. 24.

31. George W. Stocking Jr., "Franz Boas and the Culture Concept in Historical Perspective," *Race, Culture, and Evolution: Essays in the History of Anthropology, 1883-1911* (Chicago: University of Chicago Press, 1982), 195-233.

32. Franz Boas, "The Principles of Ethnological Classification," *Science* (1887), in George W. Stocking Jr., *A Franz Boas Reader*, 61.

33. For an overview, see Curtis M. Hinsley, *The Smithsonian and the American Indian*, 83-123.

34. Otis T. Mason, "Ethnological Exhibit of the Smithsonian Institution at the World's Columbian Exposition," in *Memoirs of the International Congress of Anthropology*, ed. G. Staniland Wake, 215. For a twenty-first-century reader, the regionalist temper can be defamiliarized by a different report to the Congress, Gerald M. West's "Anthropometry of American School Children," which tried to determine the "laws governing the development of children" by measuring children of different cities. Worcester children were found "markedly above the average in stature," whereas Boston children "are almost as markedly at the opposite extreme," and Milwaukee children "represent more nearly the average" (*Memoirs*, 50, 52). The transience that characterizes modernity and postmodernity hardly admits any such presumptions about geo-environmental specificity within the U.S.

35. Otis T. Mason, "Progress of Anthropology in 1890," *Annual Report of the Smithsonian Institution for the Year 1890* (Washington: Government Printing Offices, 1891), 527.

36. G. Brown Goode, "Report Upon the Condition and Progress of the United States National Museum in 1884," *Annual Report of the U.S. National Museum, 1884* (Washington, D.C.: Government Printing Office, 1885), 57; Goode, "Report Upon the Exhibit of the Smithsonian Institution and the U.S. National Museum at the Cotton States and International Exposition, Atlanta, GA., 1895," *Annual Report of the Smithsonian Institution for the Year 1896* (Washington, D.C.: Government Printing Offices, 1898), 614. One can understand Goode's commentary in terms of what Tony Bennett has called "The Exhibitionary Complex," *The Birth of the Museum* (New York: Routledge, 1995), 59-88. Goode's ideals for the field of ethnology recapitulate Louis Aggasiz's objectives in the field of natural history, as exemplified by his *Essay on Classification* (1859). For the impact of such objectives on humanistic thinking, see Lee Rust Brown, *The Emerson Museum: Practical Romanticism and the Pursuit of the Whole* (Cambridge, Mass.: Harvard University Press, 1997), especially chap. 2.

37. Michel Foucault, *The Order of Things: An Archaeology of the Human Sciences* (New York: Random House, 1973), 137.

38. "The Naturalist," *The Early Lectures of Ralph Waldo Emerson*, vol. 1, p. 75.

39. Michel Foucault, *The Order of Things*, 133.

40. Lucy Larcom, *A New England Girlhood* (1889; Boston: Northeastern University Press, 1986), 17.

41. Otis Mason, "Progress of Anthropology in 1890," 528.

42. *Sarah Orne Jewett Letters*, 19–20.

43. On realist and naturalist typology, see Lee Rust Brown, *The Emerson Museum*, who quotes from Balzac's Preface to the *Comédie humaine:* "There have always been, and always will be, social species just as there are biological species" (140); Susan Mizruchi, "Fiction and the Science of Society," *The Columbia History of the American Novel*, ed. Emory Elliott, 189–215; Mark Seltzer, *Bodies and Machines* (New York: Routledge, 1992), 106–13; Bill Brown, *The Material Unconscious: American Amusement, Stephen Crane, and the Economies of Play* (Cambridge, Mass.: Harvard University Press, 1996), 221–24.

44. My thanks to Catherine Gallagher for suggesting that a "labor theory of value" lurks within those objects that become "cultural things." I should add, though, that the study and display of objects outside the life-group seemed as fascinated by play as by work. Indeed, Stewart Culin made his reputation on the display of games at the Columbian World Exhibition. See, for instance, his "Chinese Games with Dice and Dominoes," *Report of the U.S. National Museum, 1893* (Washington: Government Printing Office, 1895), 489–538. In an a brief summary of the anthropological, psychological, and aesthetic thought of the period, I myself have argued that "play, not work," began to appear as "the mode through which a culture expresses itself" (*The Material Unconscious*, 9); the life-group exhibits, though, don't participate in this shift. On the life-group in relation to the tableau in the work of Edith Wharton, see Nancy Bentley, *The Ethnography of Manners: Hawthorne, James, Wharton* (New York: Cambridge University Press, 1995), 163–76.

45. One needs to qualify the sentimental here because it is aesthetic rather than instrumental. As Brodhead crucially puts it, in an effort to interrupt the genealogy of women's writing in America, "literary writing is a *different thing* from the work of piety or nurture, an activity they have no part in" (*Cultures of Letters*, 161).

46. I'm borrowing the phrase "sentimental materialism" from Lori Merish, who reads, in Caroline Kirkland's sketches of frontier life, above all *A New Home, Who'll Follow?* (1839), the literary origin of the "partially secular belief in the psychological and social significance of common household objects and the import of these objects in the symbolic ecology of the self" (*Sentimental Materialism: Gender, Commodity Culture, and Nineteenth-Century American Literature* [Durham: Duke University Press, 2000], 115).

47. Mark B. Sandberg, "Effigy and Narrative: Looking into the Nineteenth-Century Folk Museum," in *Cinema and the Invention of Modern Life*, ed. Leo Charney and Vanessa R. Schwartz (Berkeley: University of California Press, 1995), 345.

48. Jewett did indeed attend the fair, and "The Flight of Betsey Lane" (*Novels and Stories*, 787–808), which she published in *Scribner's* in 1893, concerns not the Chicago fair of that year but its Philadelphia predecessor. A sixty-nine-year-old woman who "looked much older" (789) leaves the Bayfleet Poor-house and manages to get to Philadelphia, where what impresses her most is that "you feel's if you'd be'n all round the world" (807) because of the people you meet: "I've talked with folks from Chiny an' the back o'Pennsylvany; and I see folks way from Australy that 'peared as well as anybody" (807). Given the way writers described fairgoers, Betsey Lane herself might have been the object of fascination, but it is she who is fascinated by others. And if these characters all seem to be the object of a kind of

ethnographic attention it may well be because people—as life-groups or as living groups—were increasingly displayed as part of international expositions. Rebecca Harding Davis reported that "Thousands of poor teachers, farmer's daughters, young girls from the West and New England, with eager brains and almost empty pockets, come every week, take a room at some cheap neighboring hotel, and eat where and how they can" ("A Rainy Day at the Exposition," *Harper's Weekly*, 18 November 1876, 930). Davis's article is an interesting instantiation of the ethnographic genre that fairs typically produce: the account of fairgoers' habits and customs. It more importantly suggests that the Centennial marked a moment when single women could enter a public space by themselves, thus anticipating the function of such amusement sites as Coney Island and movie theaters. See Kathy Peiss, *Cheap Amusements: Working Women and Leisure in Turn-of-the-Century New York* (Philadelphia: Temple University Press, 1986) and Miriam Hansen, *Babel and Babylon: Spectatorship in American Silent Film* (Cambridge, Mass.: Harvard University Press, 1991).

49. Donald G. Mitchell, "In and About the Fair," *Scribner's Monthly* 12 (October 1876): 891.

50. James D. McCabe, *The Illustrated History of the Centennial Exhibition* (Philadelphia: National Publishing, 1876), 618–19.

51. G. Brown Goode, "Report Upon the Exhibit of the Smithsonian Institution," 634.

52. Franz Boas, quoted by Ira Jacknis, "Franz Boas and Exhibits: On the Limitations of the Museum Method of Anthropology," in George W. Stocking Jr., *Objects and Others*, 110.

53. See Curtis Hinsley, *The Smithsonian and the American Indian*, 90.

54. My dichotomy is derived from Michael Fried, *Absorption and Theatricality: Painting and Beholder in the Age of Diderot* (Chicago: University of Chicago Press, 1988).

55. See, for instance, William Leach, *Land of Desire: Merchants, Power, and the Rise of a New American Culture* (New York: Pantheon Books, 1993), 64–65; and Donna Harraway, "Teddy Bear Patriarchy: Taxidermy in the Garden of Eden, New York City, 1908–1936," *Primate Visions: Gender, Race, and Nature in the World of Modern Science* (New York, Routledge, 1989), 26–58. The American genealogy can be traced back to Peale's museum.

56. G. Brown Goode, 1893 *Report*, 56; Franz Boas quoted by Ira Jacknis, "Franz Boas and Exhibits," 102. See also Gary Kulik, "Designing the Past: History-Museum Exhibition from Peale to the Present," in *History Museums in the United States: A Critical Assessment*, ed. Warren Leon and Roy Rosenzweig (Urbana: University of Illinois Press, 1989), 10.

57. See Marie-Hélène Huet, *Monstrous Imagination* (Cambridge: Harvard University Press, 1993), 188–218.

58. Rebecca Harding Davis, "Odd Corners at the Exposition," *Harper's Weekly*, 25 November 1876, 950.

59. *Sarah Orne Jewett Letters*, 29.

60. Richard Brodhead, *Cultures of Letters*, 160–61.

61. Norman Bryson, *Looking at the Overlooked: Four Essays on Still Life Painting* (Cambridge, Mass.: Harvard University Press, 1990), 60. Bryson's point may seem

to offer a heuristic distinction between the Americans and their predecessors, but the distinction doesn't always hold up. The paintings of Cornelius Gijsbrechts, for instance, contain many of the elements of a Peto painting—pens and sheets of music, for instance, objects that evoke temporality by being utensils of a familiar activity. Alfred Frankenstein produced the path-breaking book on the American trompe l'oeil tradition, emphasizing the narrative dimension of the work (*After the Hunt: William Harnett and Other American Still Life Painters, 1870-1900* [Berkeley: University of California Press, 1969]). See also William Gerdts, *Painters of the Humble Truth: Masterpieces of American Still Life, 1801-1939* (Columbia, Mo.: University of Missouri Press, 1981). The discussion of American still-life has recently achieved a completely new historical and phenomenological dimension in Alex Nemerov, *The Body of Raphaelle Peale: Still Life and Selfhood, 1812-1824* (Berkeley: University of California Press, 2001).

62. The death of Peto's father in 1895, coupled with his own declining health, seems to have contributed to the thick nostalgia of these late paintings. Indeed, one of the objects, the knife, was a family souvenir picked up from the battlefield of Gettysburg. John Wilmerding, *Important Information Inside: The Art of John F. Peto and the Idea of Still-Life Painting in Nineteenth-Century America* (Washington, D.C.: National Gallery of Art, 1983), 172.

63. Karl Marx, *Economic and Philosophic Manuscripts*, in *Early Writings*, trans. Rodney Livingstone and Gregory Benton (New York: Penguin, 1992), 389.

64. Henry James, *American Scene* (1907; Bloomington: Indiana University Press, 1968), 383-89.

65. Of course, it is crucial that the novel recounts a *return*, which enables the narrator to appear fully accustomed to the local customs. In "From a Mournful Villager," her most explicitly nostalgic sketch about the "approaching extinction" of "village character and civilization," she emphasizes the "customs," the "old traditions," the "customs and ideas . . . [that] followed from a force of habit" (*Novels and Stories*, 585). That force of habit might be said to have materializing or dematerializing effects, about which see chap. 2.

66. Lucy Larcom, *New England Girlhood*, 148-50.

67. Gaston Bachelard, *The Poetics of Space*, trans. Maria Jolas (Boston: Beacon Press, 1969), 203; hereafter cited parenthetically.

68. Elizabeth Ammons, "Material Culture, Empire, and Jewett's *Country of the Pointed Firs*," in *New Essays on the Country of the Pointed Firs*, ed. June Howard (New York: Cambridge University Press, 1993), 81-82. Ammons quotes St. George.

69. See, for instance, Thomas J. Schlereth, "Pioneers of Material Culture: Teaching History with American Things," *Cultural History and Material Culture: Everyday Life, Landscapes, Museums* (Charlottesville: University Press of Virginia, 1990), 331-45. For a contemporary field-constituting definition, see Jules David Prown, "Mind in Matter: An Introduction to Material Culture Theory and Method," *Winterthur Portfolio* 17 (Spring 1982): 1-19. For approaches to the study of material culture, see Ian M. G. Quimby, ed. *Material Culture and the Study of American Life* (New York: Norton, 1978); Simon J. Bronner, *Grasping Things: Folk Material Culture and Mass Society in America* (Lexington: University of Kentucky Press, 1986); and Steven Lubar and W. David Kingery, *History from Things: Essays on Material Culture* (Washington, D.C.: Smithsonian Institution Press, 1993). For the most sig-

nificant collection of essays from the turn-of-the-century, see Simon J. Bronner, ed. *Folklife Studies from the Gilded Age: Object, Rite, and Custom in Victorian America* (Ann Arbor: UMI Research Press, 1987).

70. Anon., "Recent Studies in American History," *Atlantic Monthly,* June 1896, pp. 837–40.

71. Theodore Roosevelt, "History as Literature" (1912), in *Theodore Roosevelt: An American Mind—A Selection from His Writings,* ed. Mario R. DiNunzio (New York: Penguin, 1995), 112–13.

72. Edward Eggleston, *The Beginners of a Nation: A History of the Source and Rise of the Earliest English Settlements in America With Special Reference to the Life and Character of the People* (New York: D. Appleton and Co., 1896). In a summary that neglects the work of Eggleston, but represents the dominant attitude of the American Historical Association that was formed in 1884, Gary Kulik writes that "the first professional historians had no interest in things. They were preoccupied with words—constitutions, charters, treaties—and they defined their subject in ways that precluded the study of ordinary people" ("Designing the Past," 12).

73. Thomas J. Schlereth, "Pioneers of Material Culture," 335. On the living history museum, see Warren Leon and Margaret Pitt, "Living-History Museums," in *History Museums in the United States,* ed. Warren Leon and Roy Rosenzweig, 64–97.

74. Eggleston, *Beginners of a Nation,* 59–60. For a separate account of Eggleston's work on the James River, see "Nathaniel Bacon, the Patriot of 1676," *Century* 40 (July 1890): 418–35.

75. Michael Kammen, *Mystic Chords of Memory: The Transformation of Tradition in American Culture* (New York: Knopf, 1991), 96, 141.

76. Constance Cary Harrison, "A Little Centennial Lady," *Scribner's Monthly* 12 (July 1876): 301.

77. Henry C. Mercer, *Tools of the Nation Maker* (1897), in *Folklife Studies,* ed. Simon J. Bronner, 281.

78. Sarah Orne Jewett, "The Queen's Twin," in *Novels and Stories,* 505; hereafter cited parenthetically.

79. When, writing to Annie Fields, Jewett lamented the diminishing length of her sketches, she described them in terms of smaller and smaller material objects: "They used to be as long as yardsticks, they are now as long as spools, and they will soon be the size of old-fashioned peppermints, and have neither beginning or end, but shape and flavor may still be left them" (*The Letters of Sarah Orne Jewett,* ed. Annie Fields [Boston: Houghton Mifflin, 1911], 81). Rather than a fragile object that one admires always from a slight distance, she offers an object that must be consumed physically, and not *seen* at a distance but touched and tasted—the sense of taste, like that of smell, in fact denying size as an important determinant, giving sensuous access to something like what Bachelard considers the vastness of the miniature (161). As the peppermint in your mouth gets smaller and smaller, the taste gets bigger.

80. *Sarah Orne Jewett Letters,* 81.

81. Donald G. Mitchell, "In and About the Fair," *Scribner's Monthly* 12 (September 1876): 747. Karal Ann Marling, who describes the exhibit at some length, notes that the idea was borrowed from the Vienna Exposition of 1873, where ethnic food was served by people in ethnic dress (*George Washington Slept Here: Colonial Re-*

vivals and American Culture 1876–1986 [Cambridge, Mass.: Harvard University Press, 1988], 37).

82. Anon., "The Centennial," *Harper's Weekly,* 23 September 1876, p. 781.

83. Otis T. Mason, "Ethnological Exhibit of the Smithsonian Institution at the Wolrd's Columbian Exposition," 215.

84. Stewart Culin, "The Road to Beauty," *Brooklyn Museum Quarterly* 14 (April 1927): 46. Quoted by Simon J. Bronner, "Object Lessons: The Work of Ethnological Museums and Collections," in *Consuming Visions: Accumulation and Display of Goods in America, 1880–1920,* ed. Simon J. Bronner (New York: Norton, 1989), 231. For an account of his award-winning exhibit at the Columbian Exposition, see Culin, "Exhibit of Games in the Columbian Exposition," *Journal of American Folklore* 6 (1893): 205–27.

85. Karl Marx, *Capital* (New York: Penguin, 1990), vol. 1, pp. 209, 1054.

86. Stewart Culin, quoted by Simon Bronner, "Object Lessons," 232.

87. L. Frank Baum, *The Art of Decorating Dry Goods Windows and Interiors* (Chicago: National Window Trimmers' Association, 1900), 86.

88. Stuart Culver, "What Manikins Want: *The Wonderful Wizard of Oz* and *The Art of Decorating Dry Goods Windows,*" *Representations* 21 (Winter 1988): 97–116. See also William Leach, *Land of Desire,* 55–61, 247–60. As Leach puts it, in a separate essay, Baum's fiction is "the literary apotheosis of commodity flow. In the Land of Oz, things are always animated, always metamorphosing" ("Strategists of Display and the Production of Desire," in *Consuming Visions,* ed. Bronner, 108).

89. L. Frank Baum, *The Wizard of Oz,* in *The Wonderful World of Oz* (New York: Penguin, 1998), 96.

90. See, for instance, Christopher Flint, "Speaking Objects: The Circulation of Stories in Eighteenth-Century Prose Fiction," *PMLA* (March 1998): 212–26; and Jonathan Lamb, "Modern Metamorphoses and Disgraceful Tales," *Critical Inquiry* 28 (Autumn 2001): 133–67.

91. Herbert Spencer, *The Principles of Sociology,* 3d ed. (1897; Westport, Conn.: Greenwood Press, 1975), vol. 1, p. 311.

92. See William Pietz's influential history of the concept of fetishism, especially "The problem of the fetish, IIIa: Bosman's Guinea and the enlightenment theory of fetishism," *Res* 16 (Autumn 1988): 106. Also parts 1 and 2, *Res* 9 (Spring 1985): 5–17, and *Res* 13 (Spring 1987): 23–45.

93. On the power of the sentimental artifact, see Gillian Brown, *Domestic Individualism: Imagining Self in Nineteenth-Century America* (Berkeley: University of California Press, 1990), 41–53; Lynn Wardley, "Relic, Fetish, Femmage: The Aesthetics of Sentiment in the Work of Stowe," *Yale Journal of Criticism* 5 (Fall 1992): 165–91; Joanne Dobson, "Reclaiming Sentimental Literature," *American Literature* 69 (June 1997): 263–88. On Colombia, see Michael T. Taussig, *The Devil and Commodity Fetishism in South America* (Chapel Hill: University of North Carolina Press, 1980). Positing fetishism as a means of disrupting the institutional systems by which objects are displayed, James Clifford writes that this personal fetishism "would accord to things in collections the power to fixate rather than simply the capacity to edify or inform." The objects would become "sources of fascination with the power to disconcert. Seen in their resistance to classification they could remind us of our *lack* of self-possession, of the artifices we employ to gather a world around us" (*The*

Predicament of Culture: Twentieth-Century Ethnography, Literature, and Art [Cambridge, Mass.: Harvard University Press,1988], 229).

94. Charles W. Chesnutt, *The Conjure Woman* (1899; Ann Arbor: University of Michigan Press, 1969), 57.

95. Karal Ann Marling, *George Washington Slept Here*, 36, 33.

96. As Ira Jacknis describes the museum disputes, Boas found himself faced, all over again, with administrators eager to display material according to functional typology or material typology, and convinced that the museum was responsible for exhibiting the evolution of man from the primitive to the complex. ("Franz Boas and Exhibits," 107).

97. In response to the narrator's neglect of the Indian relics, readers have pointed out how the violence against Native Americans remains suppressed in Jewett's fiction. The work of "historicizing Jewett," which qualified a feminist celebration of her, drew attention to her complicity in the racist, nativist, exclusionist ideology of a threatened New England genteel culture. See June Howard, ed., *New Essays on the Country of the Pointed Firs*. Jewett's treatment of the Indian relics, as I'm trying to focus it through historical epistemology, belongs to a somewhat more remote story in American culture, the story of how culture (and the individual within culture) can or cannot be known. The trajectory of Jewett criticism has become the object of considerable scrutiny. See June Howard, "Unraveling Regions, Unsettling Periods: Sarah Orne Jewett and American Literary History," *American Literature* 68 (1996): 365–84; and Marjorie Pryse, "Sex, Class, and 'Category Crisis': Reading Jewett's Transitivity," *American Literature* 70 (1998): 517–49. Jacqueline Shea Murphy has conducted a compelling literary-critical experiment of integrating Jewett's tales with Native American tales, working to fashion a more palimpsestic history of the region's American cultures ("Replacing Regionalism: Abenaki Tales and 'Jewett's' Coastal Maine," *American Literary History* 10 [1998]: 664–97).

98. G. Brown Goode, quoted by Gary Kulik, "Designing the Past," 9.

99. Walter Benn Michaels, *Our America: Nativism, Modernism, and Pluralism* (Durham: Duke University Press, 1997).

100. F. W. Putnam, "The First Notice of the Pine Grove or Forest River Shellheap," *Bulletin of the Essex Institute* 15 (1883): 86–92. For an account of Putnam's own work, in the company of geologists and naturalists, see Jeffries Wyman, "An Account of Some Kjoekkenmoeddings, or Shell-Heaps, in Maine and Massachusetts," *The American Naturalist* 1 (January 1868): 561–83. For a brief overview of early excavation, see Andrew L. Christenson, "The Identification and Study of Indian Shell Middens in Eastern North America: 1643–1861," *North American Archaeologist* 6, no. 3 (1985): 227–43.

101. Rossiler Johnson, ed., *A History of the World's Columbian Exposition Held in Chicago in 1893*, 4 vols. (New York: Appleton and Co., 1897), vol. 2, p. 320.

102. Henry David Thoreau, *The Maine Woods*, in Thoreau, *A Week on the Concord and Merrimack Rivers; Walden, or, Life in the Woods; The Maine Woods; Cape Cod*, ed. Robert F. Sayre (New York: Library of America, 1985), 646.

103. S. Weir Mitchell, "The Scientific Life," *Lippincott's Magazine* 15 (March 1875): 356.

104. Charles Egbert Craddock [Mary Murfree], *In the "Stranger People's'"* *Country* (New York: Harper and Brothers, 1891), 90, 15.

105. Sarah Orne Jewett, "Looking Back on Girlhood," 754.

106. Hannah Arendt, *The Human Condition* (Chicago: University of Chicago Press, 1958), 167-74.

107. Harriet Beecher Stowe, *The Minister's Wooing* (Hartford: Stowe-Day Foundation, 1994), 650-51.

108. See Marshall Sahlins, *Culture and Practice: Collected Essays* (New York: Zone Books, 2000), 541-47.

109. James Chandler, *England in 1819: The Politics of Literary Culture and the Case of Romantic Historicism* (Chicago: University of Chicago Press, 1998), xiii.

110. The most sustained account of this post-romantic project is still J. Hillis Miller, *Poets of Reality: Six Twentieth-Century Writers* (Cambridge, Mass.: Belknap Press, 1965).

111. See, for example William Rubin, ed., *"Primitivism" in 20th Century Art: Affinity of the Tribal and the Modern*, 2 vols. (New York: Museum of Modern Art, 1984); and James Clifford, "On Ethnographic Surrealism," in *The Predicament of Culture*, 117-51.

112. *Contact* 1 (December 1920): 10.

113. John Dewey, "Americanism and Localism," *The Middle Works, 1899-1924*, (Carbondale: Southern Illinois University Press, 1982), vol. 12, pp. 13-16.

114. Steven Conn, *Museums and American Intellectual Life*, 31. Recent claims (from the university) that discursive iteration effects materiality thus begin to sound like the inevitable telos of this fundamental shift in the scene of knowledge production: an inversion—or specular completion—of the faith that matter might express a "proposition," "several propositions."

115. Boas quoted by Ira Jacknis, "Franz Boas and Exhibits," 87.

116. Lewis Mumford, for instance, celebrates the novel because of its capacity to exhibit both the scientist's passion for fact and the symbolist's passion for meaning (*Herman Melville* [New York: Harcourt, Brace, and Co., 1929], 162-64). On Melville's cannonization, see Clare L. Spark, *Hunting Captain Ahab: Psychological Warfare and the Melville Revival* (Kent, Ohio: Kent State University Press, 2001).

117. Herman Melville, *Moby-Dick or, The Whale* (New York: Penguin, 1992), 22.

118. For a detailed analysis of the novel in the context of antebellum ethnology and other social sciences, see Samuel Otter, *Melville's Anatomies* (Berkeley: University of California Press, 1999), 101-71.

119. On the diminishment of local-color fiction, see Louis A. Renza, *"A White Heron" and the Question of Minor Literature* (Madison: University of Wisconsin Press, 1984).

120. Willa Cather, *The Professor's House* (New York: Knopf, 1925), 16; hereafter cited parenthetically.

121. Eve Kosofsky Sedgwick rightly calls this "the gorgeous homosocial romance of two men on a mesa in New Mexico" (*Tendencies* [Durham: Duke University Press, 1993], 174).

122. Willa Cather, "Paul's Case: A Study in Temperment," in *Five Stories* (New York: Vintage Books, 1956), 169.

123. Tom does not, however, "play Indian" as white Americans did throughout the nineteenth century (see Philip Deloria, *Playing Indian* [New Haven: Yale University Press, 1998]). Nor does he "become" an Indian by assimilating within a tribe, as did Frank Hamilton Cushing. Rather, he has a feel for ancestry among the rocks of the ruin; this is a spiritual connection, not a physical enactment.

124. Walter Benn Michaels, *Our America*, 44.

125. The basic story is told by Don Watson, *Indians of the Mesa Verde* (Mesa Verde, Colo.: Mesa Verde Museum Association, 1959), 9–28. Watson voices all the passionate convictions about the life of the past remaining artifactually present: "Each storage bin is chinked with a farmer's prayers for a bountiful harvest. In each plastered kiva wall is an ancient priest's reverence for his gods. A pot is not just a piece of baked clay: it is an ancient potter's moulded prayer for beauty and strength" (4). Cather not only follows this history closely—the original sighting of Cliff Palace in the snow, the discovery of mummified humans—she all but quotes the account of the discovery offered by Charles Mason, published in the Denver *Post* in 1917 (see, for instance, Watson, 18–21). See also Florence C. Lister and Robert H. Lister, *Earl Morris and Southwestern Archaeology* (Albuquerque: University of New Mexico Press, 1968), 1–23. In the same era, because of the tourism promoted by the railroad, the competition for artifacts provoked the "mass production" of pottery, "and the beginning of a stylistic revival" among the Hopi (Edwin L. Wade, "The Ethnic Art Market in the American Southwest 1880–1980," in *Objects and Others*, ed. George W. Stocking Jr., 171).

126. Walter Benn Michaels, *Our America*, 35.

127. Gail Levin, "American Art," in *"Primitivism" in 20th Century Art*, ed. William Rubin, vol. 2, pp. 453–73. Marsden Hartley, "Red Man Ceremonials: An American Plea for American Esthetics," *Art and Archeology* 9 (January 1920): 14.

128. Edward Sapir, "Culture, Genuine and Spurious" (1924), in Sapir, *Selected Writings on Language, Culture, and Personality*, ed. David G. Mandelbaum (Berkeley: University of California Press, 1985), 318. See also Sapir, *The Psychology of Culture: A Course of Lectures*, ed. Judith T. Irvine (New York: Mouton de Gruyter, 1994).

129. Gail Levin, "American Art," 456.

CHAPTER FOUR

1. *Henry James: Letters*, vol. 3 (1883–1895), ed. Leon Edel (Cambridge, Mass.: Belknap Press, 1980), 43, 42, 9.

2. Lewis Mumford, *The Golden Day* (New York: Boni and Liveright, 1926), 203, 200–201.

3. For details about the Curtis family, see Stanley Olson, *John Singer Sargent: His Portrait* (New York: St. Martin's Press, 1986), 84–86; and Elaine Kilmurray and Richard Ormond, *John Singer Sargent* (Princeton: Princeton University Press, 1998), 14.

4. In *Henry James 1882–1895: The Middle Years* (Philadelphia: Lippincott, 1962), Leon Edel quotes this expression of James's attachment from a letter to Elizabeth Boot, 2 June 1984 (108). In his edition of the *Letters*, though, the line does not appear in this letter (vol. 3, pp. 41–44), which remains nonetheless the best published source for appreciating James's first reactions to Sargent.

5. Henry James, "John S. Sargent," *Harper's New Monthly Magazine* 75 (October 1887): 682. James changed this formulation in his revised version of the essay, from which I quote below.

6. For instance, Stanley Olson writes of Sargent's portrait of Mrs. Henry Marquand: "His Mrs. Marquand was sober, refined, kindly but undemonstrative. She has seated comfortably in a cushioned Chippendale chair, wearing black, with a delicate lace fichu, collar and cuffs. The colouring was sombre and restrained. He turned her into a fine piece of reproduction Hepplewhite" (*John Singer Sargent: His Portrait,* 137). About the slightly later work of the Boston School, and in particular the paintings William McGregor Paxton painted from 1910 to 1916, Jean-Christophe Agnew writes of the "figurative dissolution" of the human subjects "into a more lively background of household objects" ("A House of Fiction: Domestic Interiors and the Commodity Aesthetic," in *Consuming Visions: Accumulation and Display of Goods in America, 1880–1920,* ed. Simon J. Bronner [New York: Norton, 1989], 146).

7. Henry James, "John S. Sargent" (1887, revised 1893), in *The Painter's Eye: Notes and Pictorial Essays,* ed. John L. Sweeney (Cambridge, Mass.: Harvard University Press, 1956), 217.

8. *Letters,* vol. 3, p. 43. For James's concern with Sargent's brilliance, see also Henry James, "The Guildhall and Royal Academy," in *The Painter's Eye,* 256–57; and see Leon Edel, *Henry James 1882–1895: The Middle Years,* 110.

9. From a review in *Art Amateur,* July 1883, quoted in Kilmurray and Ormond, *John Singer Sargent,* 98. Subsequent art criticism has remarked, in passing, how the children assume a thing-like status: Albert Boime, for instance, describes the "decorative reduction of the dispersed sisters to the level of the blue and white Chinese vases" ("Sargent in Paris and London: A Portrait of the Artist as Dorian Gray," in *John Singer Sargent,* ed. Patricia Hills [New York: Whitney Museum of American Art, 1986], 79); and David Lubin insists (somewhat curiously) that the central, youngest girl "must be viewed as a part of that rug" (*Acts of Portrayal: Eakins, Sargent, James* [New Haven: Yale University Press, 1985], 83).

10. Henry James, *Portrait of a Lady,* in *Henry James: Novels 1881–1886* (New York: Library of America, 1985), 560.

11. In Leon Edel's words, the two "must have seemed to each other, in certain respects, mirror-images" (Leon Edel, *Henry James 1882–1895: The Middle Years,* 109).

12. Guy Debord, *Society of the Spectacle* (Detroit: Black and Red, 1983), no. 17.

13. William James, *Principles of Psychology* (1890; Cambridge, Mass.: Harvard University press, 1983), 279.

14. Henry James, "Preface" to *Portrait of a Lady, Literary Criticism, Volume Two* (New York: Library of America, 1984), 1071.

15. In what remains an interesting overview of the topic, see Charles R. Anderson, *Person, Place, and Thing in Henry James's Novels* (Durham, N.C.: Duke University Press, 1977). And see, for a historical range of approaches to the novels I consider in this chapter: Lotus Snow, "'A Story of Cabinets and Chairs and Tables': Images of Morality in *The Spoils of Poynton* and *The Golden Bowl,*" *ELH* 30 (1963): 413–35; Adeline R. Tinter, "'The Old Things': Balzac's *Le Curé de Tours* and James's *Spoils of Poynton,*" *Nineteenth Century Fiction* 26 (1972): 436–55; Judith Ryan, "Validating the Possible: Thoughts and Things in James, Rilke, and Musil,"

Comparative Literature 40, no. 4 (Fall 1988): 1–13; Stephen D. Arata, "Object Lessons: Reading the Museum in *The Golden Bowl*," in *Famous Last Words: Changes in Gender and Narrative Closure*, ed. Alison Booth (Charlottesville: University Press of Virginia, 1993), 199–229; Fotios Sarris, "Fetishism in *The Spoils of Poynton*," *Nineteenth Century Literature* 51, no. 1 (June 1996): 53–83; and Eric Savoy, "The Jamesian Thing," *The Henry James Review* 22 (Fall 2001): 268–77.

16. See J. Hillis Miller, *The Ethics of Reading: Kant, de Man, Eliot, Trollope, James, and Benjamin* (New York: Columbia University Press, 1987), 104–5; Fotios Sarris, "Fetishism in *The Spoils of Poynton*"; Eric Savoy, "The Jamesian Thing."

17. Henry James, *Picture and Text* (New York: Harper and Brothers, 1893), 5–6.

18. Willa Cather, "Frank Norris" (1899), in Cather, *Stories, Poems, and Other Writings* (New York: Library of America, 1992), 920, 922.

19. Willa Cather, "On 'The Professor's House,'" in Willa Cather, *Stories, Poems, and other Writings*, 974.

20. Willa Cather, "The Novel Démeublé," in *Not Under Forty* (New York: Alfred A. Knopf, 1936), 43.

21. Le Corbusier, *Towards a New Architecture* (1923), trans. Frederick Etchells (New York: Dover, 1986), 91. The book was originally translated in 1931.

22. Frank Lloyd Wright, "The Architect and the Machine," in *Frank Lloyd Wright: Collected Writings*, vol. 1 (New York: Rizzoli, 1992), 22–24.

23. Edith Wharton and Ogden Codman, Jr., *The Decoration of Houses* (1897; New York, W. W. Norton, 1997), 1–3.

24. Wharton and Codman are blunt about their rationale for directing attention to the well-to-do. "It is a fact recognized by political economists that changes in manners and customs, no matter under what form of government, usually originate with the wealthy or aristocratic minority, and are thence transmitted to the other classes" (*The Decoration of Houses*, 7).

25. Lewis Mumford, *The Brown Decades: A Study on the Arts in America, 1865–1895* (New York: Dover, 1955).

26. See David E. Shi, *The Simple Life: Plain Living and High Thinking in American Culture* (New York: Oxford University Press, 1985), 181–89, 204–7. Among the many American precursors, Thoreau developed an especially biting attack on American material excess. As part of his call to "Simplify, simplify," he described the "nation itself, with all its so called internal improvements" (which he understood as "external and superficial") as an "unwieldy and overgrown establishment, cluttered with furniture" like "the million households in the land" that didn't recognize the benefit of a "rigid economy." He believed in the custom of the Mucclasse Indians (as described by Bartram) where the ritual destruction of unwanted possessions was taken to be a fully rejuvenating practice. "Furniture!," he declared, "Thank God, I can sit and I can stand without the aid of a furniture warehouse." He considered American houses to be "cluttered and defiled" by furniture. Henry David Thoreau, *Walden; or, Life in the Woods* (1854), in *A Week on the Concord and Merrimack Rivers; Walden, or, Life in the Woods; The Maine Woods; Cape Cod*, ed. Robert F. Sayre (New York: Library of America, 1985), 395, 374–76, 351.

27. Candace Wheeler, ed., *Household Art* (New York: Harper and Brothers, 1893).

28. Candace Wheeler, "The Philosophy of Beauty Applied to House Interiors," in *Household Art*, ed. Wheeler, 30.

29. Florence Morse, "About Furnishings," in *Household Art*, ed. Candace Wheeler, 181, 188, 187.

30. Lucia Gilbert Runkle, "The Limits of Decoration," in *Household Art*, ed. Candace Wheeler, 172.

31. Walter Benjamin, "Paris, Capital of the Nineteenth Century" (1939), *The Arcades Project*, trans. Howard Eiland and Kevin McLaughlin (Cambridge, Mass.: Harvard University Press, 1999), 17; "Bric-A-Brac," *The Curio* 1, no. 4 (December 1887): 192.

32. For an overview of this discourse, see Karen Halttunen, "From Parlor to Living Room: Domestic Space, Interior Decoration, and the Culture of Personality," in *Consuming Visions*, ed. Simon J. Bronner, 157–89. Needless to say, a more straightforward account of James's aesthetics would contextualize his thinking within a British milieu. See Jonathan Freedman, *Professions of Taste: Henry James, British Aestheticism, and Commodity Culture* (Stanford: Stanford University Press, 1990).

33. Henry James, *The Spoils of Poynton*, *The Novels and Tales of Henry James*, vol. 10 (New York: Scribner's, 1908), 6; hereafter, the novel and its Preface will be cited parenthetically.

34. "Cultural capital" is Pierre Bourdieu's term for the accumulated knowledge that allows an individual to decipher aesthetic codes and thus to demonstrate "taste," securing legitimacy within a particular class. See, above all, *Distinction: A Social Critique of the Judgment of Taste*, trans. Richard Nice (Cambridge, Mass.: Harvard University Press, 1984) and *The Field of Cultural Production: Essays on Art and Literature*, ed. Randal Johnson (New York: Columbia University Press, 1993). See also John Guillory, *Cultural Capital: The Problem of Literary Canon Formation* (Chicago: University of Chicago Press, 1993). In *The Golden Bowl*, James writes of Charlotte Stant that "Nothing in her definitely placed her; she was a rare, a special product. Her singleness, her solitude, her want of means, that is her want of ramifications and other advantages, contributed to enrich her somehow with an odd, precious neutrality, to constitute for her, so detached yet so aware, a sort of small social capital" (Henry James, *The Golden Bowl*, *The Novels and Tales of Henry James*, vols. 23 and 24 [New York: Scribner's, 1909], 1:53–54; references to the novel and its Preface will be cited parenthetically by volume [1 and 2] and page number). James's point—in Bourdieu's terms—is that social capital *does not* depend on the cultural capital described by the sociologist.

35. Vernon Lee (Violet Paget), *Art and Life* (East Aurora, N.Y.: Roycroft Print Shop, 1896), 55. Quoted by Rémy G. Saisselin, *The Bourgeois and the Bibelot* (New Brunswick: Rutgers University Press, 1984), 160. As Saisselin importantly comments, because "the mental image" is always preferred to the "tangible object," Lee's aesthetics could be used to prevent the rich from feeling guilty about possessing art.

36. Susan Stewart, *On Longing: Narratives of the Miniature, the Gigantic, the Souvenir, the Collection* (Baltimore: Johns Hopkins University Press, 1984), 164.

37. Jean Baudrillard, *The System of Objects*, trans. James Benedict (London: Verso, 1996), 91.

38. Adeline R. Tinter, "'The Old Things': Balzac's *Le Curé de Tours* and James's *The Spoils of Poynton*," 440.

39. Although James believed that "the insolence of the picture book" threatened "the negation of all literature" (Letter to William Dean Howells Feb. 22, 1894, *Letters of Henry James*, ed. Percy Lubbock [New York, Scribners, 1920], vol. 1, p. 231), he nonetheless incorporated frontispieces for the New York edition, photographs by Alvin Langdon Coburn, produced with considerable direction from James himself. In the case of the frontispiece for *Spoils*, it somewhat shockingly specifies a referent, but even the photograph remains sufficiently indistinct to emphasize effect at the expense of detail. On the Coburn photographs for the New York edition, see Charles Higgins, "Photographic Aperture: Coburn's Frontispieces to James's New York Edition," *American Literature* 53, no. 4 (January 1982): 661–75; Carol Shloss, *In Visible Light: Photography and the American Writer, 1840–1940* (New York: Oxford University Press, 1987), 59–89; and Ira B. Nadel, "Visual Culture: The Photo Frontispieces to the New York Edition," in *Henry James's New York Edition: The Construction of Authorship*, ed. David McWhirter (Stanford: Stanford University Press, 1995), 90–108.

40. Mrs. M. G. Van Rensselaer, "The Development of American Homes," in *Household Art*, ed. Candace Wheeler, 46.

41. Mieke Bal, *Double Exposures: The Subject of Cultural Analysis* (New York: Routledge, 1996), 5.

42. Such a superstition got considerably updated in 1968, when Roland Barthes published "L'effet du réel" in *Communications*, his second effort in that journal to account for the "superfluous" details in prose narrative, an account that he recognized as exceeding the limit of his own structuralism, given that, with respect to structure, "these details are scandalous" ("The reality effect," trans. R. Carter, in *French Literary Theory Today*, ed. Tzvetan Todorov [New York: Cambridge University Press, 1982], 11.) As he puts it, "notations" that have "no function"—what we might call the overspecified and undermotivated—function solely to register "the *having-been-there* of things" (12, 15). The difference between "the old 'vraisemblance,'" which depended on a level of generality, and "modern realism" (realism as such), "which accepts statements whose only justification is their referent," is that the latter conflates signifier and referent, effacing the signified and thus the structure of the sign; the absence of a signified "becomes the true signifier of realism" (15–16). See also, Barthes, "Introduction à l'analyse structurale des récits," *Communications* 8 (November 1966): 1–27.

43. Honoré de Balzac, *The Wild Ass's Skin* (1831), trans. Herbert J. Hunt (London: Penguin Books, 1977), 34; *Cousin Pons* (1848), trans. Herbet J. Hunt (London: Penguin Books, , 1968), 239, 24.

44. Honoré de Balzac, *Eugénie Grandet* (1833), trans. Marion Ayton Crawford (London: Penguin Books, 1955), 50. When a contrastingly underspecified barometer appears in Flaubert's *Un Coeur simple*, it occasions Roland Barthes's theory of the "reality effect." I have argued elsewhere, though, that Flaubert's barometer may have considerably more thematic significance than Barthes thinks (Bill Brown, *The Material Unconscious: American Amusement, Stephen Crane, and the Economies of Play* [Cambridge, Mass.: Harvard University Press, 1996], 13–19).

45. Georg Lukács, "Narrate or Describe: A Preliminary Discussion on Naturalism and Formalism" (1936), *Writer and Critic and Other Essays*, ed. and trans. Arthur

D. Kahn (New York: Grosset & Dunlap, 1970), 116–17. Hereafter cited parenthetically.

46. Henry James, "Honoré de Balzac" (1875), *Literary Criticism, Volume Two*, 50.

47. Thus, in his Preface to *Roderick Hudson*, James writes in one paragraph that the novelist, "embarks, rash adventurer, under the star of 'representation,' and is pledged thereby to remember that the art of interesting us in things—once these things are the right ones for the case—can *only* be the art of representing them"; he then writes, in the next paragraph, that "one nestled, technically, in those days, and with yearning, in the great shadow of Balzac" (*Literary Criticism, Volume Two*, 1044).

48. Henry James, "Honoré de Balzac," 67, 33.

49. See, for instance, Werner Muensterberger's chapter on "Two Collectors: Balzac and His *Cousin Pons*," in *Collecting: An Unruly Passion* (New York: Harcourt Brace and Co., 1994).

50. Henry James, *Washington Square*, in *Henry James: Novels 1881–1886*, 13–14. Hereafter cited parenthetically.

51. A more extensive reading of the doctor's deciphering skills would locate his work within the paradigm charted by Lawrence Rothfield, in *Vital Signs: Medical Realism in Nineteenth-Century Fiction* (Princeton: Princeton University Press, 1992).

52. Georg Lukács, *History and Class Consciousness*, trans. Rodney Livingstone (Cambridge, Mass.: MIT Press, 1971), 92. Carolyn Porter is the Americanist literary critic who has deployed Lukács's notion of reification most extensively, in *Seeing and Being: The Plight of the Participant Observer in Emerson, James, Adams, and Faulkner* (Middletown: Wesleyan University Press, 1981). Arguing that the world of the late James is one where "reification has penetrated to a level so deep as to constitute the limits of the knowable" (122), she concentrates on *The Golden Bowl* with a particular emphasis on vision.

53. Walter Benjamin, "Unpacking My Library," trans. Harry Zohn, in Benjamin, *Selected Writings*, vol. 2, *1927–1934*, ed. Michael W. Jennings, Howard Eiland, and Gary Smith (Cambridge, Mass.: Harvard University Press, 1999), 492.

54. Jean Baudrillard, *The System of Objects*, 16.

55. This is to say that James's understanding of things, and of the objectification of people, could be read in relation to his understanding of—or suppression of—the politics of race in America. The question of race and of racism in James has become a crucial topic within James criticism. See, for instance, Kenneth Warren, *Black and White Strangers: Race and American Realism* (Chicago: University of Chicago Press, 1993); and Sara Blair, *Henry James and the Writing of Race and Nation* (New York: Cambridge University Press, 1996).

56. Jean-Christophe Agnew, "A House of Fiction," in *Consuming Visions*, ed. Simon J. Bronner, 133–55. Specific page references will be provided in the text.

57. Walter Benjamin, "Paris, Capital of the Nineteenth Century," 19.

58. As Susan Stewart, among others, has argued, collections may depend on the economy, but the "economy of collecting" is "fantastic," fostering it own principles of value, exchange, and substitution (*On Longing*, 132–69).

59. The image of the Prince as a coin out of circulation ought to be read in relation to Trina McTeague's effort to keep her gold from circulating. See chapter 2.

60. In a chapter on "Art and America," Charles Edward Jerningham and Lewis

Bettany declare the three "R's of British History: Reformation, Revolution, and Removal," by which they mean the transfer of treasures to the U.S. With surprising admiration for the taste of both the American collectors and their agents "scouring the land," they conclude that in time "the vast mass of old-world work will be in the United States" (*The Bargain Book* [London: Chatto and Windus, 1911], 310–13). For an account of the premiere agent of the era, see Rémy G. Saisselin's chapter on Bernard Berenson in *The Bourgeois and the Bibelot*, 135–68. And see W. G. Constable, *Art Collecting in the United States of America: An Outline of a History* (London: Thomas Nelson, 1964); Neil Harris, "Collective Possession: J. Pierpont Morgan and the American Imagination," in *Cultural Excursions: Marketing Appetites and Cultural Tastes in Modern America* (Chicago: University of Chicago Press, 1990); Aline B. Saarinen, *The Proud Possessors: The Lives, Times, and Tastes of Some Adventurous American Art Collectors* (New York: Random House, 1958); Kathleen D. McCarthy, *Noblesse Oblige: Charity and Cultural Philanthropy in Chicago, 1849–1929* (Chicago: University of Chicago Press, 1982). For a reading of *The Golden Bowl* in the context of the museum movement in America, see Stephen D. Arata, "Object Lessons: Reading the Museum in *The Golden Bowl*."

61. William Carew Hazlitt, *The Confessions of a Collector* (London: Ward and Downey, 1897), 2.

62. *The Curio* 1 (September 1887): 47, 1.

63. Caroline Frear Burk, "The Collecting Instinct" (1900), in *Aspects of Child Life and Education*, ed. G. Stanley Hall (Boston: Ginn and Company, 1907), 236–37.

64. Sharon Cameron, *Thinking in Henry James* (Chicago: University of Chicago Press, 1989), 85.

65. James produces a similar effect, early in the novel, with his elaborate (unfocalized) conceit that describes the Prince's place within Adam and Maggie's relationship. That relationship resembles "a good deal some pleasant public square, in the heart of an old city, into which a great Palladian church, say—something with a grand architectural front—had suddenly been dropped. . . . The Palladian church was always there, but the *piazza* took care of itself . . . the way round was easy" (1:135). Only after the conceit do we suddenly learn, in an account of Fawns, that there was in fact a "little old church, 'on the property,' that our friend often found himself wishing he were able to transport, as it stood, for its simple sweetness, in a glass case, to one of his exhibitory halls" (1:152).

66. The deictic, I want to emphasize, functions to locate "objects" in a "spatiotemporal context." See J. Lyons, *Semantics*, (New York: Cambridge University Press, 1977), vol. 2, p. 657.

67. Balzac's writing of the novel was inseparable from his own passions as a collector. When he took possession of his luxurious new house on Paris's Rue Fortunée, he filled the house with his possessions, and he set out to find new acquisitions that would amplify what he took to be his important and supremely valuable collection. With an obsession far more pathological than Twain's, Balzac plunged himself into debt, and then schemed to get out of debt with get-rich-quick fantasies. His collecting obsession and fantasies of grandeur clearly derive from his deeply troubled childhood. See Werner Muensterberger, who considers Balzac a manic depressive for whom collecting was an obsessional defense, and for whom "grandiosity" was

meant to compensate for the novelist's "self-doubt" and "the narcissistic wound dealt him by his indifferent, uncaring mother" (*Collecting: An Unruly Passion*, 101–34).

68. Eugenio Donato, "The Museum's Furnace: Notes Toward a Contextual Reading of Bouvard and Pécuchet," in *Textual Strategies: Perspectives in Post-Structuralist Criticism*, ed. Josué Harari (Ithaca, N.Y.: Cornell University Press, 1979), 216, 223.

69. Tony Bennett, *The Birth of the Museum: History, Theory, Politics* (New York: Routledge, 1995), 63.

70. This is really to argue, in Elaine Scarry's terms, that the pagoda attains a far greater "givenness," its description achieves a far greater reality-effect, than other buildings depicted in the novel. See, for instance her account of Levin's motion in *Anna Karenina*, and the way that a character's motion through or around something seems to grant that something its physical thingness (*Dreaming by the Book* [New York: Farrar, Straus & Giroux, 1999], 227–29).

71. Henry James, *Letters*, vol. 3, p. 264.

72. Tony Bennett, *The Birth of the Museum*, 63.

73. Henry James, Preface to *Portrait of a Lady*, *Literary Criticism, Volume Two*, 1075. Further references will be provided parenthetically.

74. Edith Wharton, *A Backward Glance* (New York: D. Appleton-Century, 1934), 191.

75. Jacques Lacan, *The Ethics of Psychoanalysis 1959–1960: The Seminar of Jacques Lacan Book VII*, trans. Dennis Porter (New York: Norton, 1992), 118. Further references will be provided in the text.

76. The image thus completes, by inverting, James's account of his discomfort as he posed for Matthew Brady in the daguerreotype parlor, keenly embarrassed by the "single row of buttons" on his "sheath-like jacket" that had been the object of Thackery's attention and had made Henry James as a boy recognize that "we were somehow *queer.*" See *A Small Boy and Others* (New York: Charles Scribner's Sons, 1913), 87–88.

77. Leon Edel, *Henry James 1901–1916: The Master* (Philadelphia: Lippincott, 1972), 485.

78. *Henry James: Selected Letters*, ed. Leon Edel (Cambridge, Mass.: Harvard University Press, 1987), 409.

79. On James's life-long sensitivity to his popularity, see Michael Anesko, *"Friction with the Market": Henry James and the Profession of Authorship* (New York: Oxford University Press, 1986).

CODA

1. Henry James, *The American Scene* (1907; Bloomington: Indiana University Press, 1968), 8. Hereafter cited parenthetically.

2. On the critical reputation of *The American Scene*, see Leon Edel's introduction to the Indiana University Press edition, vii–xxiv.

3. W. H. Auden, "Introduction" to Henry James, *The American Scene* (New York: Charles Scribner's Sons, 1946), xi.

4. Thoreau writes: "I was suddenly sensible of such sweet and beneficent society in Nature, in the very pattering of the drops, and in every sound and sight

around my house, an infinite and unaccountable friendliness all at once like an atmosphere sustaining me, as made the fancied advantages of human neighborhood insignificant, and I have never thought of them since. Every little pine needle expanded and swelled with sympathy and befriended me." Henry David Thoreau, *Walden; or, Life in the Woods* (1854), in Thoreau, *A Week on the Concord and Merrimack Rivers; Walden, or, Life in the Woods; The Maine Woods; Cape Cod*, ed. Robert F. Sayre (New York: Library of America, 1985), 427. One might very well conclude that James means to extend something like Thoreau's environmental imagination to the modern city. On Thoreau's environmentalism, see Lawrence Buell, *The Environmental Imagination: Thoreau, Nature Writing, and the Formation of American Culture* (Cambridge, Mass.: Harvard University Press, 1995).

5. Jean Baudrillard, *Fatal Strategies*, trans. Philip Beitchman and W. G. J. Niesluchowski (New York: Semiotext(e), 1990), 111.

6. Hugh Kenner, *The Pound Era: The Age of Ezra Pound. T. S. Eliot, James Joyce, and Wyndham Lewis* (London: Faber and Faber, 1975), 14–15. Hereafter cited parenthetically.

7. F. S. Flint, "Imagisme" (1913), *Imagist Poetry*, ed. Peter Jones (London: Penguin, 1972), 129. Ezra Pound, "A Few Don'ts By An Imagiste," *Imagist Poetry*, 131. William Carlos Williams, *Spring and All* (1923), in *Imaginations* (New York: New Directions, 1970), 95.

8. William Carlos Williams, *Spring and All*, 102.

9. William Carlos Williams, *Spring and All*, 123. Of course, one *could* say that James's ventriloquism dramatizes a potency of objects that comes to fruition in Williams's early verse, where objects are given not aural but bodily presence. Indeed, this is how James repeatedly ends up theorizing a modernism he himself never practiced. Kenneth Burke, whose dramatistic thinking is so indebted to James, uses the preface to *The Spoils of Poynton* as a way to define the work of Marianne Moore. "'The thing is to lodge somewhere at the heart of one's complexity an irrepressible *appreciation*,'" Burke quotes by way of describing how, for Moore, the chosen particular becomes an "objective replica of the subjective" and thus the way that the objects in her verse "have the property not simply of things, but of volitions" (*A Grammar of Motives* [New York: Prentice-Hall, 1945], 491, 496). And yet, in what Burke calls Moore's "objectivism" (which we would now call ocular objectivism), "an object may be chosen for treatment because of its symbolic or subjective reference," but "once it has been chosen it is to be studied in its own right" (486). This is the kind of studying that James nowhere adopts, perhaps least of all in *The Spoils of Poynton*, where subjective reference in fact obscures the objects themselves (see above, chapter 4). There is nothing of Moore's "attempt to report and judge of a thing's intrinsic qualities, to make us feel its properties as accurately as possible" (488).

10. Kevin Lynch, *The Image of the City* (Cambridge, Mass.: MIT Press, 1960), 10.

11. Fredric Jameson, *Postmodernism, or, The Cultural Logic of Late Capitalism* (Durham: Duke University Press, 1991), 38. Lynch's *Image of the City* provides the link between Jameson's personal disorientation in Los Angeles and the problem of cognitively mapping postmodern global space (51).

12. Jameson, *Postmodernism*, 38; Georg Simmel, *The Philosophy of Money*, trans. Tom Bottomore, David Frisby, and Kaethe Mengelberg (New York: Rout-

ledge, 1990), 448–52. Simmel's students—notably Siegfried Kracauer and Walter Benjamin—were able to express this disjuncture in a mode of materialist phenomenology.

13. In a more recent effort to align James not with the modernism of Williams but with the modernism of Critical Theory, Ross Posnock argues that objects in *The American Scene* enjoy a sustained potency and priority. James "sets aside conventions of control," Posnock asserts in *The Trial of Curiosity: Henry James, William James, and the Challenge of Modernity* (New York: Oxford University Press, 1991), "as he lets the world of objects take the lead" and finds himself "invaded by the external world" (86). Above all, he wants to make it clear that James does not subsume the otherness of objects. In a book successfully devoted to seeing beyond the Frankfurt School's vilification of pragmatism, and to tracking the resistance to a logic of identity that both William and Henry James share with Adorno and Benjamin, Posnock posits the *American Scene*'s "immanent, antisubjectivist, and materialist" response to modernity as a Benjaminian mode where "the subject immerses itself in the particularity of the preexisting object (to avoid idealism) without extinguishing its own creative imagination (to avoid positivism)" (146). Impressive as Posnock's argument is, this assessment not only falls short of explaining how the particularity of urban Baltimore and rural New Hampshire, say, disappear before the subjective impression. It also never confronts Benjamin's own attraction to a "new barbarism" (manifest in Le Corbusier's architecture, as in Klee's painting) that rejects "the traditional, solemn, noble image of man, festooned with all the sacrificial offerings of the past"; his belief that people "long to free themselves from experience," from the burden of culture and tradition; and his celebration of Atget's ability to "cleanse" objects of "atmosphere," the photographer's "emancipation of object from aura" (Walter Benjamin, "Experience and Poverty," trans. Rodney Livingstone, *Selected Writings*, vol. 2, *1927–1934*, ed. Michael Jennings, Howard Eiland, and Gary Smith [Cambridge, Mass.: Harvard University Press, 1999], 734; "Little History of Photography," 518). In *One-Way Street* (1928), where Benjamin too plays the role of *flâneur* (a word both he and James used for themselves), and which he wrote as a revisiting spirit in Berlin, a "Construction Site" provokes his most moving account of the human interaction with the inanimate world. Children "are irresistibly drawn by the detritus generated by building," he writes, and "in waste products they recognize the face that the world of things turns directly and solely to them," enabling them to bring the materials into a "new, intuitive relationship" (Walter Benjamin, *One-Way Street*, trans. Edmund Jephcott, in *Selected Writings*, vol. 1, *1913–1926*, ed. Marcus Bullock and Michael W. Jennings [Cambridge, Mass., Harvard University Press, 1996], 449–50). While James emphasizes preservation as opposed to waste, Benjamin emphasizes the redemption of waste.

14. Michel de Certeau provides an account of walking through the city that could readily provoke a reading of this episode energized by the convergence of psychoanalytical and existentialist insights: "In this place that is a palimpsest, subjectivity is already linked to the absence that structures it as existence and makes it 'be there,' *Dasein*. But as we have seen, this being-there . . . must ultimately be seen as the repetition, in diverse metaphors, of a decisive and originary experience, that of the child's differentiation from the mother's body" (*The Practice of Everyday Life*, trans. Steven Rendall [Berkeley: University of California Press, 1984], 109). This is

the point to say, too, that a very different reading of *The American Scene* would find its engagement with buildings—at the expense of engagement with persons—to be pathological.

15. With a similar logic, Cornelius Castoriadis has argued against the psychoanalytic understanding of desire as defined by the lack of a desired object, when in fact the object must be present to the psyche as desirable, meaning that the psyche has in fact already fashioned the object. *The Imaginary Institution of Society* (1975), trans. Kathleen Blamey (Cambridge, Mass.: MIT Press, 1987), 288–90.

16. Benjamin worked toward a more extended understanding of the anesthetization that shields consciousness. See Susan Buck-Morss, "Aesthetics and Anaesthetics: Walter Benjamin's Artwork Essay Reconsidered," *October*, no. 62 (Fall 1992): 3–41.

17. Theodor Adorno, "Subject and Object," *The Essential Frankfurt School Reader*, ed. Andrew Arato and Eike Gebhardt (New York: Continuum, 1982), 500. On the subject/object dialectic and the importance of recognizing the alterity of things, see Adorno, *Negative Dialectics*, trans. E. B. Ashton (New York: Continuum, 1997), 173–94.

18. Karl Marx and Friedrich Engels, *Manifesto of the Communist Party*, in *The Marx-Engels Reader*, ed. Robert C. Tucker (New York: Norton, 1978), 476.

19. I am simplifying Walter Benjamin's notion of aura, which he conceptualizes most fully in his "Little History of Photography," trans. Edmund Jephcott and Kingsley Shorter, *Selected Writings*, vol. 2, *1927–1934*, pp. 507–30; and "The Work of Art in the Age of its Technological Reproducibility," trans. Howard Eiland, *Selected Writings*, vol. 4 (Cambridge, Mass: Harvard University Press, forthcoming).

20. Walter Benjamin, "One-Way Street," 454. Similarly, Benjamin's friend Siegfried Kracauer reported that "objects have been struck dumb" ("Farewell to the Linden Arcade," *The Mass Ornament: Weimar Essays*, trans. Thomas Y. Levin [Cambridge, Mass.: Harvard University Press], 342). In perhaps the most famous modernist instance of the animation of the physical environment, Sartre's *Nausea*, the animation of things emphasizes their radical otherness. See Fredric Jameson, *Sartre: The Origins of a Style* (New York: Columbia University Press, 1984), 73–78. James's commitment to leaving the buildings undescribed prevents any such confrontation.

21. Theodor W. Adorno, "Portrait of Walter Benjamin," *Prisms*, trans. Samuel and Shierry Weber (Cambridge: MIT Press, 1983), 233.

22. Benjamin scholars will notice that I avoid using the word "innervation" here, which Benjamin comes to deploy as a way of describing a productive internalization of new technology. For the most successful unpacking of this Benjaminian term (and a lexical genealogy that touches on William James's psychology), see Miriam Bratu Hansen, "Benjamin and Cinema: Not a One-Way Street," *Critical Inquiry* 25 (Winter 1999): 306–43.

23. Bruno Latour, *We Have Never Been Modern*, trans. Catherine Porter (Cambridge, Mass., 1993), 10–11. He insists that "things do not exist without being full of people" and that considering humans necessarily involves considering things ("The Berlin Key or How to Do Words with Things," trans. Lydia Davis, in *Matter, Materiality, and Modern Culture*, ed. P. M. Graves-Brown [London, 2000], 10, 20). See

also Michel Serres, *Statues* (Paris: François Bourin, 1987); Miguel Tamen, *Friends of Interpretable Objects* (Cambridge, Mass.: Harvard University Press, 2001).

24. Alexsandr Rodchenko, quoted by Christina Kiaer, "Rodchenko in Paris," *October* 75 (Winter 1996): 3.

25. Louis Aragon, "On Décor," trans. Paul Hammond, in *French Film Theory and Criticism*, vol. 1, *1907–1929*, ed. Richard Abel (Princeton: Princeton University Press, 1988), 165, 167.

26. Siegfried Kracauer, *Theory of Film: The Redemption of Physical Reality* (Princeton: Princeton University Press, 1997), 297.

27. William Carlos Williams, *Paterson* (New York: New Directions, 1963), 6.

28. Georges Bataille, "Architecture," *Critical Dictionary*, ed. Bataille, in *Encyclopedia Acephalica*, ed. Alastair Brotchie, trans. Iain White et al. (London: Atlas Press), 36.

29. From Bataille's point of view, architecture is an expression, foremost, of society's "authoritative command and prohibition"; the attack on the Bastille is thus a paradigmatic attack on the social force of the architectural ("Architecture," 35). See Denis Hollier, *Against Architecture: The Writings of Georges Bataille*, trans. Betsy Wing (Cambridge, Mass.: MIT Press, 1989). I don't mean to suggest that James's emotional investment in built space is not a longing for stability; I mean to suggest, rather, that the manifestation of this investment—the animation of the object— necessarily disrupts that stability.

30. Marcel Mauss, *The Gift*, trans. W. D. Halls (New York: Norton, 1990), 49.

31. See N. Katherine Hayles, *How We Became Posthuman: Virtual Bodies in Cybernetics, Literature, and Informatics* (Chicago: University of Chicago Press, 1999).

INDEX

Adorno, Theodor: on modernism, 193n.48; on objects, 2; on the otherness of the physical world, 18; on phenomenology, 184; on things, 4, 78, 186

aesthetics, 2, 35, 227n.32; commodity, 13, 27, 198n.25; of decorating, 143–50; Kantian, 26, 196n.16; modernist, 74–76, 125, 143–44, 180; national, 133–35; physiological, 26, 196n.17

Agnew, Jean-Christophe, 156–57, 205n.79, 225n.6

Allen, Grant, 196n.17

Amariglio, Jack, 198n.26

Ammons, Elizabeth, 106

Anderson, Charles R., 225n.15

Anderson, Margo J., 201n.43

Anderson, Sherwood, 127

Andrews, Kenneth R., 195n.2

Anesko, Michael, 231n.79

animism, 64, 114–15. *See also* fetishism

anthropology, 54; materialist, 5; museal, 16, 81–99, 118; and natural sciences, 89–91; objects in, 85–89; regionalization of, 85–89. *See also* ethnography; ethnology

Apollinaire, Guillaume, 125

Appadurai, Arjun, 190n.16

Aragon, Louis, 187

Arata, Stephen, 225n.15, 229n.60

Arendt, Hannah, 33, 122, 200n.36

Aristotle, 44, 45

Arnold, Matthew, 82

art, as an object, 2

artifacts, 18, 81; absence of, 123; legible, 104, 124; Native American, 118–24, 129–35; 224n.125; traffic in, 133, 224n.125

Auden, W. H., 178

Auerbach, Eric, 16

Ayer, A. J., 208n.20

Bachelard, Gaston, 4, 190n.15; on objects and human interiority, 7, 112

Baetzhold, Howard G., 202n.55

Bal, Mieke, 228n.41

Baldwin, Mark, 1–2

Balzac, Honoré de, 19, 170; collecting in, 166; and Henry James, 150–55, 229n.47; and passion for things, 14–15, 84, 151–52, 230n.67; on typology, 217n.43

Barnum, P. T., 21

Barthes, Roland, 16; on the reality-effect, 207n.5, 228n.42

Bataille, Georges, 3, 235n.28

Baudelaire, Charles, 6, 18, 182

Baudrillard, Jean, 17–18, 146, 179

Baum, L. Frank, 115

beauty, 26–27

Beckett, Samuel, 54

Beer, Gillian, 207nn. 5, 10

Benjamin, Walter, 4, 18, 190n.15; on collecting, 156–57; on commodity fetishism, 30–31, 144; on literature, 11; on photography, 9, 234n.20; on things, 177, 186, 213n.62, 233n.13; on toys, 6

Bennett, Tony, 166, 216n.36

Benson, Susan Porter, 198n.27

Bentley, Nancy, 217n.44

Berenson, Bernard, 229n.60

Berlant, Lauren, 205n.85

Bettany, Lewis, 229n.60

bicycle, 34–35

Made in the USA
Lexington, KY
16 January 2012